Psychology of Mental Health

Psychology
of Mental Health

FIRST EDITION

Naomi Fisher

OXFORD
UNIVERSITY PRESS

OXFORD
UNIVERSITY PRESS

Great Clarendon Street, Oxford, OX2 6DP,
United Kingdom

Oxford University Press is a department of the University of Oxford.
It furthers the University's objective of excellence in research, scholarship,
and education by publishing worldwide. Oxford is a registered trade mark of
Oxford University Press in the UK and in certain other countries

Published in the United States of America by Oxford University Press
198 Madison Avenue, New York, NY 10016, United States of America

British Library Cataloguing in Publication Data

Data available

Library of Congress Control Number: 2023950712

ISBN 978–0–19–886298–7

Printed in the UK by
Bell & Bain Ltd., Glasgow

Links to third party websites are provided by Oxford in good faith and
for information only. Oxford disclaims any responsibility for the materials
contained in any third party website referenced in this work.

Brief Contents

Table of Contents

Acknowledgements

Many people were very generous with their time when I was writing this book.

I am immensely grateful to those who talked to me for Chapter 7, and who allowed me to use their stories. Many of them remain anonymous and so I will not name them here, but this book would be far weaker without them.

The case studies which you will find throughout the book are not based on real people. All the experiences you will hear about are real, but I have made up composite people as illustrative examples. Any resemblance to a real person is purely accidental.

It is the nature of writing a book like that that I drew on the expertise of others. I talked to several colleagues and researchers when I was putting this together, and I would like to thank Melissa Black, Mary Boyle, Lucy Johnstone, Jill Newby, and John Read, who all took the time to share their thoughts with me and to point me in the direction of relevant research. Lucy Johnstone also read an early version of Chapter 4 and helped me to get my understanding of the Power Threat Meaning Framework straight.

As a PhD student, I studied at the Social, Genetic, and Developmental Psychiatry (SGDP) Centre at the Institute of Psychiatry, Kings College London. This inter-disciplinary programme was ground-breaking in requiring an experimental psychologist (as I was at the time) to also gain an understanding of genetics and social psychology. We were encouraged to make connections across disciplines and a lifelong interest in behavioural genetics and thinking across disciplines was one of the outcomes for me. I was surrounded by an inspiring group of people, some of whose research you will hear about in this book. I would like to particularly thank Francesca Happé, Judy Dunn, Robert Plomin, Terri Moffit, Avshalom Caspi, Claire Hughes, Alex Cutting, Rhonda Booth, Rebecca Charlton, Louse Arsenault, Julia Kim-Cohen, Greg Wallace, John Rogers, and Essi Viding.

As a clinical psychologist both inside and outside the NHS, I have worked with many inspiring and dedicated colleagues. There are too many to name you all here but I deeply appreciate all that I have learnt from you. I have also had the privilege to work with and hear the stories of many individual clients. I have learnt from every one of you. Thank you.

Many thanks to the anonymous reviewers who took the time to tell me what you thought. Your comments were extremely useful and constructive. I hope that I have done them justice in the final version.

Martha Bailes was the first editor of this primer, and had a significant role in shaping the book that it has become. Marcus Munafo has been extremely helpful in the later stages. Both have made suggestions which have strengthened the book in many ways. Thank you. All mistakes are mine.

Preface

A short primer on the psychology of mental health. When I was first asked to write a proposal for this book, it seemed like a reasonable proposition. That illusion lasted until I started to think about it in depth and do some reading. It quickly becomes clear that nothing in this area is straightforward. Not even the language used—an early discussion asked whether the book should refer to 'mental health', since this implied that these experiences belonged firmly in the domain of 'health'? What about using 'mental ill-health', a term which was less euphemistic, but which put the topic even more clearly in the domain of illness and disease? What would it be called if we didn't use 'health' at all and we used 'distress' or 'unusual behaviour and experiences'—was there a risk that people wouldn't know what it was about at all if we used different terminology?

It became quickly clear to me that the psychology of mental health is highly politicised. Working as a clinical psychologist (as I have since 2006) it's possible to miss that. To a certain extent I just got on with the job, which was usually to offer individual assessments and psychological interventions to people in distress. *CBT / EMDR*

However, once I started to look more deeply into current ideas about mental health I discovered that there were drawn battles on social media over what a psychiatric diagnosis really means, or whether taking a trauma-informed approach could be damaging for clients. I learnt that to criticise the biomedical model risks a person being called 'anti-psychiatry', and that once someone gets that label, everything they say may be dismissed as biased. I discovered that there are people who find diagnoses extremely helpful, and others who find them extremely unhelpful, and many in between. I saw that, unsurprisingly, for many people, the way that we talk about mental health felt deeply personal. Some people regard their psychiatric diagnosis as an essential part of their identity and say that receiving it was a transformatory experience. Online communities have formed around diagnostic categories and there are 'mental health influencers' on TikTok and YouTube. Asking whether there might be other ways to understand their experiences or questioning the validity of a diagnosis feels like an attack on their whole way of life.

This was a difficult atmosphere in which to write a book. I had to put aside my fears of how social media might react to what I wrote, because it became clear that there were certain things I needed to say. This is particularly because of my perspective, which is that of a applied psychologist. I use psychology in clinical practice on a daily basis. I use a variety of approaches, including CBT, EMDR, and ACT, all of which are explained further in this book. The longer I do this, the more complexity I see.

When I first considered writing this primer, I had a look at the books available for undergraduates and talked with colleagues who taught at this level. I was surprised. They seemed to exist in a different world to the one I inhabited. They were often called 'Abnormal Psychology' or 'Psychopathology', both words which immediately defined the experiences that we were talking about as outside the norm and an indication that something was wrong. Yet a lot of the work I did with my clients was normalising their emotional reactions to the (often difficult) events of their lives, and research shows that it may be more common to have mental health problems at some point in your life than not. Most clinical and counselling psychologists in the UK do not apply the words 'abnormal' or 'pathology' to their clients, and yet undergraduates were being taught that these were the appropriate terms, right across the front of their textbooks.

These books also often listed different mental health diagnoses (or 'disorders') chapter by chapter, describing the symptoms and then treatment. They largely presented a world where there was certainty about these categories and their usefulness. The main challenge for psychologists working in mental health, viewed from the perspective of these books, seemed to be how to effectively categorise people so they could be offered the right intervention. Students were encouraged to memorise diagnostic criteria and treatments. It all seemed to be so well understood.

This was entirely different to the messy and rather unpredictable real world within which I worked. Most of the time I work without a formal diagnosis and I plan psychological interventions based on an individual understanding of the person's experience. I have to change direction when it becomes clear that what I had planned isn't quite right for this individual. Real life often gets in the way and we have to help sort out people's benefits or housing before any type of psychological intervention is appropriate. Categorising people is far less important in my clinical work than understanding and responding to their difficulties. That didn't come across in the textbooks.

Those books are still there and you can go and read them. There was no need to repeat that in this book, and so I decided to do something different. I wanted to present some of the complexities and contradictions which are inherent when working with mental health, and I wanted to put psychology at the heart of the book. For, at the most basic level, I think that the applied psychology of mental health is about the way that people interpret and make meaning of the world around them. Clinical and Counselling Psychology involve working with the way that people think and feel about the world. Which means that the way that we talk about people's experiences matter, because it has an impact on how they make sense of what is happening to them.

If we apply this to mental health, then using the term 'abnormal psychology' or 'psychopathology' means that we have already decided what the meaning of a person's experiences is. There's something wrong with them, something different to the norm. The same applies to the biomedical model of mental health. When we accept the biomedical model without question, then we have already decided what meaning should be given to a person's experiences. They have a medical condition or disorder, which needs to be diagnosed and treated. We may make that decision without even thinking about it, because we haven't even realised that we are making an assumption. We might think that the assumptions are just 'how things are', a reflection of objective reality rather than an interpretation.

That's why this book takes a step back, and asks you to start by considering the assumptions which our society (and perhaps you) makes about mental health. For me, this is the psychology of mental health. How we interpret the world matters, and so how we interpret the experiences which we call 'mental health problems' also matters. You'll read about different theories and models, so you can critically evaluate other texts that you read. I hope that you'll start to ask yourself what unstated assumptions might be coming into play, in this book as with every other. There's a lot of uncertainty in the real world, and that lack of certainty can initially feel confusing or even destabilising. I hope that you'll be able to embrace that as part of the process.

This book includes the voices of experts by experience, both professionals and service users. This was because I felt that it was important for this not to just be a book about how psychologists and other professionals see mental health problems from the outside, but also how it is experienced from the inside. Often in textbooks the people who we are talking about are only seen in case studies, written to illustrate a point. Real-life experiences can offer different ways of understanding but they can also illustrate how very diverse people's experiences can be.

One task of an applied psychologist is to listen to the stories of people's lives, and to resist the urge to reach for easy answers. We can never assume that one solution will work for all, and the more experienced we are, the more we see that. One person's panacea can be another person's pain. This means that sitting with uncertainty and complexity is an important part of the psychology of mental health. I hope this book will help you to understand that, and that you find it both interesting and challenging.

Chapter 1
What is Mental Health?

Learning objectives

When you have completed this chapter, you should be able to do the following:

1.1 Explain the complexities involved in the language used around mental health.

1.2 Discuss the main issues around classifying mental health problems.

1.3 Outline several alternatives to the psychiatric diagnostic system.

Introduction

It's rare to come to the topic of mental health anew. You may have had your own experience of intense distress and unusual experiences, or you may know someone who has been diagnosed with a mental health problem. In addition, you will have been exposed to many messages about the appropriate way to understand distressing experiences and behaviour. There are storylines on popular TV shows about self-harm and eating disorders, and there are billboards at train stations telling us that people like us get depression. Awareness campaigns tell us mental health problems are illnesses just like cancer or diabetes. Some people declare their diagnoses in their social media profiles, showing us that they consider this to be an important part of their identity.

In this chapter, I will discuss what is meant by the term 'mental health' and take a critical look at the language that is often used to describe distress. I will summarise the experiences and behaviours which are usually included under the umbrella term 'mental health problems'. I will describe how mental health problems are categorised and understood, introducing the dominant system—often called the psychiatric or biomedical approach—and alternatives. These include dimensional approaches and frameworks which conceptualise mental distress in a different way altogether. This book comes from a particular perspective, which is that whilst the medical model of mental health can be helpful, it is not the only way to understand mental distress and unusual experiences and it can have drawbacks as well as advantages.

> **CASE STUDY 1.1**
>
> ### Ana's Story
>
> Ana is feeling very sad. She keeps crying for no apparent reason and doesn't enjoy reading or playing music anymore. She feels hopeless about the future, and about what will happen if her life doesn't improve. She can't sleep at night but feels exhausted all day. She can't be bothered to go out and meet friends and drags herself through each day.
>
> She goes to her GP who diagnoses her with mixed depression and anxiety and prescribes her an anti-depressant.
>
> Later, Ana rings her mother and tells her how unhappy she is feeling. Her mother tells her to stop being silly, to pull herself together and have a bath.
>
> Ana is distressed. The people she talks to have their own theories as to why that might be. The GP thinks she has a mental disorder which can be treated with medication. Her mother thinks she's being self-indulgent and oversensitive.
>
> Ana doesn't know what to think. She just wants to feel better. Is she ill, as the GP says? Or is it her fault, as her mother seems to think? Or is there another reason for why she feels so terrible?

1.1   What is mental health?

Mental health is a complex topic, and one of the ways in which it is complex is that the language we use is often controversial. In the UK we talk about 'mental health services' when we describe what were previously (and sometimes still are) called **psychiatric services**. Having '**mental health problems**' is a phrase widely used when we talk about people who are also sometimes described as mentally ill, mentally disordered, or suffering from mental health difficulties. '**Mental health**' can be used to describe a continuum, where some people are in good mental health and others are not. The word 'mental' is often used informally in a derogatory way, to discredit what someone says or how they feel.

The term 'mental health problems' is not without its critics. Some prefer to use '**distress**' or '**unusual experiences and behaviour**'. This is because the term 'mental health problems' implies that these experiences belong in the domain of health (and illness) rather than being a natural human response to life events and circumstances. Talking about 'mental health' may lead us to assume that we should seek to understand what is happening on an individual level, rather than looking at wider society and the impact on humans of living in the world as it is today. It's also the case that the term 'mental health' has been more widely used in general speech in recent times, describing a much larger spectrum of experiences than would have been the case a few years ago. Academic psychologist Lucy Foulkes argues that we are losing the language to distinguish between those who are seriously

unwell, and those who are experiencing a level of distress that is part of the typical range of human experience. She suggests that this blurring of boundaries is leading many people to think that they are ill when in fact they are experiencing the typical range of human emotions. She favours the term **mental illness** for this reason (Foulkes, 2021). Others argue that this distinction is misguided, and that even the most severe mental health difficulties are not helpfully understood as illness (Cooke and Kinderman, 2018). With the caveat that there is no way to talk about this topic which cannot be critiqued, the term 'mental health problems' is widely used and understood, and I will use it in this book alongside other terms.

Prevalence of mental health problems

What proportion of the population have mental health problems? Working this out—or estimating **prevalence**—is not straightforward. One way is to assess the number of people who seek help from the mental health system, but this will miss those who have dealt with their problems in a different way or have sought help privately. Another way is to survey a large group of people in the general population, but this then creates the problem of how exactly to decide whether someone has a mental health problem or not. Diagnostic interviews require extensive time and training to carry out. For this reason, many large-scale studies rely on self-report questionnaires or questionnaires completed by non-clinically trained researchers, which may overestimate how many people would reach diagnostic threshold.

The Adult Psychiatric Morbidity Surveys are carried out every seven years and are large-scale attempts to measure the prevalence of mental health problems in the UK (McManus et al., 2020). Their data indicates that 1 in 4 people reported experiences which could be diagnosed as a mental health problem in the last year and that 1 in 6 reported a common mental health problem in any given week (McManus et al., 2016).

These surveys are retrospective and carried out at a single time point, meaning that they ask people to remember past experiences. Another (and more expensive) approach is to follow people over time. An ongoing large-scale longitudinal cohort study in New Zealand found that over 85% of their population-representative sample met diagnostic criteria for a 'mental disorder' at some point by the time they reached their mid-40s (Caspi et al., 2020). According to this study, 'enduring mental health' as these researchers call it, is the exception, rather than the norm.

The most recent studies have the complicating factor of the COVID-19 pandemic, meaning that their findings may reflect the impact of the pandemic rather than a general change in prevalence. The UK Household Longitudinal Study 'Understanding Society' collects data from thousands of families each year in order to track changes over time. Their data shows that the prevalence of mental health problems rose during the COVID-19 pandemic, with the percentage of people being classified as experiencing mental health problems rising from 23% in 2017–2019 to 37% in April 2020 (Daly et al., 2020). This study used a very widely used self-report questionnaire, the General Health Questionnaire 12 (GHQ-12). In April 2020 the UK was in full lockdown due to the COVID-19 pandemic, which means that this data was collected in a unique and highly distressing set of circumstances.

I recall my A-level reading

Why not Abnormal Psychology?

↑ This

Typically, textbooks in this area are called *Abnormal Psychology* or *Psychopathology*. There will often be a list of chapters named for different diagnoses. You may be expecting that in this book too. You want to know how different disorders are diagnosed and treated. You want me to get on with what you might see as the real substance of the book.

This approach is variously called the diagnostic or psychiatric model of mental health. From this perspective, the priority when faced with people in distress is to work out what disorder they have based on the difficulties they report, which are defined as **symptoms**. Mental health problems are seen as equivalent to physical diseases and are sometimes called brain diseases or mental disorders (APA, 2013). The **diagnosis** decided on informs the choice of treatment or intervention, as it does with a physical health problem.

There are several reasons why this book takes a different approach. Over the last fifteen years research has seriously called into doubt the diagnostic system around which many books, university courses, and clinical services are structured (Kotov et al., 2017, Caspi et al., 2014, Insel et al., 2010). Those who argue that we need a new approach to classifying and responding to mental health problems come from many different perspectives, and I will discuss these later on in the book.

Then there are the words themselves. The terms **abnormal** or **pathological** imply that the reason for a person's experiences is that they have something wrong with them, and that those who do not have these experiences are '**normal**'. They locate the problem in the person. There is a growing disquiet about the implications of labelling people's experiences as abnormal or pathological and the long-term impact that this may have. Many psychologists say we should be looking to understand the behaviour and experiences of people in their social context, rather than diagnosing them with disorders (Johnstone and Boyle, 2018). Others argue that there is no reason to believe that 'abnormal' psychological processes must be involved when someone has a breakdown in their mental health, and that the same processes of learning and behaviour apply to everyone (Kinderman, 2019).

Another way the word 'abnormal' is understood is as a description of infrequency, the state of being outside the norm. If a person's behaviour is **atypical** or unusual in their community, then the person themselves or their behaviour may be considered to be abnormal, with potential long-term consequences. If we understand the word 'abnormal' in 'Abnormal Psychology' to refer to frequency, then that would indicate that experiencing mental health problems is an atypical experience. In fact, recent research indicates that it may be more common to experience a mental health problem at least once during your life than not (Schaefer et al., 2017). 'Abnormality' also has the disadvantage of defining what most people do as 'normal', by default. In the past, it was normal for women have few opportunities to work outside the home after marriage, and those who pursued professional careers were statistically rare, so those who did could have been considered 'abnormal'. People from minorities due to their culture or sexuality may by default be viewed as outside the norm, simply because they are different. A change in context can lead to someone who was previously seen as normal becoming 'abnormal'. As one example, hearing the voices of angels in a church might well be seen as normal and even desirable whilst hearing voices when in a psychiatric unit will be perceived very differently.

I've referred several times already to the psychiatric model of mental health, but this is a book about psychology. **Psychiatrists** and **psychologists** are often confused by the general public. Psychiatrists are medical doctors who have trained in general medicine and have specialised in mental health through studying **psychiatry**. They are able to prescribe medication and often (but not always) take a diagnostic approach to mental health. **Applied psychologists** are not medical doctors although they often have doctoral degrees and therefore can use the title 'Dr'. They have completed an undergraduate degree in **psychology**, followed by a postgraduate degree in using applied psychology with different groups of people. They specialise in human behaviour, emotions, and thoughts, and often (but not always) seek to understand someone's experience by understanding their psychological processes in the context of their life, rather than by diagnosing them.

Applied psychologists, including clinical, counselling, health, forensic, and sports psychologists, are sometimes called **scientist-practitioners**. They are interested in how people make sense of what happens to them, and how this then affects their lives (Kinderman, 2019). They generally assume that different psychological responses to events can lead to different outcomes (Beck, 1979). In other words, the meaning we make of things which happen to us matters. If we apply this to mental health, then a psychological approach should start with examining the way we make sense of people's behaviours and experiences. We cannot assume that these should inevitably be understood as mental disorders. Figure 1.1 illustrates the basic psychological model which underpins much of the work of applied psychologists working in mental health.

Considering alternatives to the diagnostic model of mental health can be controversial. Those who seek to understand difficulties in a non-medicalised framework are sometimes accused of suggesting that the mental

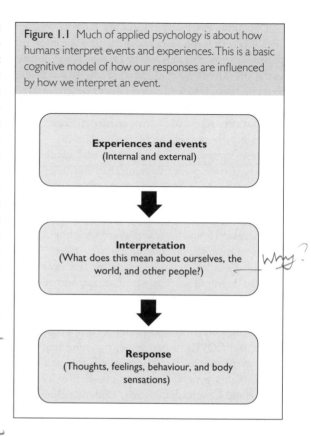

Figure 1.1 Much of applied psychology is about how humans interpret events and experiences. This is a basic cognitive model of how our responses are influenced by how we interpret an event.

Experiences and events
(Internal and external)

Interpretation
(What does this mean about ourselves, the world, and other people?)

why?

Response
(Thoughts, feelings, behaviour, and body sensations)

health problems that people describe don't really exist. The argument is that we *need* to categorise people's experiences and behaviour as illnesses and disorders, because the only alternative is that they will be held responsible and blamed for their experiences. This has been called the 'brain or blame' dichotomy (Boyle, 2013). As an example of this, some psychiatrists argue that finding biological causes for mental health problems is the only way to reduce stigma and shame (Rosenberg, 2017), implying that those who focus on psychological or social causes will inevitably come across as blaming. This is not proven, and others argue that **psychosocial** causes are less stigmatising and naturally make sense to more people (Longden and Read, 2017).

It's important to make clear that questioning how we interpret and respond to mental health problems doesn't mean denying the reality that many people have extremely distressing and disabling experiences. These are real, but this does not have to mean they are best understood as medical disorders. For example, being pregnant is a real (and often difficult) experience which is not a disorder or disease. After bereavement, the distress that people feel is often very intense,

IN THE REAL WORLD 1.1

No More Mualagh

Several years ago, many Afghan refugees were landing in Australia, to an uncertain future and hostile reception. They were interned in rural camps whilst the government decided what to do with them.

In 2005 Multicultural Mental Health Australia started a programme for them called 'No More Mualagh'. Mualagh is a Dari word meaning 'a deep sad feeling like being suspended in the air'. After research in the camps the interventions decided

on were a factsheet in Dari about mental health for the Afghan people, a factsheet about the needs and expectations of the Afghan people for health care providers, and an audio tape in Dari about mental health issues for those who were not literate.

In this way the distress that the refugees felt, interned in these camps with no control over their future, was framed as a treatable mental health problem called depression. Now the refugees had something wrong with them which could be treated, rather than the situation itself being what needed to change (Summerfield, 2012, Pillar, 2011).

but most people would not consider it to be a sign of a medical disorder. The story in the text box about Afghan refugees gives a real-life example. Is the distress felt by these refugees due to a mental disorder?

Language

The language used around mental health is subject to intense debate. This is because the way we talk about things affects how we think about and understand them. The main difference is between those who think that talking about disease and disorder when we think about mental health is useful, and those who think that it is harmful.

In 2013, the Division of Clinical Psychology of the British Psychological Society (BPS) released a position statement, calling for a move away from what they called the psychiatric disease model of mental health. They argued that the language of disease (words such as **disordered**, ill, impairment, and pathological) is unhelpful and increases stigma (BPS, 2013). Many (but not all) applied psychologists take this approach. They avoid using terms such as 'disorder', preferring to use substitutes like 'condition' or 'difficulty'.

Many people, including eminent psychiatrists, argue that by describing the experience of so many as 'disordered' we are restricting what is meant by 'normal'. This has consequences for everyone in our society (Frances, 2013). In the *No More Mualagh* campaign, could we really say that a high **incidence** of sadness and uncertainty whilst interned in a refugee camp means that people are not reacting normally?

Medicalised language infuses mental health practice. We routinely talk of symptoms, illness, and

treatment. When we refer to people who use mental health services as **patients**, we evoke hospitals, wards, and beds as well as a passive rather than active role. Some like the word 'patients' (and indeed, the medical model) because they feel it emphasises that mental health problems should be taken as seriously as physical health problems. Most psychologists and psychotherapists use 'clients' instead, but others protest that this sounds commercialised. In the UK it's common to use 'service users', particularly for those who have more serious mental health problems. There are people who dislike this term as they point out that many people are not choosing to use the system. Many people who have had experience of the mental health system call themselves **survivors** (Davies, 2013). No term suits everyone.

1.2 How are mental health problems classified?

Many people present to mental health services looking for help with overwhelming distress. At other times they are sent or brought by others who have noticed that their behaviour is unusual or troubling—often because it falls outside the norm, or because it poses a risk to themselves or to others. This poses a problem for the health system. How can we decide which difficulties fall into the category of a 'mental health problem' (and therefore require **intervention**) and which are simply a normal reaction to circumstances? This problem is not just one which affects mental health—the physical health system has similar problems. How is it decided when something becomes a problem which requires treatment? One way to do this is through diagnosis.

Diagnosis: Dividing experience into disorders

Mental health services in the UK are usually organised along diagnostic lines, and people who present to services will have an assessment to see which diagnostic category their problems fit into (if they fit into any category at all), and therefore what sort of service would be appropriate. There might be a centre for anxiety disorders, another for depression, and a different service for post-traumatic stress disorder (PTSD). Services are also divided by severity. If someone is diagnosed with a mild disorder, they may be offered guided self-help over the phone or an online therapy programme. For those with the most severe problems there are residential facilities. This process of deciding on the appropriate service can range from a short consultation with a General Practitioner (GP) to a lengthy diagnostic interview with a psychiatrist, psychologist or multi-disciplinary team.

In order to standardise diagnoses, manuals are used. There are two major **diagnostic manuals** used in the NHS. The **Diagnostic and Statistical Manual of Mental Disorders**, Fifth Edition (DSM-5) is published by the American Psychiatric Association (APA), and the **International Classification of Disorders**, Eleventh Edition (ICD-11) is published by the World Health Organization (WHO). Both DSM and ICD take a similar approach. Symptoms are grouped together to describe 'mental disorders'. If a person has enough symptoms and these are thought to be severe enough, then they are given a diagnosis.

Not all diagnoses are done **formally**—that is, by using a structured interview designed to cover all the symptoms listed in the manuals. Many people will be **informally** and relatively quickly diagnosed by a GP or other health professional. This may be done using one of the many brief self-report standardised questionnaires.

Diagnoses are important because they can determine a person's access to services; but they also influence how a person thinks about themselves and how the people around them react to them. Some diagnoses, particularly those of severe and enduring mental health problems, carry **stigma** which can lead to poor access to healthcare, poverty, and homelessness (Henderson, Potts, and Robinson, 2020).

This stigma can be hard to shift, with there being a perception that once a person has a diagnosis of a severe mental health problem, they will have it for life. This can literally be the case, as once a diagnosis is on a person's medical records it is extremely difficult to get it removed.

You can easily find online widely used self-report questionnaires such as the Patient Health Questionnaire (PHQ-9; used to assess depression) and Generalised Anxiety Disorder 7-item scale (GAD-7; used to assess anxiety). Questionnaires such as these are used to decide who should get help and who shouldn't, and what level of support they will receive (Levis et al., 2019). These checklists come with a health warning; if you look them up you may well start to see the symptoms described in yourself and others. It's common for students of psychology to start to see psychological problems all around them. Describing these problems in a particular way makes us more likely to see them through that lens.

The diagnostic system divides behaviours and experiences into groups, the main ones of which are briefly described below. As you'll see, some of these categories describe distress, whilst others describe non-conformity to culturally expected behaviour or unusual experiences. In all cases, the difficulties are not unique to those who receive that diagnosis. They vary on a continuum across the whole population, and when enough difficulties come together and last for long enough, a person reaches the diagnostic threshold.

Depression

Pervasive low mood is perhaps the most common form of distressing experience. Sleep problems, appetite problems, lack of motivation, loss of enjoyment in activities, low energy, and suicidal thoughts are all seen as symptoms of **depression**.

DSM and ICD have slightly different criteria for the diagnosis of depression. In DSM-5, a person must experience five or more symptoms from a list of eight during a two-week period, and one of the symptoms must be either depressed mood or loss of interest and pleasure in life. This means that two people can receive the same diagnosis with very different experiences.

Over 300 million people are said to suffer from depression across the world and depression is said to be the leading cause of disability worldwide (World Health Organization). Many people who go to their doctor in the UK with low mood will be offered an anti-depressant (Iacobucci, 2019). At least 50% of the people who meet diagnostic criteria for depression will also meet criteria for an anxiety disorder (Hirschfeld, 2001).

Anxiety

Anxiety takes many forms, but the common experience is a heightened fear response to a situation which is not objectively dangerous. Uncontrollable worrying, difficulty sleeping, trouble concentrating, feeling irritable, and feeling restless or on edge are defined as symptoms of anxiety disorders.

Anxiety diagnoses range from **phobias** (e.g., fear of bees or spiders) to **panic disorder**, **obsessive–compulsive disorder** (OCD), **social anxiety**, and **post-traumatic stress disorder** (PTSD). Post-traumatic stress disorder is the only diagnosis for which the social context is vital. In order to get this diagnosis someone must have been exposed to a traumatic event. Generalised anxiety disorder (GAD) is the most diagnosed anxiety disorder, with the main symptom being excessive worrying about a range of things.

People who are highly anxious often avoid situations which make them fearful. This reduces the symptoms they experience through limiting their lives. For example, someone with agoraphobia may not experience any anxiety until they try to leave the house, whereupon they have a panic attack, so, they reduce the occasions on which they leave the house. For this reason, assessing the effect of someone's experiences on their life is an important part of assessment—a person may not report feeling anxious because they have severely restricted their life in order to avoid the anxiety.

Anxiety is extremely common, with 8.2 million people meeting criteria for a diagnosis of an anxiety disorder in 2013 in the UK (Fineberg et al., 2013).

Addictions

Drinking alcohol, including heavy drinking, is normal in many cultures—so when does it become a problem? A person, their family, and a doctor may well disagree about what constitutes a problematic use of alcohol. Diagnostic criteria include alcohol causing problems with work or family life, having withdrawal symptoms, and cutting down on other activities in order to drink.

The terminology used in the health service is that of '**substance use**' which covers both drugs and alcohol. Excessive use of substances such as drugs and alcohol can have devastating effects on people's lives.

People can develop a physiological and psychological need for the substance, called an **addiction**. Over time, serious physical and social problems can be caused by use of alcohol and drugs (Fox et al., 2013). The diagnoses given by DSM-5 are those of 'substance use disorders' and they are divided by the type of substance.

Addictions are not only related to substances. Many people have problems with gambling which they cannot control and cannot afford, and which can leave them financially and personally devastated. Recently there has been research interest in the idea of internet or technology addiction (Przybylski, Weinstein, and Murayama, 2017), and 'gaming disorder'—an addiction to video games—was added to the most recent version of ICD.

Eating problems

Problems with eating are wide-ranging, from restricting eating to the point of life-threatening weight loss to over-eating to the point of dangerous weight gain. People who restrict their eating often do not consider themselves to be 'disordered' and in some cases will be admitted to hospital against their will in order to increase their weight. These people will often get diagnoses of **anorexia nervosa**. Online communities sometimes support people in severely restricting their eating, promoting it as a lifestyle choice (Wang et al., 2018).

Eating problems are not restricted to those who have either dangerously low or high weight. **Binge-eating disorder** and **bulimia nervosa** involve eating a large amount of food in a short space of time and feeling a lack of control over the eating. In bulimia, this is followed by what is called 'compensatory behaviour', meaning behaviours to prevent weight gain. This can involve self-induced vomiting, misuse of medications, or excessive exercise.

Sexuality and gender

Psychology and psychiatry have a troubled history with sexuality and gender. It's perhaps the area where it's easiest to see how a society's prejudices can be given legitimacy through labelling a person with a disorder.

Homosexuality was listed in DSM-II (published in 1968) as a mental disorder. People were treated with **conversion therapy**, which attempted to change their sexual orientation. In 1973, the issue of whether homosexuality was a disorder was decided by a vote by the psychiatrists attending the American Psychiatric Association convention. The vote was passed by 5854 votes to 3810, and thus homosexuality was declared to no longer be a reason to consider someone mentally ill.

Gender dysphoria is a diagnosis given to people who feel distress and incongruence with their biological sex. It has been diagnosed in much greater numbers in children and teenagers in the last ten years, with the Gender Identity Development Service (GIDS) at the Tavistock in the UK reporting an increase in referrals from 134 in 2010–2011 to 2565 in 2019–2020. The treatment of these young people has become highly politicised, with advocacy groups arguing that off-label drugs to block puberty and then cross-sex hormones should be given to alleviate psychological distress, whilst others argue that there has not been enough research on the long-term effects of these drugs (Malone et al., 2021). In 2022, an independent review by Dr Hilary Cass into GIDS found that there was a lack of high-quality evidence of the **effectiveness** of using puberty blockers

and cross-sex hormones to treat gender dysphoria in adolescents and the long-term consequences are unknown (Cass, 2022).

Unusual experiences and behaviour

Psychosis is the term used to describe the experience of hearing, believing, or seeing things which other people do not. Traditionally this was contrasted with **neurosis**, which described people in distress who did not show signs of a disconnection with reality. There is now evidence that this division may be artificial (Kelleher and Cannon, 2014). In the language of diagnostic manuals, these experiences are called auditory and visual **hallucinations**, and **paranoid delusions**. Many of these people get diagnoses of **schizophrenia**, **bipolar disorder** (previously called manic depression), or depression with psychotic features if they present to mental health services.

People with psychosis are sometimes said to be 'lacking in **insight**' which means that they do not realise that their experiences are psychological in origin. They may, for example, believe that the

---

CASE STUDY 1.2

Chinwe: Diagnosis in Action

The longer that people remain in mental health services, the more diagnoses they tend to acquire. The next case study is of a woman, Chinwe, who was given several different diagnoses over her time in mental health services. It contains distressing information, including child abuse. As you're reading, think about what each diagnosis means for Chinwe. How are the diagnoses helping or not helping her? What would a 'normal' reaction be to her experiences?

Chinwe was physically and emotionally abused by her father when she was growing up. Then, when she was eighteen she got pregnant by her first boyfriend. Her father was furious and threw her out the house.

She was referred to the psychologist when she was forty. This was not the first time she had had contact with mental health services, as she had had several episodes in the past of being quite unwell. Her daughter, whom she had raised as a single parent, was leaving home and Chinwe had started to get scared about the idea of being alone. She had worked hard to give her daughter a happy childhood. Now that she was leaving Chinwe found herself with lots of time to think.

Chinwe had flashbacks to her father hitting her when she was nine, as well as nightmares and intrusive thoughts. She heard a

male voice telling her that she was bad and dirty and that she deserved to be punished. Sometimes, Chinwe would see dirt everywhere in her house. She would throw away food because she thought it was inedible. She would scrub her hands until they bled.

These experiences felt real to Chinwe. Because of this, she was given a diagnosis of schizophrenia and was prescribed antipsychotics. A doctor in the past had queried whether she might have emotionally unstable personality disorder (EUPD), as she would take scalding hot baths to try to clean the dirt off, which was seen as deliberate self-harm.

As Chinwe talked to the psychologist, she explained that she had previously received a diagnosis of an eating disorder due to her restriction of food. A different psychiatrist had diagnosed her with obsessive-compulsive disorder because of the rituals that she used to keep her food and house clean. She was described as 'complex'.

There was no service which could look at her problems as a whole, and so she was referred to a series of different services, a specialist trauma service, an outpatient clinic for OCD, a therapeutic community for personality disorder, and a community psychiatric team. Chinwe wasn't hopeful that any of this would make any difference.

"Fascinating"

voices they hear come from outside themselves. This puts some people into a conflictual relationship with mental health services. When they say that they do not think they are unwell, this is sometimes seen as a sign of how unwell they are. Promoting insight is often a goal of treatment, despite evidence that those with better insight may suffer from more depression (Murri et al., 2016).

Personality

When people have long-standing and severe difficulties with managing their emotions and relating to others, they may be given the diagnosis of a **personality disorder**. DSM-5 lists ten different specific personality disorders, including borderline personality disorder (BPD, sometimes also called emotionally unstable personality disorder or EUPD), antisocial personality disorder, and narcissistic personality disorder. Borderline personality disorder was given this name because it was originally thought to be on the border between psychosis and neurosis—a distinction which is now no longer used.

Personality disorders are some of the most stigmatised and controversial diagnoses. This is particularly true of the diagnosis of BPD or EUPD, which is frequently given to women who were sexually abused as children. Some psychologists argue that a diagnosis of personality disorder is not a useful way to understand the distress of people who have typically been treated very badly by others over a sustained period of time, as it locates the issue in them rather than in the things which have happened to them (Johnstone, 2022).

Limitations of the diagnostic system

Over the last thirty years evidence has emerged from research and clinical practice that the diagnostic system used by DSM and ICD has serious limitations. People from many different perspectives (including senior psychiatrists, researchers, clinical practitioners, and service users) suggest that the present system of **categorising** mental health problems is not fit for purpose. In particular, they argue that the diagnostic categories do not reflect objective reality. Mental health problems do not fall neatly into diagnostic categories and mental health is better understood as something which varies along **dimensions**, rather than as a set of discrete disorders. Research institutes have expressed concern that using diagnostic categories are holding back progress in research, since they do not reflect real

underlying entities (Insel et al., 2010). Others argue that diagnosing people in distress with disorders isn't the only way to understand their problems (Johnstone and Boyle, 2018, Watson, 2019). These concerns are serious enough that some governments are no longer recommending use of diagnosis. In June 2019, the Belgian Governmental Superior Health Council published a report which recommended the default approach to mental distress and crises in Belgium should be non-problematising and non-medicalising.

The objections fit into three main categories. Firstly, 'disorders' cannot be reliably differentiated from normality. Secondly, 'disorders' cannot be reliably differentiated from each other and do not naturally fall into the categories described in the diagnostic manuals. And lastly, diagnoses are often stigmatising and lead us to focus on biological factors and treatments to the detriment of psychosocial explanations. They take no account of context.

Some of those who would like to rethink the diagnostic system also disagree with the biomedical model of mental health (which I will explain further in Chapter 2), but this is not the case for everyone. The diagnostic system is rooted in a biomedical approach, but diagnosis is not the only way in which mental health can be medicalised. It is possible to take both a dimensional and a biological approach to mental health. An example of this would be the suggestion that we need a biological model of mental health which starts with basic biological processes and the assumption of brain disorder rather than with the behaviour and emotional experiences used in DSM and ICD (Insel, 2015).

Thresholds

When diagnosing a person with a mental health problem, a key question is where to draw the line between what is seen as 'normal' and what is considered to be 'disordered'. In many areas of psychology and psychiatry, deviation from the statistical norm is used to define disorder. However, this means that **qualitative** experiences—emotions and behaviour—have to be turned into **quantitative** measures. Diagnostic manuals solve this problem with symptom lists and structured interviews. They create cut-off lines—if a person has five or more symptoms of depression, then they get a diagnosis. If they have four or less, they do not. However, this can appear to be arbitrary (Johnstone, 2022), and varies over time when diagnostic manuals are rewritten. This makes it hard to compare diagnoses in the present with those in the past, since the criteria have changed. Dr Ginny Russell, a sociologist who researches changing rates of autism diagnosis over time illustrates this with this simile 'Autism is not like a continent awaiting discovery' (Gallagher, 2021). She means that the concept itself is not fixed, it is defined and redefined each time a new diagnostic manual is published. In 2013, the diagnostic criteria for autism changed to include a wider group of people. Diagnostic rates for autism went up by 787% between 1998 and 2018 (Russell et al., 2022), leading Uta Frith, professor of cognitive development at UCL, to say that this suggests that the diagnosis has been stretched to breaking point and outgrown its purpose (Gallagher, 2021). What it means to be diagnosed with autism in the present day is something different to what was meant 20 years ago.

Diagnostic thresholds have always been influenced by culture, time, and place. 'Normality' is generally defined by the more powerful people in a society, leading to the **pathologising** of less powerful groups. Becoming pregnant outside marriage was enough reason for a woman to be pathologised and detained in Ireland until relatively recently (Finnegan, 2004). In 1851, a physician in New Orleans described a 'disorder' which was particular to Black enslaved people which he called 'drapetomania'. The main 'symptom' was that enslaved people persisted in trying to run away from their 'owners' (Cartwright, 1851). 'Normality' therefore was therefore defined as submitting to slavery without trying to escape, something which could only ever be seen as 'normal' from the perspective of a slave-owner.

When researchers look at particular experiences, rather than at diagnostic categories, then 'normality' (or at least the typical range of human experience) seems to be a much wider spectrum that might otherwise be assumed. Experiences which are thought of as symptoms of 'mental disorder' in some contexts exist widely in people who do not consider themselves to be unwell (Baumeister et al., 2017). These include experiences such as hearing voices.

Differentiation

There is a substantial amount of research which finds that the disorders of DSM and ICD do not reflect naturally separate entities (Forbes et al., 2016, Haslam, Holland, and Kuppens, 2012). Borders between diagnoses are hard to define and people with the same diagnosis may have entirely different experiences (Hengartner and Lehmann, 2017). Over 50% of people who qualify

for a diagnosis of one 'mental disorder' also qualify for another (Hirschfeld, 2001, Kessler et al., 2005). This is often called 'co-morbidity', a term meaning that a person has two illnesses at the same time. Some argue that this term is misleading, because it implies that someone has several distinct 'disorders' (Forbes et al., 2016), rather than the diagnostic categories not adequately describing their experiences, or the diagnostic categories having significant overlap.

Researchers in behavioural genetics have found that genetic risk factors for mental health problems are general rather than specific. This means that the same genes are identified as risk factors when people are diagnosed with a range of disorders, including attention deficit hyperactivity disorder (ADHD), bipolar disorder, and schizophrenia. This makes it unlikely that separate genetic causes will be found for different diagnostic categories, again making it harder to claim that the diagnostic boundaries reflect an underlying biological reality (Caspi et al., 2014).

Despite this, diagnoses are widely used in the health service and in research, and different interventions have been successfully developed for those with different diagnoses. It is necessary to have some way of identifying commonalities in people's experience in order to develop new interventions or try out different drugs, and diagnostic categories provide a pragmatic way to do this.

Stigma

In 2001, the World Health Organization wrote 'the single most important barrier to overcome in the community is the stigma and associated discrimination toward persons suffering from mental and behavioural disorder' (WHO, 2001).

Stigma involves the negative stereotyping of people with mental health problems and is widespread, as is prejudice against those who are perceived to be 'mentally ill'. The effects are wide-ranging, with people struggling to get jobs, form relationships, and find safe housing. This means that many people face a double problem—not only do they have distressing experiences, but others are biased against them due to those distressing experiences. Some feel that this stigma is due to negative assumptions about a mental health diagnosis, whilst others argue that this is due to the unusual way in which a person behaves and would be there whether they had a diagnosis or not.

Opinions differ as to how stigma can be best addressed. Many anti-stigma campaigns have focused on educating people in the biomedical model, using the 'illness like any other' model. The underlying assumption of this is if the public would accept that mental health problems were 'real illnesses', stigma would be reduced. However, there is a lack of evidence for long-term behaviour change as a result of these programmes, and there is some evidence of unintended consequences, such as finding that those who accept that people with mental health problems are 'ill' tend to see them as more different to themselves (Johnstone and Foster, 2021).

Context

Diagnostic systems locate the problem inside a person. They identify a person's reactions as disordered, regardless of the circumstances of a person's life. Some clinical psychologists argue that the very act of defining someone's experiences as disordered ignores context and can be actively harmful (Johnstone, 2019, Johnstone and Boyle, 2018).

Social scientists argue that by focusing on diagnosis and treating apparent 'mental disorders', we ignore the problems in society which lead to mental health problems. We instead locate the problem and the solution in individuals (Wilkinson and Pickett, 2018, Marmot, 2015). This is something I will return to in Chapter 2.

1.3 Alternatives to the diagnostic system

The diagnostic system has disadvantages but there are pragmatic reasons why it continues. It provides a way for people to understand their problems, and for professionals to communicate with each other. Most research uses diagnostic categories and these guide professionals when choosing interventions. However, alternatives are actively being developed by researchers, clinicians, and service users.

Dimensional frameworks

One alternative which is increasingly popular with research scientists is to understand mental health problems within a **dimensional framework**. Categorical systems such as diagnosis focus on qualitative differences in order to create distinct groups. Several alternatives have been proposed which use dimensional variation instead (Kotov et al., 2017, Insel et al.,

2010). These are not yet used clinically and have been developed for research purposes. These are discussed in more detail in Chapter 9.

Dimensional models are easy for many people to accept when it comes to depression and anxiety. We recognise that anxiety and mood vary across the whole population, including people who don't reach a diagnostic threshold. However, many believe that this is different from the experiences (such as hearing voices) which are often taken to be symptoms of serious 'mental illness' and therefore something which is outside the range of normal experience (Cooke and Kinderman, 2018).

Research indicates that symptoms such as hearing voices are in fact common in people in the general population (Beavan, Read, and Cartwright, 2011). Other studies have found that nearly one in three people hold beliefs that clinicians might consider paranoid (Bebbington et al., 2013). Isobel Clarke, consultant clinical psychologist and researcher, looks at the intersection between psychosis and spirituality. She argues that psychosis and the experience of spiritual awakening come from the same place, the feeling of being taken out of oneself (Clarke, 2010). At the extreme, this can result in anomalous experiences and losing touch with reality.

Different ways to understand distress

Another alternative to diagnosis is to ask why someone might be feeling and behaving the way that they are, and how their life experiences have affected them.

Eleanor Longden, a research scientist, author, and activist who hears voices, says that the most important question to ask someone in distress shouldn't be 'What's wrong with you?' but instead 'What happened to you?'. You can see her TED talk, *Living with Voices in Your Head* on YouTube. She still hears voices, but she does not consider herself to be mentally ill.

Longden is part of a movement which seeks to redefine many of the experiences which are considered symptoms of 'mental disorder'. The Hearing Voices Network has been active since the first chapter *Stichting Weerklank* was started in the Netherlands in 1987. There are now networks in at least 29 countries. The Hearing Voices Network starts from the perspective that hearing voices is a meaningful experience, and advocates for more involvement of voice-hearers in research (Corstens et al., 2014).

'Drop the Disorder' and 'Mad in America' are examples of organisations which seek a paradigm shift in our understanding of mental distress. Mad in America has a global section, including Mad in Norway, Mad in Sweden, and Mad in the UK. They take a critical approach to the psychiatric model of mental health and promote alternatives. They argue that when we understand someone's story, their experiences and behaviour often make sense (Kinderman, 2019, Bentall, 2009). They point out that some circumstances, for example living with the threat of violence, abuse or in a war zone, it might be more unusual to **not** feel intense distress.

→ ? is why some do/some don't:

A trauma-informed perspective

A **trauma-informed** approach to mental health is one that looks at the experiences a person has had and how they have had to adjust. Imagine an adult who comes to mental health services and describes a deep anxiety around other people, so extreme that they avoid all social contact and hardly leave the house. From a diagnostic perspective, this behaviour could be seen as a symptom and a diagnosis such as social anxiety or agoraphobia might be given.

In a trauma-informed assessment, the person would be asked about their earlier experiences. We might discover that they were severely bullied as a child, and found that withdrawing from other people was the best way to avoid being hurt. They became **hypervigilant** in order to keep themselves safe. As an adult, they still jump at the slightest noise and find their heart pounding when they have to talk to another person. Their body continues to respond as if it is in imminent danger. A trauma-informed approach sees these reactions as the body's natural **survival response**, triggered too easily due to previous experiences (Fisher, 2017).

Many of the people who come to mental health services in the UK have had traumatic things happen to them. They include refugees who have fled war zones, those who were abused as children, military veterans, and people who have experienced oppression and discrimination. Every event such as the terrorist attacks in cities across the world results in an increase in referrals to mental health services. New services are set up to cope with demand, as with the 2017 Grenfell Tower disaster in West London (Adhyaru, 2018).

Research shows that childhood **adversity** is associated with a higher chance of developing serious mental health difficulties in adulthood (Read et al., 2014, Varese et al., 2012). Experiencing childhood sexual abuse appears to increase the risk of later psychotic problems by 15-fold (Bebbington et al., 2013). Peter Kinderman, Professor of Clinical Psychology at Liverpool University points out that this order of magnitude is comparable to the increased risk of lung cancer afflicting smokers (Kinderman, 2019).

Seeing distress in context

Trauma is one thing, but less newsworthy events such as relationship breakdown, bullying, bereavement, or losing a job also cause human misery. Alongside these are chronic stressors such as poverty, discrimination, work instability, illness, and disability.

In 2020, the outbreak of COVID-19 was at the forefront of everyone's minds. Many people reported difficulty sleeping, high anxiety and low mood, and a preoccupation with hand-washing and hygiene. Overnight, avoiding social contact and isolating yourself at home went from being symptoms of mental disorders to the actions of responsible citizens. People across the world were put on lockdown and were told to stay at home. Many lost their jobs or were unable to work. Schools closed and children were not allowed to play with each other.

It would be surprising if this huge change in people's lives did not affect their emotional and psychological experiences, and there is evidence that it did so (Bonati et al., 2022). Many people started to experience distress, and the media responded with articles about a 'second pandemic' of mental health problems. It is clear that more people have experienced and reported distress during the pandemic, and also that the isolation and difficulties in accessing services have made the situation worse for many people who already had mental health problems. However, we might reasonably ask what constitutes a normal psychological response to a global pandemic, and whether being distressed in these circumstances is a sign of disorder or pathology.

Coping mechanisms

Many of the behaviours which are labelled as symptoms can also be seen as **coping mechanisms**. Difficulties in emotion regulation underlie many mental health problems. People find it hard to regain their emotional equilibrium, and so develop a set of ways to manage their emotions. These coping mechanisms might include drinking, taking drugs, avoiding stressful situations, self-harm, and withdrawing socially. In the short term these strategies work but in the long term they cause other problems (Moorey, 2010).

Seeing behaviour as a coping mechanism means that we can see unusual behaviour as a logical response to difficult experiences. A person might rock themselves whilst banging their head on the wall to provide sensory stimulation in order to calm themselves, whilst someone else might cover their ears or hide under the bed because they are very sensitive to noise. Seeing behaviour as a response to experience means that an intervention can be targeted more appropriately. For example, if someone is rocking themselves as a calming strategy, they could be offered other ways to calm themselves which do not involve head banging (and therefore harm), or their environment could be changed so they do not get so aroused.

This approach can be particularly useful when thinking about people who have had very difficult experiences in the past. An abused child might, for example, learn to cut off from their feelings and what is happening to them because they have no other way to escape. In adulthood, they continue to use this strategy even though they are now out of the abusive situation. They 'zone out' or dissociate from experiences in their daily life. What started out as a coping mechanism has become the problem.

Culturally sanctioned expressions of distress

There is evidence that different cultures express their distress in different ways. When I worked in a central London service for people with traumatic stress, it was recognised among clinicians that people from some countries expressed their distress in physical terms. At the time we saw many refugees from Albania who had gone through terrible war-time experiences. They often presented with severe disabling headaches rather than (or in addition to) the symptoms we would usually recognise as post-traumatic stress disorder. It seems that in some cultures, distress is more likely to be expressed physically. *and some people*

Medical historian Edward Shorter (Shorter, 1997) described the powerful role that culture can play in the way that distress is expressed. This also applies to physical health, where culture has been shown to affect both symptoms and how medical doctors respond to physical health problems (Payer, 1996). Shorter uses the metaphor of the '**symptom pool**'. He argues that each culture has a metaphorical pool of culturally acceptable symptoms from which people in that society will draw to express their distress. This process is mostly not a conscious one, and the symptom pool can change over time (Davies, 2013). Ethan Watters tracked how features of anorexia nervosa became part of the symptom pool in Hong Kong following widespread media coverage of the death of a young girl from an eating disorder. Prior to this event anorexia nervosa was very rare in Hong Kong, but prevalence levels quickly rose until they were comparable to other developed countries. The rapid rise in gender dysphoria in the last ten years could also be seen as a change in the symptom pool, meaning that young people who might in previous generations have expressed their distress in other ways currently do so through gender.

One implication of this is that campaigns which purport to be raising mental health awareness may change the way that people in that society experience and express distress through changing the symptom pool (Watters, 2011). This doesn't signify that this distress is not real, it simply indicates that people are highly complex and influenced by the culture around them.

1.4 What about Ana?

Let's come back to Ana, with whom I started the chapter.

That evening Ana met up with a friend, and the friend asked her what was going on in her life. Ana told her that she'd just split up with her boyfriend, that she was struggling at work, and she felt overwhelmed. The friend listened, said she'd gone through something similar recently and had felt terrible for a while. They discussed how Ana might improve her situation at work, and how the boyfriend clearly hadn't properly appreciated her. Her friend suggested they met up the next day to go running together and to chat.

Ana decided to get her prescription but to delay starting the anti-depressants for a while as she recovered from the breakup. She also decided to talk to her boss at work about her workload and to spend some more time with her friends and see how that went.

Ana still felt very low, but she felt she had made sense of why that might be and felt hopeful that things might change.

Chapter Summary

- Talking about mental health requires that we think carefully about language and about the way in which we conceptualise distress.

- Mental health problems are usually defined by reference to the diagnostic or psychiatric model. This is widely used in the health service and in research.

- There is growing consensus that there are scientific and clinical limitations to the diagnostic approach.

- Research scientists have found that the categories in diagnostic manuals do not reflect underlying biological or genetic categories, and have proposed dimensional models as an alternative.

- Some service user movements and clinicians say that the diagnostic system is pathologising and leads us to focus unhelpfully on individual disorders, at the expense of considering societal and contextual factors.

- The psychiatric diagnostic model is widely used and well accepted, meaning that any attempt to think differently is often seen as controversial and is framed as denying the severity of people's experiences.

? QUESTIONS

1. What are some of the ways to define who has a mental health problem? Explain the advantages and disadvantages of different approaches.

2. What are the reasons why some psychologists do not use the terms 'psychopathology', 'abnormal psychology' and 'normality'?

3. What are the DSM and ICD? What are the advantages and disadvantages of the diagnostic system for psychologists?

4. Look at the websites for several different mental health organisations. You could start with the Hearing Voices Network, Mind, Drop the Disorder, Mental Health UK, Mad in America, the Royal College of Psychiatrists, and the British Psychological Society. How do they talk about mental health? What language do they use? What are the differences between them and why do you think these differences exist?

5. Explain and contrast several different ways of understanding and explaining a person's distress. You could include diagnosis, the symptom pool, coping mechanisms, and a trauma-informed perspective.

FURTHER READING

Bentall, R. (2009). *Doctoring the Mind: Why Psychiatric Treatments Fail.* London: Allen Lane.

This book is by a clinical psychologist who works with people with severe and enduring mental health problems. He gives an overview of psychiatry and argues that we need a new way to think about mental health.

Foulkes, L. (2021). *Losing Our Minds: What Mental Illness Really Is … And What It Isn't.* New York: Vintage.

This brings together the author's (an academic psychologist) own experience of mental health problems with a look at our changing understanding of mental health over time.

Frances, A. (2013). *Saving Normal, An Insider's Revolt Against Out-of-Control Psychiatric Diagnosis.* New York: William Morrow & Company.

This account by the psychiatrist who led the taskforce for DSM-IV argues that psychiatric diagnoses have become over-inclusive but still have utility when properly applied.

Watters, E. (2011). *Crazy Like Us: The Globalization of the Western Mind*. New York: Robinson Publishing.

This book looks at the spread of Western ideas about mental health through a series of case examples in different countries.

REFERENCES

Adhyaru, J.S. (2018). *Trauma Therapies for Grenfell Survivors, Grenfell Health and Wellbeing Services*. Presentation. Retrieved 14 November 2019. https://www.rcpsych.ac.uk/docs/default-source/improving-care/ccqi/quality-networks/psychological-therapy-appts/2-trauma-therapies-for-grenfell-survivors.pdf?sfvrsn=934a4f0c_4

American Psychiatric Association (2013). *Diagnostic and Statistical Manual of Mental Disorders: Fifth Edition*. Arlington, VA: American Psychiatric Association.

Baumeister, D., Sedgwick, O., Howes, O., and Peters, E. (2017). Auditory verbal hallucinations and continuum models of psychosis: A systematic review of the healthy voice-hearer literature. *Clinical Psychological Review*, 51, 125–141.

Beavan, V., Read, J., and Cartwright, C. (2011). The prevalence of voice-hearers in the general population: A literature review. *Journal of Mental Health*, 20, 281–292.

Bebbington, P.E., McBride, O., Steel, C., Kuipers, E., Radovanovic, M., Brugha, T., and Freeman, D. (2013). The structure of paranoia in the general population. *British Journal of Psychiatry*, 202, 419–427.

Beck, A.T., Rush, A.J., Shaw, B.F., and Emery, G. (1979). *Cognitive therapy of depression*. New York: Guilford Press.

Bentall, R. (2009). *Doctoring the Mind: Why Psychiatric Treatments Fail*. London: Allen Lane.

Bonati, M., Campi, R., and Segre, G. (2022). Psychological impact of the quarantine during the COVID-19 pandemic on the general European adult population: A systematic review of the evidence. *Epidemiology and Psychiatric Sciences*, 31, E27. doi:10.1017/S2045796022000051

Boyle, M. (2013). The persistence of medicalisation: Is the presentation of alternatives part of the problem? In S. Coles, S. Keenan, and B. Diamond (eds), *Madness contested: Power and practice*. Ross-on-Wye, UK: PCCS Books, pp. 3–22.

British Psychological Society (2013). *Division of Clinical Psychology Position Statement*. doi:10.53841/bpsrep.2013.inf212

Cartwright, S.A. (1851). Report of the diseases and physical peculiarities of the Negro race. *The New Orleans Medical and Surgical Journal*, May, 691–715.

Caspi, A., Houts, R.M., Belsky, D.W., et al. (2014). The p Factor: One general psychopathology factor in the structure of psychiatric disorders? *Clinical Psychological Science*, 2(2), 119–137. doi:10.1177/2167702613497473

Caspi, A., Houts, R.M., Amber, A., Danese, A., Elliott, M., Hariri, A., Harrington, H., Hogan, S., Pouton, R., Ramrakha, S., et al. (2020). Longitudinal assessment of mental health difficulties and comorbidities across 4 decades among participants in the Dunedin birth cohort study. *JAMA Network Open*, 3(4): e203221. doi:10.1001/jamanetworkopen.2020.3221

Cass, H. (2022). *Independent Review of Gender Identity Services for Children and Young People*. NHS England. https://www.england.nhs.uk/commissioning/spec-services/npc-crg/gender-dysphoria-clinical-programme/implementing-advice-from-the-cass-review/independent-review-into-gender-identity-services-for-children-and-young-people/

Clarke, I. (ed.) (2010). *Psychosis and Spirituality*, Second Edition. Oxford: Wiley.

Cooke, A., and Kinderman, P. (2018). 'But what about real mental illness?' Alternatives to the disease model approach in 'schizophrenia'. *Journal of Humanistic Psychology*, 58(1), 47–71.

Corstens, D., Longden, E., McCarthy-Jones, S., Waddingham, R., and Thomas, N. (2014). Emerging perspectives from the hearing voices movement: Implications for research and practice. *Schizophrenia Bulletin*, 40, S285–S294. doi:10.1093/schbul/sbu007

Davies, J. (2013). *Cracked: Why Psychiatry is Doing more Harm than Good*. London: Icon Books.

Daly, M., Sutin, A.R., and Robinson, E. (2020). Longitudinal changes in mental health and the COVID-19 pandemic: Evidence from the UK Household Longitudinal Study. *Psychological Medicine*, 2020, 13 October, 1–10. doi:10.1017/S0033291720004432

Fineberg, N., Haddad, P., Carpenter, L., Gannon, B., Sharpe, R., Young, A., Joyce, E., Rowe, J., Wellsted, D., Nutt, D., and Sahakian, B. (2013). The size, burden and cost of disorders of the brain in the UK. *Journal of Psychopharmacology*, 27(9), 761–770.

Finnegan, F. (2004). *Do Penance or Perish: Magdalen Asylums in Ireland*. Oxford: Oxford University Press.

Fisher, J. (2017). *Healing the Fragmented Selves of Trauma Survivors: Overcoming Internal Self-Alienation*. New York: Routledge.

Forbes, M.K., Tackett, J.L., Markon, K.E., and Krueger, R.F. (2016). Beyond comorbidity: Toward a dimensional and hierarchical approach to understanding psychopathology across the life span. *Development and Psychopathology*, 28(4pt1), 971–986. doi:10.1017/S0954579416000651

Foulkes, L. (2021). *Losing Our Minds: What Mental Illness Really Is ... And What It Isn't*. New York: Vintage.

Fox, T.P., Oliver, G., and Ellis, S.M. (2013). The destructive capacity of drug abuse: An overview exploring the harmful potential of drug abuse both to the individual and to society. *ISRN Addiction*, 2013, 450348. doi:10.1155/2013/450348

Frances, A. (2013). *Saving Normal: An Insider's Revolt Against Out-of-Control Psychiatric Diagnosis*. New York: William Morrow & Company.

Gallagher, P. (2021). Autism Diagnosis 'stretched to breaking point' with numbers jumping 20-fold over last two decades. *iNews*. Retrieved 13 October 2021. https://inews.co.uk/news/health/autism-diagnosis-figures-stretched-breaking-point-increase-1219876

Haslam, N., Holland, E., and Kuppens, P. (2012). Categories versus dimensions in personality and psychopathology: A quantitative review of taxometric research. *Psychological Medicine*, May, 42(5), 903–920.

Hengartner, M.P., and Lehmann, S.N. (2017). Why psychiatric research must abandon traditional diagnostic classification and adopt a fully dimensional scope: Two solutions to a persistent problem. *Frontiers of Psychiatry*, 8, 101.

Henderson, C., Potts, L., and Robinson, E. (2020). Mental illness stigma after a decade of Time to Change England: Inequalities as targets for further improvement. *European Journal of Public Health*, 30(3), 497–503. doi:10.1093/eurpub/ckaa013

Hirschfeld, R.M. (2001). The comorbidity of major depression and anxiety disorders: Recognition and management in primary care. *Primary Care Companion to the Journal of Clinical Psychiatry*, 3(6), 244–254.

Iacobucci, G. (2019). NHS prescribed record number of antidepressants last year. *BMJ*, 364, l508.

Insel, T., Cuthbert, B., Garvey, M., Heinssen, R., Pine, D.S., Quinn, K., and Wang, P. (2010). Research domain criteria (RDoC): Toward a new classification framework for research on mental disorders. *American Journal of Psychiatry*, 167(7), 748–751.

Insel, T. (2015). Psychiatry is reinventing itself thanks to advances in biology. *New Scientist*. Retrieved 19 August 2015. https://www.newscientist.com/article/mg22730353-000-psychiatry-is-reinventing-itself-thanks-to-advances-in-biology/

Johnstone, L. (2022). *A Straight Talking Introduction to Psychiatric Diagnosis*, Second Edition. Monmouth: PCCS Books.

Johnstone, L. (2019). Do you still need your psychiatric diagnosis? Critiques and alternatives. In J. Watson (ed.), *Drop the Disorder.* Monmouth: PCCS Books.

Johnstone, L. and Boyle, M., with Cromby, J., Dillon, J., Harper, D., Kinderman, P., Longden, E., Pilgrim, D., and Read, J. (2018). *The Power Threat Meaning Framework: Overview.* Leicester: British Psychological Society.

Kelleher, I., and Cannon, M. (2014). Whither the psychosis–neurosis borderline. *Schizophrenia Bulletin*, 40(2), 266–268. doi:10.1093/schbul/sbt230

Kessler, R.C., Berglund, P., Demler, O., Jin, R., Merikangas, K.R., and Walters, E.E. (2005). Lifetime prevalence and age-of-onset distributions of DSM-IV disorders in the National Comorbidity Survey Replication. *Archives of General Psychiatry*, 62(6), 593–602. doi:10.1001/archpsyc.62.6.593

Kinderman, P. (2019). *A Manifesto for Mental Health. Why We Need a Revolution in Mental Health Care.* New York: Palgrave Macmillan.

Kotov, R., Krueger, R.F., Watson, D., Achenbach, T.M., et al. (2017). The Hierarchical Taxonomy of Psychopathology (HiTOP): A dimensional alternative to traditional nosologies. *Journal of Abnormal Psychology*, 126(4), 454–477. doi:10.1037/abn0000258

Levis, B., Benedetti, A., and Thombs, B.D. (2019). Accuracy of Patient Health Questionnaire-9 (PHQ-9) for screening to detect major depression: Individual participant data meta-analysis. *BMJ*, 365, l1476.

Longden, E., and Read, J. (2017). 'People with problems, not patients with illnesses': Using psychosocial frameworks to reduce the stigma of psychosis. *The Israel Journal of Psychiatry and Related Sciences*, 54(1), 24–28.

Malone, W., D'Angelo, R., Beck, S., Mason, J., and Evans, M. (2021). Puberty blockers for gender dysphoria: The science is far from settled. *The Lancet Child & Adolescent Health*, 5(9), e33–e34.

Marmot, M. (2015). *The Health Gap: The Challenge of an Unequal World.* London, Bloomsbury Publishing PLC.

McManus, S., Bebbington, P., Jenkins, R., and Brugha, T. (eds) (2016). *Mental Health and Wellbeing in England: Adult Psychiatric Morbidity Survey 2014.* Leeds: NHS Digital.

McManus, S., Bebbington, P.E., Jenkins, R., Morgan, Z., Brown, L., Collinson, C., and Brugha, T. (2020). Data resource profile: Adult Psychiatric Morbidity Survey (APMS). *International Journal of Epidemiology*, 49(2), 361–362e. doi:10.1093/ije/dyz224

Moorey, S. (2010). The six cycles maintenance model: Growing a 'vicious flower' for depression. *Behavioural and Cognitive Psychotherapy*, 38(2), 173–184. doi:10.1017/S1352465809990580

Murri, M., Amore, M., Calcagno, P., et al. (2016). The 'Insight Paradox' in schizophrenia: Magnitude, moderators and mediators of the association between insight and depression. *Schizophrenia Bulletin*, 42(5). doi:10.1093/schbul/sbw040

Payer, L. (1996). *Medicine and Culture.* New York, Holt McDougal.

Pillar, I. (2011). *Intercultural Communication, A Critical Introduction.* Edinburgh: Edinburgh University Press.

Przybylski, A.K., Weinstein, N., and Murayama, K. (2017). Internet gaming disorder: Investigating the clinical relevance of a new phenomenon. *American Journal of Psychiatry*, 174, 230–236.

Read, J., Fosse, R., Moskowitz, A., and Perry, B. (2014). The traumagenic neurodevelopmental model of psychosis revisited. *Neuropsychiatry*, 4(10), 65–79.

Rosenberg, D. (2017). How seeing problems in the brain makes stigma disappear. *The Conversation.* https://theconversation.com/how-seeing-problems-in-the-brain-makes-stigma-disappear-83946

Russell, G., Stapley, S., Newlove-Delgado, T., Salmon, A., White, R., Warren, F., . . . Ford, T. (2022). Time trends in autism diagnosis over 20 years: A UK population-based cohort study. *Journal of Child Psychology and Psychiatry*, 63(6), 674–682.

Schaefer, J.D., Caspi, A., Belsky, D.W., Harrington, H., Houts, R., Horwood, L.J., Hussong, A., Ramrakha, S., Pouton, R., and Moffitt, T.E. (2017). Enduring mental health: Prevalence and prediction. *Journal of Abnormal Psychology*, 126, 212–224.

Shorter, E. (1997). *A History of Psychiatry: From the Era of the Asylum to the Age of Prozac*. New York: Wiley.

Summerfield, D. (2012). Afterword: Against 'global mental health'. *Transcultural Psychiatry*, 49(3–4), 519–530.

Varese, F., Smeets, F., Drukker, M., et al. (2012). Childhood adversities increase the risk of psychosis: A meta-analysis of patient-control, prospective- and cross-sectional cohort studies. *Schizophrenia Bulletin*, 38(4), 661–671.

Wang, T., Brede, M., Ianni, A., and Mentzakis, E. (2018). Social interactions in online eating disorder communities: A network perspective. *PloS ONE*, 13(7), 0200800.

Watters, E. (2011). *Crazy Like Us: The Globalization of the Western mind*. New York: Robinson Publishing.

Watson, J. (ed.) (2019). *Drop the Disorder: Challenging the Culture of Psychiatric Diagnosis*. Monmouth: PCCS Books.

Walsh, D., and Foster, J. (2021). A call to action. A critical review of mental health related anti-stigma campaigns. *Frontiers of Public Health*, 8 January, 569539. doi:10.3389/fpubh.2020.569539

Wilkinson, R., and Pickett, K. (2018). *The Inner Level: How More Equal Societies Reduce Stress, Restore Sanity and Improve Everyone's Wellbeing*. London: Allen Lane.

World Health Organization (2001). *Mental Health: New Understanding, New Hope*. Geneva: World Health Organization.

Chapter 2
Conceptualising Mental Health

Learning objectives

When you have completed this chapter, you should be able to do the following:

2.1 Explain what a model of mental health is and the purpose of a theoretical model.

2.2 Describe how the issues currently understood as 'mental health' were approached before the advent of modern psychiatry and psychology.

2.3 Outline the assumptions underpinning the biomedical model.

2.4 Explain how the biopsychosocial and stress–diathesis models are different and similar to the biomedical model.

2.5 Compare different psychological models of mental health.

2.6 Explain what is meant by a social or sociocultural model of mental health.

2.7 Contrast multi-level interactional models with other models of mental health.

2.8 Evaluate the wider implications of the different models of mental health.

Introduction

When seeking to understanding mental health, we construct theories as to what is going on. These theories are called **models**. Models are not always stated explicitly, but they underpin all conversations about mental health. Interventions and research are planned based on the model which clinicians and researchers use, which means that these models affect the reality of people's lives.

In this chapter you will be introduced to some of the different theories and models that are used to understand distress. You will read about some of the different ways in which mental distress has been conceptualised throughout history and in the present day. We will start with the biomedical model and will then cover the biopsychosocial and stress–diathesis model. There will be a discussion of psychological, social and socio-cultural models of understanding mental distress. Each model has advantages, and each can be criticised. These models are not necessarily in opposition to each other, although some do rest on very different and contradictory assumptions. Many psychologists will take an integrated approach, drawing on a range of models when appropriate.

Before you start, read the case study that follows. How do the different people involved conceptualise Penny's problems and how does it affect the interventions they offer?

CASE STUDY 2.1

Penny's Story

Penny was referred by her GP to her local trauma service. The letter was brief. It explained that she had post-traumatic stress disorder and needed cognitive behaviour therapy.

When Penny came to the clinic she started crying the moment she saw the psychologist. She told the psychologist that she was jumpy all the time and could never relax. She had very poor sleep and had nightmares of being chased. She had been assaulted as a teenager by an older cousin and experienced flashbacks whenever she saw a man who looked like him.

The GP had already prescribed Mirtazapine (an anti-depressant) which Penny was taking. She said this made some difference, but she was still very distressed. The psychologist formulated her problems as a post-traumatic response to the assault, and planned a course of cognitive behaviour therapy, starting with

treating her low mood and then moving onto trauma-focused work.

Three sessions in, Penny came in more distressed than usual. She told the psychologist that she had not had enough to eat for several days, and that her husband was restricting her food to punish her for not being a good wife. It emerged that after her assault she had quickly married an older man, who had been physically and emotionally abusive to her ever since. He had brought her to the appointment and was currently sitting in the waiting room. She had no work and no income of her own. She was too scared to leave, particularly since they had a three-year-old daughter and she was frightened that she would lose her.

'Please help me' she said. 'I don't want to feel like this anymore, I want therapy to stop me having nightmares. Or is there another medicine that will help me?'.

Keep Penny's story in mind as you read this chapter. What do the different models offer her?

2.1 What is a theoretical model?

Models are theories with explanatory and predictive power. They are used to plan interventions and research, and to justify how people are treated. The **biomedical model** is the dominant model currently used in services in the UK and USA. This is reflected in the dominance of medication as the frontline treatment. Various psychological, social, and socio-cultural models also exist, and these offer explanations on a different level.

It is not always obvious that a particular explanation is a model, rather than simply fact, because they are often presented as 'just the way something is'. The biomedical model is particularly prone to this, with people in mental health services often being told with certainty that their experiences are due to an illness, rather than being offered this explanation as one possible theory out of several.

The model we use to understand a person's problems has serious implications. If a person is understood to be possessed by demons, for example, then it is logical to perform an exorcism. If they are thought to be physically ill, then medication or surgery might be offered or even insisted on. If problems are seen

as primarily psychological in origin, people may feel pressured to undergo psychological therapy even if they do not want to talk to a professional, and sometimes psychological therapy is made a condition of a court order. When one model is presented as truth, or when professionals only see things from one perspective, people are not able to choose for themselves how to think about their problems, but instead have a meaning imposed on them by others (Johnstone and Boyle, 2018). This is one of the reasons why psychologists try to remain open-minded and curious about the origin and meaning of a person's difficulties.

2.2 Distress and unusual behaviour before psychiatry and psychology

Unusual behaviours and experiences are not new phenomena. We have accounts dating back thousands of years describing people whose behaviour and experiences were unusual. '**Madness**' is referred to in the Bible as a curse whilst the ancient Greeks and Romans described melancholia, mania, hysteria, and people hearing voices.

For most of human history unusual behaviour was probably explained by supernatural forces. This explanation could make people the object of fear or veneration, with some people being labelled as witches and subject to cruel punishments whilst others were thought to have supernatural powers of healing. When distress was viewed as a moral failing or as a sign of demonic possession, religion was often considered to be the appropriate intervention, with distressed people being subject to exorcisms or prayer.

2.3   The biomedical model

The biomedical model understands unusual experiences and behaviours as the result of a biological disorder or disease. The current dominant form of this model is the psychiatric diagnostic system. This seeks to categorise experiences into disorders, diagnosable through their 'symptoms'.

The modern diagnostic conceptual system can be traced back to 1883, when the German psychiatrist Emil Kraepelin (1856–1926) published his *Compendium of Psychiatry*. His ground-breaking innovation was to group symptoms by patterns, which he believed to be related to underlying clinical disorders.

Kraepelin's system had three key assumptions. These were that mental health problems were congenital (i.e., genetic in origin), that they could be divided into separate naturally occurring **categories**, and that they were fixed and would get worse over time (Pilgrim, Kinderman and Tai, 2008). His ideas were enormously influential, and he is considered by many to be the founder of scientific psychiatry. Modern-day diagnostic manuals continue to group symptoms by patterns, and then to assume that this defines an underlying medical disorder. These assumptions have shaped how people in distress have been treated throughout the twentieth and into the twenty-first centuries.

Working from a premise of biological disorder meant that it was logical to try physical interventions in search of a cure. On this basis, doctors in the early 20th century attempted to cure people with invasive and frequently dangerous treatments. One particularly brutal neurosurgical treatment, the leucotomy, was instigated in 1935 by a Portuguese neurologist, Egas Moniz (1874–1955). This involved deliberately damaging the frontal lobes of the brain. He reported good results in decreasing negative thoughts. Two Americans, Walter Freeman and James Watts, developed a quicker and easier (for the surgeon) alternative. This they called the **lobotomy**, and they carried it out in fifteen minutes without an operating theatre. They used a tool somewhat like an ice pick and severed

the nerve fibres in the frontal lobes through the eye sockets. The results of lobotomy were unpredictable. Some people became incontinent and lost their ability to speak. Rosemary Kennedy, sister of the American president John F Kennedy, was one of these unfortunate people (Kessler, 1996). By 1951, 18,601 people had had lobotomies in the USA (Davidson et al., 2015) and Moniz was awarded the Nobel Prize for his invention. There are people still alive today who had this procedure and who have written about their experiences. One such is Howard Dully, operated on in 1960 aged twelve (Dully and Fleming, 2008).

In this context of these unpredictable interventions, modern psychiatric medications started to appear and offered a less invasive alternative. Lithium was introduced for bipolar affective disorder in 1949. **Anti-psychotics** appeared in the early 1950s and first-generation anti-depressants (the tricyclics) in 1956. Second generation anti-psychotics have now largely but not entirely replaced the early drugs as they have more tolerable side-effects. **Selective serotonin reuptake inhibitors** (**SSRIs**) have mostly replaced the earlier tricyclic anti-depressants.

Prescriptions for these drugs have risen steadily ever since. A study looking at trends between 1998 and 2010 found that prescriptions for **anti-depressants** went up by 10% each year, whilst anti-psychotic prescriptions increased by 5.1% each year (Ilyas and Moncrieff, 2012). More than 70 million prescriptions for anti-depressants were given out by the NHS in 2018, almost double the number than in 2008 (Iacobucci, 2019).

Drug-centred and disease-centred models

The emergence of these drugs have themselves had an impact on how people think about mental health. If the drugs have a particular effect on **neurotransmitters** such as serotonin and that relieves people's symptoms, went the logic, perhaps those drugs were correcting an imbalance of neurotransmitters in the brain. This is called the **'chemical imbalance' theory** (or model) and has been widely promoted by pharmaceutical companies (Bentall, 2009). Recent reviews have found no evidence of an association between the neurotransmitter serotonin and depression (Moncrieff et al., 2022).

Joanna Moncrieff, consultant psychiatrist and senior researcher at UCL, distinguishes two ways of thinking about drugs and mental health. In a **disease-centred model**, people are assumed to have a brain disorder which drugs rectify. Alternatively, a **drug-centred model** sees the drugs as chemical substances which affect the way people think and feel, and which may or may not be helpful. For example, taking caffeine makes many people feel more alert, but lack of alertness is not thought to be due to an imbalance in caffeine. In a drug-centred model, the drugs are not seen as healing a disease. The disease-centred model is far more prevalent in mental health and is reflected in the names of the commonly used drugs. The names 'anti-depressants' and 'anti-psychotics' contain within them the assumption that the drugs are correcting a disorder.

2.4 The biopsychosocial and stress–diathesis models

A concern that a focus on biology alone was not leading to effective treatment led to the development of new models which put biology alongside social and psychological factors. Two frameworks for this are the **biopsychosocial** and the **stress–diathesis models**.

The biopsychosocial model

Frustrated by what he saw as a reductionist focus on molecular biology in health, in 1977 psychiatrist George Engel proposed what he called 'a new medical model', the highly influential biopsychosocial model (see Figure 2.1). This did not just apply to mental health. In fact, Engel's early papers applied the biopsychosocial model to diabetes.

Engel proposed that all health problems needed to be understood as a combination of biological, psychological, and social factors. He suggested that doctors should see their patients as part of the wider social system, as well as focusing on treating their disease. He emphasised the importance of how clinicians relate to their patients (Engel, 1977; Engel, 1980). The biopsychosocial model was not intended as a replacement for diagnosis. Engel saw it as a widening of the

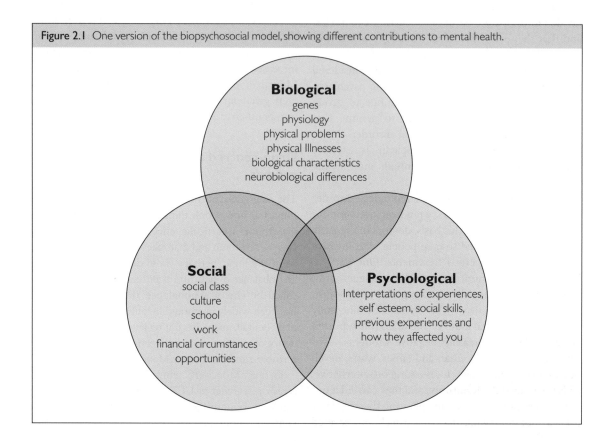

Figure 2.1 One version of the biopsychosocial model, showing different contributions to mental health.

perspective of the doctor and as an antithesis to biological **reductionism**.

The biopsychosocial model is incorporated into medical training and many believe that it is now the overarching framework in contemporary healthcare (Bolton and Gillett, 2019). It is widely used in mental health. It recognises that mental health is the result of many different factors which can all affect outcome, and suggests that focusing on any one of these to the exclusion of the others will limit effectiveness.

The biopsychosocial model has been criticised for its lack of specificity and content. Ghaemi (2009) describes it as 'mere eclecticism'. Some use it as a model of causation, whilst others use it to conceptualise how a person's experience of any health problem will always be affected by psychological and social factors as well as biology. Essentially, anyone can claim to be taking a biopsychosocial approach if they refer to anything about a person which is outside the realms of molecular biology. For example, a health professional might refer to psychology and social factors to explain why someone has developed depression, but then plan their interventions on an entirely biological level. This has led some to argue that the biopsychosocial model can be used as rhetoric to hide a fundamentally biological understanding of mental health (Read et al., 2009). Interactions between the different domains are not explicitly included in the model, meaning that these can be treated as if they are separate rather than integrated.

The stress–diathesis model

Any model of mental health needs to explain why some people develop mental health problems and others don't, even when they have had the same experiences. Some people seem to be resilient to life events, whilst others are less so, and it's not always obvious what makes the difference. One solution to this conundrum is the stress–diathesis model.

The **stress–diathesis** (also called the stress–vulnerability) model was first proposed to explain the onset of schizophrenia (Rosenthal, 1963) and has since been expanded to many other mental health problems including suicidality and depression (Colodro-Conde et al., 2018). This model provides a framework to look closely at the interactions between a person and their environment and is outlined in Figure 2.2. The central idea is that the effects of life stress on mental health

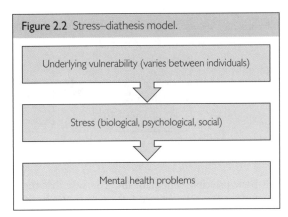

Figure 2.2 Stress–diathesis model.

Underlying vulnerability (varies between individuals)

Stress (biological, psychological, social)

Mental health problems

are dependent on a person's pre-existing vulnerability. This explains why a group of people can have similar experiences, but only some of them go on to develop mental health problems.

The stress–diathesis model, like the more general biopsychosocial model, does not fundamentally challenge a biomedical model of mental health. It integrates social or psychological factors with the idea of an underlying biological vulnerability. It has been criticised because it still carries the underlying assumption that this interaction results in the development of a 'mental disorder' which is usually considered to be biological, and because some argue that the idea of an underlying vulnerability is stigmatising and can be experienced as blaming of the individual (Johnstone and Boyle, 2018).

2.5 The development of psychological models

During the nineteenth and early twentieth century, psychiatry was focused mainly on those who today we would describe as having severe and enduring mental health problems. During the first half of the twentieth century this started to change, and the field expanded to include those whose difficulties were less disabling. Sigmund Freud (1856–1939), a neurologist and medical doctor, was one of the first to conceptualise people's problems as due to psychology, rather than biology.

Psychological models of mental health focus on a person's thoughts, feelings, and behaviour. Psychological processes are hypothesised to be the link between what happens to a person, and their emotional distress or mental health difficulties. Figure 2.3 shows

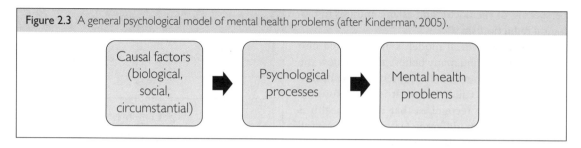

Figure 2.3 A general psychological model of mental health problems (after Kinderman, 2005).

this basic principle schematically. The way that these psychological mechanisms work can be understood in various ways, for example through psychoanalytic or cognitive theory.

Psychoanalysis and psychodynamic theories

Freud's work and the emerging field of **psychoanalysis** was a dramatic paradigm shift in mental health. Freud's focus on what his patients said and thought about (and his theories about this) led him to explain everything through psychological processes. Rather than dividing people into disordered and non-disordered, he essentially saw everyone as having some sort of **psychopathology** (Rogers and Pilgrim, 2014).

Freud used talking as treatment. He emphasised the importance of the therapeutic relationship (meaning the relationship between a therapist and their client), a focus which is a central part of many psychological therapies today. His theories were based on interpretations of his clients' case histories and gave a central role to unconscious and unresolved conflicts in explaining the human condition (Davidson et al., 2015).

Psychoanalysis laid the groundwork for many modern psychological therapies. However, psychoanalysis does not now form a central part of the work of most applied psychologists and is not a core feature of most psychology training programmes (although some go on to do further training in psychoanalysis). This is partly because psychoanalysis as Freud developed it is a lengthy process, sometimes taking years, and because it is not usually focused on symptom reduction, meaning it does not fit well into a symptom-focused health service. New perspectives and approaches have emerged from Freud's original work and these are called **psychodynamic**. Some of these are short-term and therefore more suited to use in the health service.

Psychoanalysis and psychodynamic models are often criticised for being unscientific. The evidence base has lagged behind other psychological therapies, although there are now efforts to address this problem (Leuzinger-Bohleber, Solms, and Arnold, 2020). Psychoanalysis has been criticised for coming from one very particular perspective. Freud based his theories on case studies of his clients, who were not socially or culturally diverse. His views are culturally bound and of their time, particularly in reference to women. Many of his theories are untestable through empirical means.

Behaviourism

Whilst Freud was developing his theories of the unconscious, psychologists were focused on a rather different way of understanding the human condition. Keen to establish themselves as a rigorous scientific discipline, psychologists such as John Watson (Watson, 1913) focused on what they could observe and measure. This meant behaviour. **Behaviourism** was initially based on animal models, with Ivan Pavlov and B.F. Skinner studying how dogs and rats learnt.

Behaviourism did not concern itself with the psychological or individual reasons why someone behaved the way they did. Behaviour was seen as something which happens in response to environmental stimuli, and which could be modified by changing the environment. The principles of behaviourism proved to be highly successful in treating some mental health problems and are still used today. For example, phobias are often treated by systematic desensitisation (Wolpe, 1969), a process by which people are gradually exposed to the feared object. If they are afraid of spiders, they might start by looking at pictures of spiders, then touching a toy spider, then moving onto seeing a real spider in a tank, before finally touching a spider. **Behavioural activation**, a therapeutic approach where therapists help clients engage in more valued activities, is a key element of many treatments for depression, and has a strong evidence base (Jacobson, Martell, and Dimidjian, 2001).

Behaviourism has its limitations. The emphasis on behaviour as a set of conditioned responses ignores internal processes (such as thoughts and emotions) and the role of choice. Behavioural approaches (such as Applied Behaviour Analysis, ABA) have recently been strongly criticised when applied to **autistic** children, both because abusive techniques such as pain and shock have been used to discourage particular behaviours, and because critics argue that attempting to modify autistic behaviour to fit a societal norm does psychological harm and has been done without the consent of the children (Kirkham, 2017). Critics argue that behaviourist theory frequently does not adequately distinguish between something which is done **to** a person and something which is done **by** a person and can be used as a method of social control—choosing to modify your behaviour is very different to being obliged to do so in order to avoid pain or an electric shock.

Parts of behavioural theory have been integrated with cognitive theories to create cognitive behavioural models, which I will discuss below.

Humanistic psychology

By the 1940s and 1950s, some psychologists were frustrated with psychoanalysis and behaviourism, and what they saw as a narrow focus on problems and deficits. **Humanistic** psychologists wanted to focus on potential, rather than pathology. They saw people as possessing an innate drive towards self-actualisation, which Abraham Maslow (1908–1970) defined as a state of fulfilment in which a person is achieving at their highest level of capacity.

Carl Rogers (1902–1987) applied these ideas to therapy. He thought that people could heal themselves given the right circumstances. From this perspective, the job of the therapist was to provide a therapeutic environment including unconditional positive regard, which would allow people to move towards self-actualisation. Therapists are non-directive, focusing on providing the core conditions and trusting in the ability of the client to reconnect with their sense of agency. Rogers' ideas were not met with universal acclaim. In fact, he was accused of practising medicine without a licence and attempts were made to close

his clinic down. At the time psychological therapy was seen as something which was done by medically trained doctors, not psychologists.

Humanism emphasised the unique person, and centred their experience in a way which had not happened before. It moved away from symptoms and pathology towards potential and growth. It has had an influence on therapy beyond those who use Rogerian approaches today, particularly the focus on taking a non-judgemental and curious approach. However, it has also been criticised as being inadequate for those with more serious mental health problems who may not have the resources to self-actualise in a non-directive context. The focus is different for each person and humanistic therapy may not focus on symptoms at all, making it hard to test empirically. Some argue that it is unscientific and focuses too much on the individual rather than the social context. It has been suggested that humanist theory is ethnocentric, reflecting Western individualistic ideals about what a fulfilled life involves, rather than more collective or communal ideals from other cultures.

Cognitive behavioural models

By the 1950s, a new interest was developing in the ways in which our thoughts affect emotions and behaviour. Aaron Beck (1921–2021) and Albert Ellis (1913–2007) separately developed **cognitive models** and psychological therapies which focused on how people think and feel about events. The simplest cognitive models simply outline how thoughts, feelings, behaviour, and physiological responses are all connected (Figure 2.4)

Cognitive psychotherapies positioned cognitions (or thoughts) as the primary mechanism of change. Later these were combined with behavioural therapies. These therapies (**cognitive behavioural therapies** or **CBT**) see the relationship between thoughts, feelings, and behaviour as fundamental to the development and maintenance of mental health problems. In interviews, both Ellis and Beck have said they were inspired by Stoicism (an ancient Greek philosophy), which contains the idea that it is not events that cause suffering but rather our interpretation of those events (Evans, 2017). CBT has been very successful in establishing an evidence base and has been shown to be effective for a wide range of mental health problems (David, Cristea, and Hofmann, 2018). Most research into psychological therapies is conducted into CBT, and the evidence base for CBT is growing all the time (Fordham et al.,

Figure 2.4 A basic cognitive model showing the interactions between cognitions, emotions, behaviour, and physiology. The way we think affects our feelings, behaviours, and physiology, and all of those things affect how we think. (Adapted from Greenberger and Padesky, 2015).

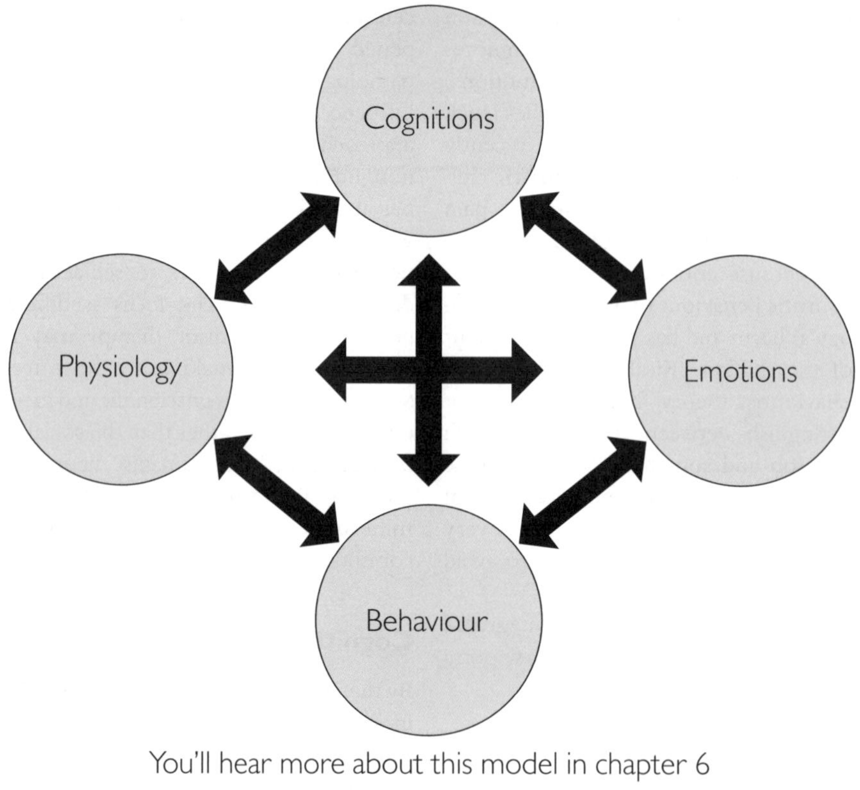

Cognitions

Physiology

Emotions

Behaviour

You'll hear more about this model in chapter 6

2021). The scientific approach is integral to CBT, with methods such as hypothesis testing, data collection, and behavioural experiments being a central part of therapy. CBT is now used for more severe problems such as psychosis as well as less serious mental health issues.

This scientific approach is also a reason why CBT has been criticised. With its focus on what is measurable and on symptom reduction, some argue that CBT is part of a neo-liberalist approach to human existence which ignores the wider complexities of life (Dalal, 2018). Because most of the evidence for the effectiveness of psychological therapies is focused on CBT, it is hard for any other therapy to build a comparable evidence base. Funding is channelled into CBT because the evidence base is strong, which then makes it even harder for other therapies to establish themselves. Some argue that therapies such as CBT

are cultural constructs which reflect the values of Western society, using rational and apparently scientific thinking to control emotions (Timimi, 2021). CBT also comes under some criticism for ignoring the reality of people's lives and instead labelling their thoughts and feelings as dysfunctional. In the COVID-19 global pandemic, for example, can it be considered dysfunctional to feel very anxious about the possibility of catching the virus and to wash one's hands many times a day? Or is it a functional response to a difficult situation? I'll come back to CBT in Chapter 6, where you can read a detailed example of how CBT works in practice.

Since the 1950s, a plethora of different approaches to **psychotherapy** has been developed. Apart from systemic or family interventions, which I will discuss in Chapter 6, they have tended to focus on the individual. In other words, they assume that psychological processes are at the core of a person's problems, and that by addressing those, their situation can be improved. Like the biomedical model, this is an explanation on a particular level and it can be criticised for focusing exclusively on the individual rather than on the circumstances of their lives. Seeing people in the context of their lives, culture, and society is a different **level of analysis**, and here we come to social and socio-cultural theories.

2.6 Social and socio-cultural theories

Social theories look at the environment a person is in, and how that affects them. **Socio-cultural theories** take a wider view of a person's life, considering the cultural context and seeking to understand their experiences from this perspective. It is widely accepted that the way in which people present when distressed does differ between cultures, and a socio-cultural perspective holds that culture is critical in understanding how we distinguish between a mental health problem, and what we consider to be 'normal' (López and Guarnaccia, 2016). Some argue that we can never ignore culture as it is the way in which we experience the world. They suggest that Western psychiatry and psychology assume that that the diagnostic model of mental health is universally applicable and culture-free, whilst seeing other perspectives as limited by culture—something which has been described as colonialism (Timimi, 2014). Others may not see distress as a result of disorder or dysfunction at all, but as an understandable response to circumstances (Johnstone and Boyle, 2018, Watson, 2019).

As with biomedical and psychological models, social theories lead to the development of interventions. The difference is that social models usually call for wider-scale, societal changes. Advocates of these models argue that tackling social problems would have a much greater effect on mental health than offering individual treatments when things have already gone wrong (Marmot, 2015, Wilkinson and Pickett, 2018).

There are several different social and socio-cultural models, including social causation, societal response, and social constructionism (Rogers and Pilgrim, 2014). They all focus on the interaction between a person and the world around them, but in different ways.

Social causation

The **social causation** theory states that social circumstances, particularly adversity, can cause mental health problems. There is a strong body of research indicating that experiencing adversity makes a person more likely to develop mental health problems (Longden and Read, 2016, Bentall et al., 2014, Varese et al., 2012).

It took a sociologist and a psychologist working together to produce the first large-scale study to look at the impact of adversity on mental health (Brown and Harris, 1978). Interviewing 458 women in Camberwell, South London, they found that in the next year 37 of them became depressed. 90% of these women had experienced trauma or serious adversity, compared to only 30% of those who did not become depressed. They also found that the presence of a confiding relationship reduced the likelihood of a woman becoming depressed.

Their important conceptual shift was the idea that people became depressed not because there was something wrong with them, but because something terrible had happened to them. There is now a large body of research looking at Adverse Childhood Experiences (ACEs), which find that having a range of difficult experiences in childhood does not only relate to later mental health problems but also to a range of physical health problems (Hughes et al., 2017).

This leads to the question as to whether some societies cause more distress than others. Epidemiologists have found that the level of inequality in a country is more important than absolute levels of poverty for predicting mental health problems, and that as a country becomes more unequal, mental health worsens (Wilkinson and Pickett, 2018, Marmot, 2015). Inequality is worsening in countries such as the USA and the UK and has been doing so since the 1970s. We would expect this to lead to an increased incidence of mental health problems in these countries, something which appears to be the case but is hard to reliably assess due to changing attitudes to mental health and changing diagnostic criteria.

A particular form of the social causation theory is the **social justice**. This model views distress as a product of social oppression, whether that is due to economic inequality, sexism, racism or homophobia, or another oppression. Through this lens, it isn't the individual who has the problem and who needs intervention, but rather society (McClelland, 2014). This model has been growing in popularity in recent years, with many arguing that factors such as systemic racism, poverty, and violence should be recognised as central to the experience of those who develop mental health problems (Finn, 2017). An analysis of how this occurs has led to a new awareness of the differing daily experiences of people from different groups, with people calling for recognition of the cumulative harm done to people by small daily injustices—called **microaggressions**—and of **unconscious bias**. Recently, some have argued that psychologists should act as social change agents, advocating for system change (Carr et al., 2023).

Critics of these models point out that when a person is experiencing severe mental health problems, it does not help to blame society, because the person's distress requires a response right now. They suggest that the focus on social factors can minimise individual agency, which leads to people feeling helpless in the face of their problems. They point out that a social causation theory alone does not explain why some people develop mental health problems in the face of adversity whilst others do not.

The social justice approach has been criticised as being more of an ideology than a theory, which when brought into psychology requires that clients and psychologists adopt progressive positions on social issues. Critics argue that encouraging people to focus on microaggressions and unconscious bias can have a detrimental effect on their mental health, as it encourages emotional fragility (Lukianoff and Haidt, 2015). They suggest that a focus on unintentional interpersonal slights and unconscious bias will not challenge social and economic inequality and injustice and in fact could deflect attention from wider societal issues.

Societal response

Another way of thinking about the interaction between a person and society is to look at **societal response** when someone is in distress or exhibiting unusual behaviour. When people have mental health problems, those around them often react negatively. This can then compound their problems through stigma and discrimination.

Erving Gottesman (1963) was one of the first to describe 'stigma'. He saw it as the process of being linked with negative stereotypes and seen as socially deviant. Stigma can affect how people and their families seek support, how they see themselves, and their prospects for recovery (e.g., Stangl et al., 2019).

Recently, large-scale anti-stigma campaigns have been launched, for example *Time to Change* in the UK and *Bring Change 2 Mind* in the USA. The aim of these campaigns is to change public attitudes, thus changing the experience of those with mental health problems. Evaluations of these campaigns show that they do have an effect, with people reporting moderate changes in attitudes (Henderson et al., 2017). However, any campaign which aims to change public perceptions must by necessity define the attitudes they want to encourage. Exactly *which* attitudes are stigmatising is a matter for debate.

Critics point out that anti-stigma campaigns often focus on the biomedical model with the premise that if only people would accept that mental health problems are an illness like any other, then stigma would be reduced (Read et al., 2006). They point out that this is not proven, and some studies have indicated that a psychosocial explanation of mental health is in fact less stigmatising (Longden and Read, 2017). Many anti-stigma and awareness campaigns are funded by pharmaceutical companies. The model which is generally presented is one which emphasises the biological nature of the problem, encourages people to seek medical help, and emphasises treatability, usually by medication (Moynihan and Cassels, 2005). This is a model that is highly profitable for pharmaceutical companies (Davies, 2013, Watters, 2011).

Anti-stigma and mental health awareness campaigns have another side. Some argue that as awareness is raised, people have started to see pathology everywhere, including emotional reactions which would previously have been seen as within the range of typical experience (Foulkes, 2021). We may have gone from a situation where mental health problems were taboo to a situation where the lens of mental health is applied to all emotional experiences, with terms such as depression, anxiety, OCD, and PTSD being used colloquially far more widely than what is described by the diagnostic criteria.

A final level of complexity is that anti-stigma campaigns generally approach stigma as something which is located in individual attitudes, ignoring societal level discrimination or structural stigma (Hatzenbuehler, 2016).

Social constructionism

Social constructionism holds that the ways in which we understand the world are always culturally and historically specific. It suggests that people construct meaning between them through their everyday social interactions, and that therefore our current understanding can never be due to an objective observation of the world (Burr, 2015). The implication of this is that there is no essential core inside a person which makes them who they are (or makes them unwell), and that all psychological and medical theories are products of their time and culture. This contrasts with mainstream psychological theory as well as psychiatric diagnosis, both of which take an essentialist view of human experiences and behaviour. This means they assume that there is an underlying reality which is described by psychological and biological models.

A social constructionist perspective would argue that diagnosing behaviour and emotional experiences as a medical disorder involves imposing a social construction, rather than identifying an underlying condition. Some argue that psychiatric disorders are constructed not just by professionals but by the general population, saying that when symptoms are described (for example in awareness campaigns) and become widely known, people start to recognise themselves in these descriptions and so the prevalence of a condition rises (Borch-Jacobsen, 2009). A person may start to see themselves as having depression when previously they just thought that they were low in mood. They now identify with the social construction of depression.

Social constructionism has come in for criticism for discounting the role of biology, and some people feel that it denies the reality of their experiences. It may not lead naturally to suggestions as to how to intervene to help a person in distress, as the focus is on conceptualisation, rather than on practical support. Recognising that diagnoses are social constructs may be useful, but working out what to do instead is complex. Others argue that a social construct is to all intents and purposes 'real', because it is recognised and used as such within society, and therefore it doesn't matter whether there is any underlying 'truth' to the construct.

world around them, but people can also affect their environment, a process called bidirectionality. The **socio-ecological model** (Bronfenbrenner, 1989) is a nested approach which attempts to capture some of the complexity of people's lives. It is an example of a socio-cultural model, where an individual is seen as embedded in their cultural context. The idea is that the individual always exists in context, and they will interact with this context in different ways.

Imagine two people who are depressed and who have identical symptoms, living next door to each other. The first person has supportive family around them, can access psychological support at work, and knows of others who have similar experiences in their wider community. Their neighbour is rejected by their family, sacked from their job, and decides there is no point in seeking support in their community because they know that others will not be sympathetic. Who is likely to have a better outcome? Context clearly matters, and will probably be the thing which makes the difference in outcomes between these people.

Figure 2.5 shows a socio-ecological model. Each circle interacts with each other—nothing is independent. It's not possible to remove the individual from their context, and therefore the socio-ecological model suggests that context and bidirectionality should always be considered when trying to understand someone's experiences.

This model can be helpful when trying to understand a person's problems and reflects the complexity of people's lives. It acknowledges how complex people's lives are, and how we cannot ignore the systems within which people live. However, complexity can make it harder to see what might be helpful, and where an intervention might start. This model does not lead to strong predictions regarding how best to help someone in distress. Some people can also experience this type of model as blaming of their culture or family context, and prefer to focus on their individual experiences.

2.7 Multi-level interactional models

Many of the models discussed here focus on one level of analysis to the exclusion of others. They may focus just on biology, or just on social factors. Even those which include different levels may not account for interactions between those levels. In practice, people's lives are complex. They are affected by the

2.8 Where's the 'pathology'?

One of the difficulties in trying to conceptualise mental health is the question of what, exactly, we are trying to understand. Biomedical models define disorder by 'symptoms', and then try to explain how these disorders occur. The language of biological disorder creeps into other theories, often resulting in social or

Figure 2.5 A socio-ecological model. The individual is affected by every level and multiple interactions will be present (for example, the way that public policy affects a person will be different depending on their individual characteristics and family system). (Adapted from Bronfenbrenner, 1989).

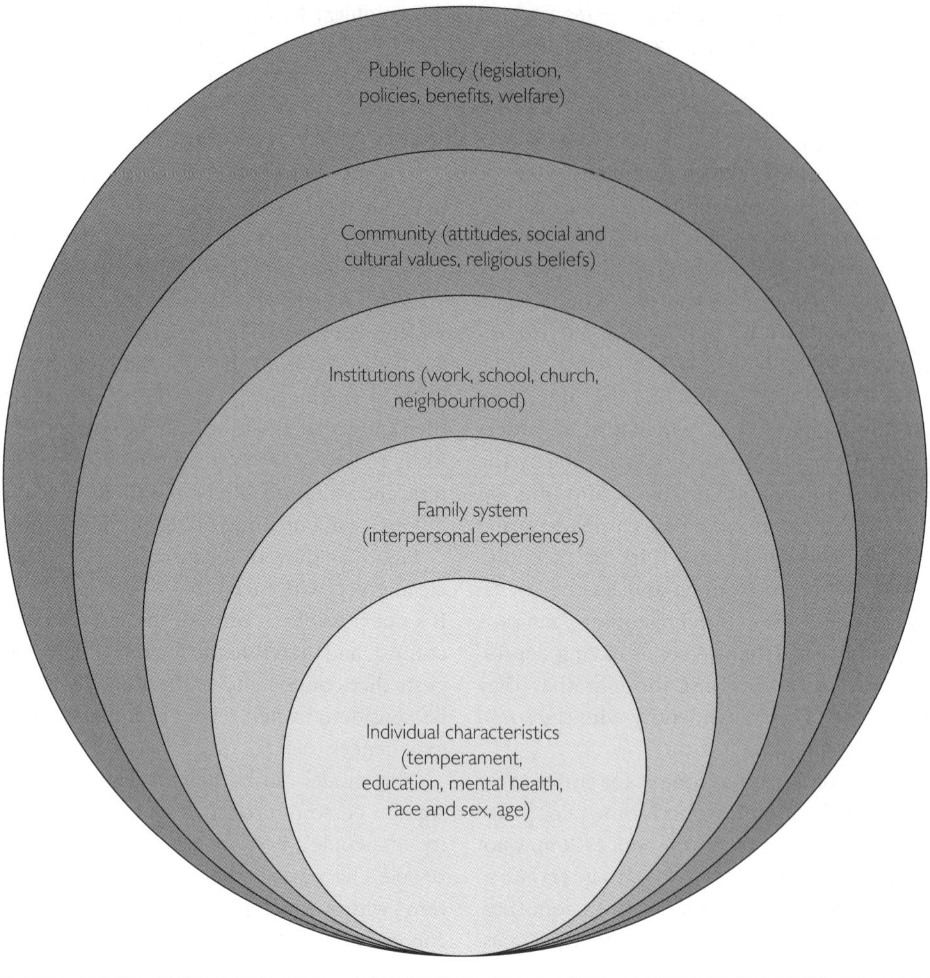

Public Policy (legislation, policies, benefits, welfare)

Community (attitudes, social and cultural values, religious beliefs)

Institutions (work, school, church, neighbourhood)

Family system (interpersonal experiences)

Individual characteristics (temperament, education, mental health, race and sex, age)

psychological theories being used as adjuncts to the biomedical model (Kinderman, 2019).

If we look at the person in context, by contrast, we may decide that there is nothing wrong with the person at all, but that their social situation is one that will naturally cause intense distress. Seeing problems like this could lead us to look for changes which could be made to social circumstances or wider society. If the structure of our society causes widespread distress, perhaps it makes more sense to put our resources towards changing society rather than treating each individual as if they were disordered (Marmot, 2005; Marmot, 2015). However, this is unlikely to help the

distressed individual in the here and now. In contrast, biomedical or psychological approaches usually focus on the individual and may ignore society. These individualised approaches may help a particular person feel better, but do not address societal causes of distress. In this way, how we understand mental health becomes political, affecting government policy and social attitudes.

This issue is particularly important because it affects the evidence base. When a study defines a successful outcome as a reduction in symptoms, then the researchers have accepted that an improvement in mental health is best measured by symptoms, a premise of the medical model. This means that all interventions will be measured by this yardstick, when in fact there may be other ways to define success. **Survivor-led movements** such as the Hearing Voices Network say that the things which make their lives worth living are not well captured by a list of symptoms. This has led to the development of interventions which are focused on living well with hearing voices rather than reducing them (Romme and Escher, 2011). However, the success of these interventions then needs to be measured in a different way, making them hard to compare with other approaches.

2.9 What about Penny?

So how about Penny, the woman whose husband was waiting outside? Penny's problems were understood by her GP on a biomedical level, and so she had been prescribed anti-depressants. The psychologist conceptualised her problems on a psychological level, and so had tried to start cognitive therapy. Penny herself just wants to feel better.

Penny's distress was understandable in the context of her life, where she had very little power and was vulnerable to mistreatment by her husband. When the psychologist talked to Penny about this, Penny became very distressed. The psychologist asked some more questions about her daughter and was satisfied that she was well cared for and not at immediate risk of harm.

The psychologist told Penny she thought it was totally understandable that she would feel like this, given the circumstances of her life, and she wondered if there was anything they could do together to help her change that. She therefore offered a social causation theory as an alternative to the biomedical or psychological approaches. This was a shock for Penny. She hadn't thought before that perhaps her feelings made sense.

The psychologist gave Penny the details for an outreach worker at the local woman's refuge. They stopped doing trauma-focused therapy for the time being and instead focused on how Penny could plan to move forward with her life, which would probably involve leaving her husband.

Seeing her problems in context made a difference to Penny. She had thought that she was ill, but now she started to think about her life and what she wanted her daughter's childhood to be like. She regained some of her sense of agency and over the next six months started making plans for an independent life and future.

Chapter Summary

- Models are theories with explanatory and predictive power.
- When applied to mental health, models either take a single level of analysis—biological, psychological, or socio-cultural—or can attempt to integrate these levels.
- Reductionist models describe a complex phenomenon in terms of simple constituents, particularly when this is said to provide a sufficient explanation. Reductionism can happen within any model; biological, psychological, or socio-cultural.
- There are many different models used to understand mental health problems, and the models used by professionals will affect the help and support that is offered as well as the way they think about the problem.

? QUESTIONS

1. How do theoretical models of mental health influence interventions? Compare and contrast three different approaches taken by psychologists.

2. Should mental distress be conceptualised as a health problem? What are the advantages and disadvantages of doing so?

3. What are the main types of social and socio-cultural models and how do they differ from each other? Should psychologists be involved with campaigning for social change? Why or why not?

4. What is reductionism and why is it a problem in mental health? Give an example of how taking a reductionist approach could affect the interventions a person is offered.

5. Find some examples of organisations describing mental health problems online. You could try Rethink Mental Illness, NHS Direct, Time 2 Change, Mind, The Hearing Voices Network, Drop the Disorder, and the National Institute of Mental Health. What models of mental health do they use? How do you know?

 FURTHER READING

Bolton, D., and Gillett, G. (2019). *The Biopsychosocial Model of Health and Disease: New Philosophical and Scientific Developments.* Cham, Switzerland: Palgrave Macmillan.

A very thorough exploration of the biopsychosocial model.

Davidson, G., Campbell, J., Shannon, C., and Mulholland, C. (2015). *Models of Mental Health.* London: Red Globe Press.

An overview of different models and how they apply to mental health, covering biological, psychological, and social.

Engel, G. (1977). The need for a new medical model: A challenge for biomedicine. *Science*, 196, 4286; and Engel, G. (1980). The clinical application of the biopsychosocial model. *American Journal of Psychiatry*, 137(5), 535–544.

Engel's original papers introducing the biopsychosocial model, well worth a read to see how he conceptualised it.

Huda, A.S. (2019). *The Medical Model in Mental Health: An Explanation and Evaluation.* Oxford: Oxford University Press.

A thoughtful exploration of the medical model and how it applies to mental health.

Porter, R. (2003). *Madness: A Brief History.* Oxford: Oxford University Press.

Read, J., Bentall, R., and Fosse, R. (2009). Time to abandon the bio-bio-bio model of psychosis: Exploring the epigenetic and psychological mechanisms by which adverse life events lead to psychotic symptoms. *Epidemiology and Psychiatric Sciences*, 18(4), 299–310.

A critique of how the bio-psycho-social model is being applied in practice—the authors argue it is reduced to 'bio-bio-bio'.

Shorter, E. (1997). *A History of Psychiatry: From the Era of the Asylum to the Age of Prozac.* Hoboken, NJ: John Wiley & Sons, Inc.

 REFERENCES

Bentall, R. (2009). *Doctoring the Mind: Why Psychiatric Treatments Fail.* London: Allen Lane.

Bentall, R.P., de Sousa, P., Varese, F., Wickham, S., Sitko, K., Haarmans, M., and Read, J. (2014). From adversity to psychosis: Pathways and mechanisms from specific adversities to specific symptoms. *Social Psychiatry Psychiatric Epidemiology*, 49(7), 1011–1022. doi:10.1007/s00127-014-0914-0

Bolton, D., and Gillett, G. (2019). *The Biopsychosocial Model of Health and Disease: New Philosophical and Scientific Developments.* Cham, Switzerland: Palgrave Macmillan.

Borch-Jacobsen, M. (2009). *Making Minds and Madness: From Hysteria to Depression.* Cambridge: Cambridge University Press.

Bronfenbrenner, U. (1989). Ecological systems theory. In R. Vasta (ed.), *Annals of Child Development: Vol. 6.* London, UK: Jessica Kingsley Publishers, pp. 187–249. [Google Scholar]

Bring Change 2 Mind https://bringchange2mind.org/learn/

Brown, G.W., and Harris, T.O. (1978). *Social Origins of Depression: A Study of Psychiatric Disorder in Women.* London: Tavistock.

Burr, V. (2015). *Social Constructionism.* Hove: Routledge.

Carr, E.R., Davenport, K.M., Murakami-Brundage, J.L., Robertson, S., Miller, R., and Snyder, J. (2023). From the medical model to the recovery model: Psychologists engaging in advocacy and social justice action agendas in public mental health. *American Journal of Orthopsychiatry*. doi:10.1037/ort0000656

Colodro-Conde, L., Couvy-Duchesne, B., Zhu, G., et al. (2018). A direct test of the diathesis-stress model for depression. *Molecular Psychiatry*, 23(7), 1590–1596.

Dalal, F. (2018). *CBT: The Cognitive Behavioural Tsumani. Managerialism, Politics and the Corruptions of Science*. Abingdon: Routledge.

David, D., Cristea, I., and Hofmann, S. (2018). Why cognitive behaviour therapy is the current gold standard of psychotherapy. *Psychopathology*, 9. doi:10.3389/fpsyt.2018.00004

Davidson, G., Campbell, J., Shannon, C., and Mulholland, C. (2015). *Models of Mental Health*. London: Red Globe Press.

Davies, J. (2013). *Cracked: Why Psychiatry is Doing more Harm than Good*. London: Icon Books.

Dully, H., and Fleming, C. (2008). *My Lobotomy: A Memoir*. New York: Crown. Reprint Edition.

Engel, G. (1977). The need for a new medical model: A challenge for biomedicine. *Science*, 196, 4286.

Engel, G. (1980). The clinical application of the biopsychosocial model. *American Journal of Psychiatry*, 137(5), 535–544.

Evans, J. (2017). *The End of History and the Invention of Happiness*. CWiPP Working Paper No.11 Centre for Wellbeing in Public Policy, University of Sheffield.

Finn, A. (2017). Our Approach to Mental Health Isn't Working. *Open Society Foundations*. Retrieved October 2017. https://www.opensocietyfoundations.org/voices/our-approach-mental-health-isn-t-working

Fordham, B., Sugavanam, T., Edwards, K., Stallard, P., Howard, R., Das Nair, R., … Lamb, S. (2021). The evidence for cognitive behavioural therapy in any condition, population or context: A meta-review of systematic reviews and panoramic meta-analysis. *Psychological Medicine*, 51(1), 21–29. doi:10.1017/S0033291720005292

Foulkes, L. (2021). *Losing Our Minds: What Mental Illness Really Is And What It Isn't*. London: Bodley Head.

Ghaemi, S.N. (2009). Editorial: The rise and fall of the biopsychosocial model. *British Journal of Psychiatry*, 195, 3–4.

Gottesman, E. (1963). *Stigma: Notes on the Management of Spoiled Identity*. New York: Simon & Schuster, Inc.

Greenberger, D., and Padesky, C. (2015). *Mind Over Mood: Change How You Feel By Changing the Way You Think*. New York: Guilford Press.

Hatzenbuehler, M.L. (2016). Structural stigma: Research evidence and implications for psychological science. *The American Psychologist*, 71(8), 742–751. doi:10.1037/amp0000068

Henderson, C., Robinson, E., Evans-Lacko, S., and Thornicroft, G. (2017). Relationships between anti-stigma programme awareness, disclosure comfort and intended help-seeking regarding a mental health problem. *British Journal of Psychiatry*, 211(5), 316–322.

Hughes, K., Bellis, M.A., Hardcastle, K.A., et al. (2017). The effect of multiple adverse childhood experiences on health: A systematic review and meta-analysis. *Lancet Public Health*, 2, e356–e366.

Huda, A.S. (2019). *The Medical Model in Mental Health: An Explanation and Evaluation*. Oxford: Oxford University Press.

Iacobucci, G. (2019). NHS prescribed record number of antidepressants last year. *BMJ*, 364, 1508.

Ilyas, S., and Moncrieff, J. (2012). Trends in prescriptions and costs of drugs for mental disorders in England, 1998–2010. *British Journal of Psychiatry*, 200(5), 393–398.

Jacobson, N.S., Martell, C.R., and Dimidjian, S. (2001). Behavioral activation treatment for depression: Returning to contextual roots. *Clinical Psychology: Science and Practice*, 8(3), 255–270. doi:10.1093/clipsy.8.3.255

Johnstone, L. and Boyle, M., with Cromby, J., Dillon, J., Harper, D., Kinderman, P., Longden, E., Pilgrim, D., and Read, J. (2018). *The Power Threat Meaning Framework: Overview.* Leicester: British Psychological Society.

Kessler, R. (1996). *The Sins of the Father: Joseph P. Kennedy and the Dynasty He Founded.* New York: Grand Central Publishing.

Kinderman, P. (2005). A psychological model of mental disorder. *Harvard Review of Psychiatry,* 13(4), 206–217. doi:10.1080/10673220500243349. PMID: 16126607

Kirkham, P. (2017). 'The line between intervention and abuse'—autism and applied behaviour analysis. *History of the Human Sciences,* 30(2), 107–126. doi:10.1177/0952695117702571

Leuzinger Bohleber, M., Solms, M., and Arnold, S.E. (eds) (2020). *Outcome Research and the Future of Psychoanalysis.* Abingdon: Routledge.

López, S.R., and Guarnaccia, P.J. (2016). Cultural dimensions of psychopathology: The social world's impact on mental disorder. In J.E. Maddoz and B.A. Winstead (eds), *Psychopathology: Foundations for a Contemporary Understanding,* Fourth Edition. New York: Routledge, pp. 59–75.

Longden, E., and Read, J. (2016). Social adversity in the etiology of psychosis: A review of the evidence. *American Journal of Psychotherapy,* 70(1), 5–33. doi:10.1176/appi.psychotherapy.2016.70.1.5

Longden, E., and Read, J. (2017). 'People with problems, not patients with illnesses': Using psychosocial frameworks to reduce the stigma of psychosis. *Israel Journal of Psychiatry and Related Sciences,* 54(1), 24–28.

Lukianoff, G., and Haidt, J. (2015). The coddling of the American mind. *The Atlantic.* Retrieved September 2015. https://www.theatlantic.com/magazine/archive/2015/09/the-coddling-of-the-american-mind/399356/

Marmot, M. (2005). Remediable or preventable social factors in the aetiology and prognosis of medical disorders. In P.D. White (ed.), *Biopsychosocial medicine: An integrated approach to understanding illness.* New York: Oxford University Press.

Marmot, M. (2015). *The Health Gap: The Challenge of an Unequal World.* London: Bloomsbury Publishing PLC.

McClelland, L. (2014). Reformulating the impact of social inequalities: Power and social justice. In L. Johnstone and R. Dallos (eds), *Formulation in Psychology and Psychotherapy: Making Sense of People's Problems,* Second Edition. London, UK: Routledge, pp. 121–144.

Moncrieff, J., Cooper, R.E., Stockmann, T., et al. (2022). The serotonin theory of depression: A systematic umbrella review of the evidence. *Molecular Psychiatry,* 28, 3243–3256. doi:10.1038/s41380-022-01661-0

Moynihan, R., and Cassels, A. (2005). *Selling Sickness: How Drug Companies are Turning Us All Into Patients.* Sydney: Allen & Unwin.

Porter, R. (2003). *Madness: A Brief History.* Oxford: Oxford University Press.

Pilgrim, D., Kinderman, P., and Tai, S. (2008). Taking stock of the biopsychosocial model in the field of 'mental health care'. *Journal of Social and Psychological Sciences,* 1, 1–32.

Read, J., Bentall, R., and Fosse, R (2009). Time to abandon the bio-bio-bio model of psychosis: Exploring the epigenetic and psychological mechanisms by which adverse life events lead to psychotic symptoms. *Epidemiology and Psychiatric Sciences,* 18(4), 299–310.

Read, J., Haslam, N., Sayce, L., and Davies, E. (2006). Prejudice and schizophrenia: A review of the 'mental illness is an illness like any other' approach. *Acta Psychiatrica Scandinavica,* 114(5), 303–318.

Romme, M., and Escher, S. (2011). *Psychosis as a Personal Crisis: An Experience Based Approach.* Abingdon: Routledge.

Rogers, A., and Pilgrim, D. (2014). *A Sociology of Mental Health and Illness.* Maidenhead: McGraw-Hill Education (UK).

Rosenthal, D. (1963). A suggested conceptual framework. In D. Rosenthal (ed.), *The Genain Quadruplets: A Case Study and Theoretical Analysis of Heredity and Environment in Schizophrenia.* New York: Basic Books, pp. 505–511.

Shorter, E. (1997). *A History of Psychiatry: From the Era of the Asylum to the Age of Prozac*. Hoboken, NJ: John Wiley & Sons, Inc.

Stangl, A.L., Earnshaw, V.A., Logie, C.H., et al. (2019). The health stigma and discrimination framework: A global, crosscutting framework to inform research, intervention development, and policy on health-related stigmas. *BMC Medicine*, 17, 31. doi:10.1186/s12916-019-1271-3

Timimi, S. (2014). No more psychiatric labels: Why formal psychiatric diagnostic systems should be abolished. *International Journal of Clinical and Health Psychology*, 14(3), 208–215.

Timimi, S. (2021). *Insane Medicine: How the Mental Health Industry Creates Damaging Treatment Traps and How You Can Escape Them*. Independently Published.

Varese, F., Smeets, F., Drukker, M., Lieverse, R., Lataster, T., et al. (2012). Childhood adversities increase the risk of psychosis: A meta-analysis of patient-control, prospective- and cross-sectional cohort studies. *Schizophrenia Bulletin*, 38, 661–671.

Watson, J.B. (1913). Psychology as the behaviorist views it. *Psychological Review*, 20(2), 158–177. doi:10.1037/h0074428

Watson, J. (ed.) (2019). *Drop the Disorder! Challenging the Culture of Psychiatric Diagnosis*. Monmouth: PCCS Books.

Watters, E. (2011). *Crazy Like Us: The Globalization of the Western Mind*. New York: Free Press.

Wilkinson, R., and Pickett, K. (2018). *The Inner Level: How More Equal Societies Reduce Stress, Restore Sanity and Improve Everyone's Well-Being*. London: Allen Lane.

Wolpe, J. (1969). *The Practice of Behavioral Therapy*. New York: Pergamon Press.

Chapter 3
What Causes Mental Health Problems?

Learning objectives

When you have completed this chapter, you should be able to do the following:

3.1 Explain the different research designs used to establish causality and outline the hierarchy of evidence.

3.2 Compare and contrast research designs which look at individual and group differences.

3.3 Summarise the research into the causes of mental health problems.

3.4 Discuss how life experiences can impact mental health.

3.5 Analyse the role of psychological factors in mental health.

3.6 Give examples of how societal factors may affect mental health.

3.7 Explain how biological factors impact mental health.

3.8 Critically evaluate the ways in which different theories of causality are used politically and the impact of this on mental health research and clinical practice.

Introduction

Humans like to understand why things happen. In everyday life, we frequently explain events in terms of their causes. We seek to understand.

This is particularly the case for complex issues such as mental health problems. When someone is distressed or has a breakdown, our first question is often why, or what happened? When we are offered an explanation which makes sense to us, we feel resolution. This is perhaps one reason why there is a tendency to explain the causes of mental health problems in simplistic (or reductionist) terms. It is reassuring to believe that we understand what has gone wrong, and why. Perhaps then we will be able to avoid it happening again.

Unfortunately, the evidence shows that when it comes to mental health, establishing **causality** is not straightforward. By the end of this chapter I hope you will understand some of the reasons why. I will start by discussing how researchers try to demonstrate causality and why this is difficult. I'll then

EXPLORING THE RESEARCH 3.1

The English and Romanian Adoptees Study

In the late 1980s the British public was shocked by images from Romanian orphanages after the fall of the Ceausescu regime. Children in these orphanages had suffered extreme deprivation. They were frequently malnourished, had very little social contact and were confined to their cots.

Hundreds of families adopted Romanian orphans. This tragedy provided a natural experimental design which researchers used in the English-Romanian Adoptees Study. The Romanian children had had a discrete period of deprivation after which they were adopted into caring families. This made them a particularly unusual group, because for most children, the effects of early deprivation cannot be separated from their later experiences. Perhaps, scientists thought, they would be able to discover how the children's early experiences affect their lives. The study would assess social, emotional, cognitive, and neurological development, visiting the children throughout their lives.

As the children grew the researchers visited regularly. Those who had spent more than six months in an institution had persistently higher rates of psychological difficulties than the comparison group. By young adulthood, those who had spent more than six months in an orphanage were more likely to be unemployed, to have low educational attainment, and to have used mental health services (Sonuga-Barke et al., 2017).

By 2020 the children were young adults, but differences were still there. The study found that the brains of the Romanian adoptees were substantially smaller than the comparison group of non-deprived adoptees, and brain volume was reduced for each month they had spent in the orphanage (Mackes et al., 2020).

Despite this extreme early deprivation, not all the adoptees were affected. A fifth of the individuals who had spent more than six months in an institution reported no problems at any of their assessments. Even this severe level of early deprivation was apparently not sufficient to cause long-term difficulties for everyone.

move on to discussing the different research designs used to investigate the causes of mental health problems, and look at their strengths and limitations. The second half of the chapter will discuss the factors which have been most consistently linked with the development of mental health problems, and some of the issues that this raises.

We may all have our own theories about mental health problems and why they happen, but how can we research something so complex? It would be unethical to set up experiments to look at the effects of many of the more difficult aspects of people's lives, so researchers instead use a range of approaches. One such way is to take advantage of naturally arising situations, such as the terrible deprivation suffered by children in Romanian orphanages under Ceausescu. Box 3.1 outlines one way in which researchers did this.

3.1 Determining causality

Establishing the causes of mental health problems is extremely complex. Multiple factors interact in unpredictable ways, and any identified cause acts in a **probabilistic**, rather than **deterministic**, fashion. In other words, something may increase or decrease the likelihood of a person developing mental health problems, but it's never a sure thing.

Another complicating factor is the different levels of explanation. On one level our biology causes everything we do. It's simply impossible for us to do anything without our brains and bodies being involved.

However, our bodies (and our thoughts and feelings) change in response to our experiences, and conversely, our biological characteristics affect the events of our lives. On another level, wider social and cultural factors shape what happens to us and affect the events of our lives, and again, our individual characteristics will affect how we experience the social and cultural context. All of these will interact with each other, meaning that causality is extremely complex and non-linear.

In scientific terms, a causal effect is said to occur if variation in an **independent variable** is followed by variation in a **dependent variable**, with all other things being equal. Establishing causality in real life

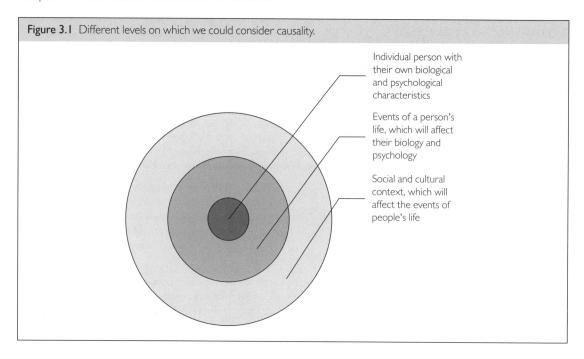

Figure 3.1 Different levels on which we could consider causality.

Individual person with their own biological and psychological characteristics

Events of a person's life, which will affect their biology and psychology

Social and cultural context, which will affect the events of people's life

is notoriously difficult. If we see causality in deterministic terms, then A should be either necessary or sufficient (or both) in order for B to occur. No factors have been shown to be either necessary or sufficient for the development of mental health problems. This means that we are always thinking in probabilistic terms, that A will increase or decrease the possibility of B occurring.

Research design

The way in which a research study is designed will make a difference to what that study can find or demonstrate. Design includes the structure of the study, the hypothesis being tested, and exactly how the researchers plan to test their hypothesis. Large-scale research designs commonly used in mental health include **experimental studies**, **quasi-experimental** designs, and **cohort studies** (which may be cross-sectional or longitudinal). Smaller-scale research designs include case studies and case series.

Experiments provide a clear and logical way in which to assess causality and are widely used in psychology. Researchers can deliberately manipulate a variable and then measure the effect of doing so, whilst attempting to hold all other factors steady. The hypothesis is outlined at the start and tested by the study. Let's take an example. In order to look at

the effect of social media usage on depression and anxiety, Hunt et al. (2018) recruited 143 students, and randomly divided them into two groups. One group was asked to limit their social media use to ten minutes a day for three weeks. The other group (the controls) continued as usual. The researchers gave the students questionnaires measuring their levels of anxiety, depression, and loneliness before and after the three-week period, and found a reduction in depression and loneliness in the experimental group. Because they had directly changed the independent variable (social media use) they could measure the effect on the dependent variable (depression and loneliness). They concluded that using less social media than usual led to decreases in depression and loneliness. The experimental design which is considered to be the 'gold standard' for establishing causality is the **randomised control trial (RCT)**, where people are assigned to different groups at random.

Experimental studies have advantages. The variables are clearly defined, and strong conclusions can often be drawn about the effects of a particular intervention. However, they also have significant weaknesses. They take a carefully selected sample and remove the events from context. We can't tell whether cutting down on social media would have the same effect for people in the wider community. We don't know what it was about limiting social media use

EXPLORING THE RESEARCH 3.2

The Dunedin Multidisciplinary Health and Development Study

In the early 1970s, the expectant mothers of Dunedin, New Zealand, were recruited to a research study. A total of 1037 babies were included. The children were visited regularly, and each time they were given medical examinations, asked in detail about what was going on in their lives, and asked to complete psychological tests and questionnaires. Keeping track of them as they grew wasn't easy. As young adults, a third of the participants emigrated and had to be flown back to New Zealand from their lives elsewhere, or visited in other countries if they couldn't travel. The study guaranteed complete confidentiality and their participants told them about criminal acts, violence, and anti-social behaviour. Participants were even visited in prison.

In 2017–2019, 94% of the living participants, by now in their mid-40s, participated. The research team has published thousands of papers. Their findings have influenced social and criminal policy and have challenged traditional conceptualisations of mental health (Caspi et al., 2014). Among their findings is the discovery that most people will meet criteria for a diagnosis of a mental health problem or disorder at some point during their lives (Schaefer et al., 2017).

With this rich longitudinal data set, their main finding is complexity. As Richie Poulton, director of the study, said 'We don't see genetic determinism or environmental determinism. Life is a complex interplay between nature and nurture.... There is never a point at which things cannot be changed'.

which causes the change—perhaps participants took more exercise, for example, because they had more time, or perhaps they talked to friends instead. Or perhaps they felt pleased with themselves for cutting down on social media use, and that cheered them up.

Experimental studies are limited by what they can manipulate. Social media use or a drug treatment can be assigned to different groups, but it is impossible to experimentally assess the impact of chronic abuse, neglect, or poverty. Here, researchers have to rely on quasi-experimental design, otherwise known as taking advantages of situations which have arisen naturally in the world. The English and Romanian Adoptee study, described at the start of this chapter, is one such study. Children were not randomised in that study, and it would never be ethical to manipulate a variable like neglect or adoption.

Given that there is so much which cannot be manipulated experimentally, other research designs are necessary in order to assess the relationship between complex variables. In **longitudinal cohort studies**, researchers follow the lives of a group of people over time without intervening. The Dunedin study, described in Box 3.2, shows how this can work in practice.

Studies like the Dunedin project are considered to be more **ecologically valid** than experimental studies. Cohort studies ideally include a wide spectrum of society, unlike many experimental studies (which frequently use a group of undergraduate students as their research participants, something which is known as a convenience sample). However, cohort studies are expensive to run, and (unless strenuous efforts are made), those participants who have more difficult lives will be more likely to drop out over time. The studies that do manage to retain their participants—like the Dunedin study—provide us with a rich archive of material. As new events arise in people's lives, it's possible to use the existing data to look back at the lives of the participants in infancy and even before birth. Studies like this can look at the relationship between how someone was parenting and their own parenting style, (for example), by using data collected at the time. This is much more accurate than asking people retrospectively about their experiences.

Some longitudinal cohort studies have continued into the next generation. The Avon Longitudinal Study of Parents and Children (ALSPAC) looked at 14,500 people born between April 1991 and December 1992, and has gone on to collect data on the children born to this cohort. A recent study looked at the mental health before and during the COVID-19 pandemic in those with diagnoses of ADHD and autism. They collected data during the pandemic and were able to compare this with data collected at earlier time points due to the longitudinal nature of the study (Shakeshaft et al., 2023).

Smaller-scale research studies are very different. Case studies look at the experience of an individual in depth, whilst case series take a group of individuals. Here, we get far more insight into the detail of a person's experience, something which can be lost in large-scale studies which rely on standardised questionnaires. However, we should be wary about drawing wider conclusions from a single case, as any findings may not generalise to others.

The hierarchy of evidence

With this plethora of research comes a problem. Studies do not all come to the same conclusions, even on very similar topics and using similar designs. Somehow it needs to be decided which evidence should be given most weight (and therefore, which findings should be used to plan and fund interventions).

To solve this, most health services use a **hierarchy of evidence**. Figure 3.2 shows one example, called Levels of Evidence (OCEBM, 2011). The highest quality evidence is considered to be those which bring together the results of multiple studies. These are called **meta-analyses** and **systematic reviews**. A randomised control design comes next, followed by high-quality cohort studies. Randomised control trials are used to test if an intervention is effective or not, and in order to reduce bias the ideal is that participants

and researchers should be **blind** as to who received the active intervention and who received a placebo.

Case-control studies come next, and these compare two groups of people. The case group will usually all share a characteristic (such as a diagnosis of depression) whilst the control group will be matched for similarity with the cases but will not have the diagnosis.

At the bottom are case series or individual case studies which are seen as lower quality and right at the bottom is expert opinion. Lower-quality evidence is seen as more likely to be influenced by bias.

This system is not without critics (e.g. Greenhalgh et al., 2018). Using a hierarchy like this means that personal accounts, whether written by service users or professionals, are relegated to the lowest rung in the evidence hierarchy. Studies at the top will be the

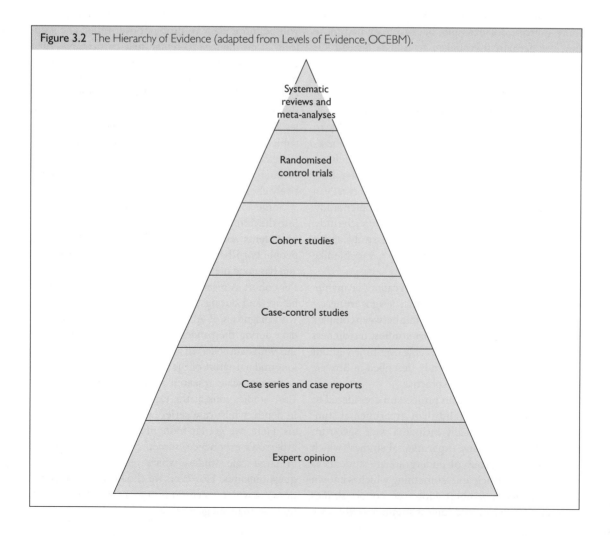

Figure 3.2 The Hierarchy of Evidence (adapted from Levels of Evidence, OCEBM).

largest and most ambitious, which generally means more expensive to run. This makes it hard for service users to become involved in research which could affect change. Whilst there are people pioneering what is called **survivor-led research** (Sweeney et al., 2009), the reality is that running a study that will be considered to be high-quality evidence usually takes funding, institutional backing, and higher degrees in research. Critics say that the hierarchy of evidence was developed for medical treatments, which means that it favours study designs where the outcome is symptom reduction. In mental health, they argue, the experience of the individual matters, something which can be lost when studies rely on large samples with standardised questionnaires and on those who share a diagnosis (Shean, 2014). Measuring the effect of a social or community intervention is much more difficult using a randomised control trial, meaning that these types of intervention have an immediate disadvantage in the evidence hierarchy.

One way to mitigate the disadvantages of a hierarchy is to **triangulate** research, meaning strategically using multiple methods to approach the same underlying question. Each method has advantages and disadvantages, so perhaps instead of ranking studies we should be clear about sources of bias and look to use a multitude of research methods which will all have different and unrelated sources of bias. In this way, causality could be established from multiple viewpoints (Munafo and Davey-Smith, 2018).

3.2 Individual and group differences

Experimental studies usually focus on group differences. Researchers will group participants together (sometimes on the basis of a diagnosis) and will compare them with a control group. In an example of a case-control design, Lieberman and colleagues looked at group differences in suicidal thinking between a group of people experiencing psychosis and a group of people with severe mental health problems, but without psychosis (Lieberman et al., 2021). They compared the two groups on a range of measures and found that as a group, those who did not have psychosis reported higher levels of suicidal thinking, as well as feeling more burdened and less like they belonged.

Group difference studies can help to identify features that a group share, but they have disadvantages. They direct our attention away from differences between group members. Differences *within* groups may be just as (or more) significant as those *between* groups, but these are masked when we look at the group average. In the past, many psychology studies have focused on looking for a 'core deficit' shared by everyone with the same diagnosis, with very little success (Astle and Fletcher-Watson, 2020). Given the issues with the psychiatric diagnostic categories, and the uncertainty over whether these categories describe meaningful groups, it is perhaps unsurprising that few core deficits have been identified.

An alternative approach is to look at individual differences. A study of individual differences seeks to understand how and why individuals differ, and how these differences predict outcome. In mental health, a study of individual differences might be set up to ask why some individuals respond well to an intervention whilst others don't, or perhaps why some people with psychosis have suicidal thoughts whilst others do not. Studies of reactions to the COVID-19 pandemic have looked at how individual differences in coping strategies and stress appraisals relate to wellbeing (Zacher and Rudolph, 2021).

For psychologists working with people with mental health problems, causality is something which they seek to understand for each individual. Psychologists use a quasi-scientific approach, called **formulation**, to come to an individual understanding of a person's distress. Formulation is discussed in more detail in Chapter 4. When working with an individual, it doesn't really matter whether (for example) the research shows that as a group, people sharing their diagnosis are less likely to have suicidal thoughts if the person in front of you does have suicidal thoughts. Research can guide and inform choices, but individual differences mean that there will never be one-size-fits-all.

3.3 Causes of mental health problems

By now you may be thinking that the task of establishing causality is so complex that we can't draw any general conclusions at all about what does cause mental health problems. Luckily, this is not the case. There are some experiences or characteristics which are consistently linked in the research with an increased likelihood of developing mental health problems.

These factors fall into broad categories. These are life experiences, psychological differences, societal factors, and biological factors. All of these factors will interact with each other and they can all exist concurrently, creating what Eric Turkheimer, psychologist and behavioural geneticist, calls 'a hypercomplex developmental network' (Turkheimer, 2011).

A recent development in mental health has been the application of a **complex systems approach** to understanding causality (Fried and Robinaugh, 2020). This approach uses computer modelling to look at the complex and multi-level interplay between neurobiological and psychosocial factors. A strength of this approach is that it can identify feedback loops which can then be used to plan more effective and multi-faceted interventions (Langellier et al., 2019). The complex systems approach suggests that it is not enough to understand the different components, we must also look at the interactions between them. The opposite of this approach could be said to be reductionism, where a complex phenomenon is reduced to its most basic parts and it is assumed that there is a single cause.

3.4 Life experiences

Many psychologists look first to life experiences when trying to understand why someone is having difficulties. This includes early experiences, trauma and adversity, and family relationships (Hughes et al., 2017). It's now well accepted that childhood trauma can make people more likely to develop mental (and physical) health problems in adulthood, but this is in fact a relatively recent discovery. It all started in 1985 in an obesity clinic run by Kaiser Permanente (a health insurance company) in San Diego, California. Doctors noticed that 50% of their patients were dropping out of the weight-loss programme, despite successfully losing weight. Wanting to solve the mystery of why this was happening, Vincent Felitti, the head of the clinic, interviewed 286 of the drop-outs. He found to his surprise that a majority of them had been abused as children, and that many of them saw a connection between this and their difficulties with their weight. Kaiser Permanente went onto conduct huge surveys with their clients of 'adverse childhood experiences' or **ACEs**. They found that ACEs were common, often occurred together, and seemed to have a 'dose-response' relationship with both physical and mental health problems (Felitti et al., 1998). ACEs include factors such as witnessing violence, having a parent in

prison whilst growing up, and having a parent with a drug or alcohol problem.

Several reviews and meta-analyses indicate that people who develop psychosis are more likely to have a history of childhood trauma than those who do not (Inyang et al., 2022, Varese et al., 2012, Matheson et al., 2013). To add complexity, recent genetically informed studies have suggested that increased exposure to trauma in childhood is positively associated with the genetic liability for receiving a diagnosis of schizophrenia (Sallis et al., 2021). Essentially this means that those who are at a higher genetic risk for developing severe mental health problems are also more likely to experience trauma in childhood, and therefore the direction of causality is unclear. The authors suggest that perhaps those individuals at higher genetic risk could benefit from early interventions to reduce their exposure to trauma. Genetic influences on mental health will be discussed later in this chapter and in Chapter 9.

3.5 Psychological differences

People vary in how they respond to different situations, and the way in which they think about and experience the world. Some people may have more of a tendency to think and react in ways which may make them vulnerable. Studies have found that having a ruminative thinking style, for example, is a risk factor for developing depression as well as being a symptom of depression (Whisman et al., 2020). Others have found that low self-esteem is a vulnerability factor for developing depressive symptoms during adolescence (Masselink et al., 2018).

Different psychological models have different ways of thinking about causality. A cognitive model suggests that mental health problems are caused by the way in which people have interpreted and responded to their life experiences, forming beliefs about themselves which then act as vulnerability factors. In contrast, a psychoanalytic model suggests that unconscious emotions and thoughts drive behaviour, and that developing an awareness of these recurring patterns can promote insight and allow healing. Systemic theory sees humans in the context of those around them—usually their family—and seeks to understand thoughts and behaviour by looking at the dynamics and interactions. The different theories will affect the way in which psychologists understand a person's problems, and also the explanations that they offer to the people that they see.

Psychological factors are influenced by the environment and biology, and there is some debate over whether psychological factors can really be considered as causal, or whether they are in fact better thought of as mediators between biology, social factors, and a person's response.

3.6 Societal factors

Most life experiences aren't random. The society you live in and your social status in that society affect what happens to you. Social context affects the life experiences a person has, their opportunities, and the way in which they think about themselves and the world around them. There are some specific societal factors which have been shown to have an impact on mental health on a group level, including socioeconomic inequality, sex differences, and racial discrimination.

Inequality

There is strong evidence that living in an unequal society affects mental health (Wilkinson and Pickett, 2018). Wilkinson and Pickett argue that inequality directly creates distress, as people at all levels of income worry about their social status and what will happen to them or their children if they lose status. Income inequality in a country is associated with a higher incidence of problems such as depression (Patel et al., 2018). This holds regardless of how high incomes are in the country as a whole—a lower income country with a more equal income distribution will have better mental health overall than a higher income country with a less equal distribution.

Being in a lower socioeconomic position is related to a significantly higher probability of developing mental health problems. Children and adults who are in the lowest 20% for income in the UK are two to three times more likely to experience difficulties than those in the top 20% (Marmot et al., 2010). Marmot describes a 'social gradient' of mental health which is more extreme in less equal societies. Critics argue that it is possible that this social gradient exists because mental health problems make someone more likely to live in poverty, rather than poverty making it more likely for someone to experience mental health problems. It is of course possible for both these things to be true.

Sex differences

Men and women live different lives side by side, even in higher income countries, and this affects both their experiences and how they express distress. Girls are significantly more likely to be sexually abused than boys, with three times as many girls than boys experiencing sexual abuse before the age of 16 in the UK (Office for National Statistics, 2020a). As adults, men are more likely to serve in armed conflict, whilst women are more likely to be victims of domestic abuse. In many parts of the world, women are still not allowed to make choices about their lives and have very limited opportunities in life when compared to men. Bearing children brings its own risks, with studies finding that up to 30% of women become depressed in the perinatal period (Dagher et al., 2021) and a very small number of women developing postpartum psychosis (VanderKruik et al., 2017).

In addition to their different life experiences, men and women report different symptoms of distress. Women are more likely to get diagnoses of eating disorders, anxiety, depression, and emotionally unstable personality disorder, whilst men are more likely to be given diagnoses of alcohol or substance misuse and anti-social personality disorder. Explanations for this vary, from biological differences between the sexes, to the different social roles expected of men and women and the lower social status of women in most countries in the world.

Racism and racial inequality

The effects of racial inequality on people's lives caught the attention of the global media in 2020. The COVID-19 pandemic had a disproportionate effect on people from ethnic minorities, particularly Black people (Office for National Statistics, 2020a). The *Black Lives Matter* movement swept major cities across the world following the videoed murder of George Floyd (who was Black) by a white police officer. Anger was expressed about the differential and discriminatory treatment of Black people by the police, the criminal justice system, the health system, and the education system.

There are strong indications that the experience of being Black or in a minoritised racial group in the UK or the USA causes distress. Community survey data from the UK indicates that being Black in the UK is associated with a higher risk of developing psychosis, even when unemployment and socioeconomic position are controlled for (Qassem et al., 2015). Belonging to an ethnic minority group (particularly Black Caribbean or Black African) in the UK is associated with a higher rate of involuntary admission to psychiatric hospital (Barnett et al., 2019). Being a migrant (whatever your skin colour) is also associated with an increased likelihood of being detained by the mental health system on compulsory grounds. Discrimination against minorities causes ongoing distress which for some will result in severe mental health problems.

One recent change is the growing recognition of the cumulative and damaging effects of apparently small acts of racial discrimination. An earlier focus on highly visible events such as racist attacks rather than on effects of ongoing 'lower level' discrimination may have led researchers to underestimate the effect that racism has on mental health (Wallace, Nazroo, and Becares, 2016). In Chapter 7, personal accounts illustrate how people make sense of these experiences for themselves.

Intersectionality

A recent development in mental health (related to the social justice model I discussed in Chapter 2) has been an interest in **intersectionality**. This approach suggests that different factors can combine to create unique circumstances which can be missed if we look at separate categories. The term was coined by an American lawyer, Kimberlé Crenshaw, who successfully argued in a legal case that Black women were being uniquely discriminated against in a way which was missed by focusing on race and sex separately. Since then, the term intersectionality has been used very widely, far beyond the original context, and it is sometimes used to make generalisations which may or may not be true for a given individual.

Through an intersectional lens, a Black woman on a low income is at the intersection of social inequality and sex and racial discrimination, all of which are risk factors for developing mental health problems and could result in her being discriminated against in ways in which a Black woman on a high income, or a white woman on a low income, would not experience. Her specific vulnerability may not be reflected by research which looks at race, sex, and income factors separately.

Critics argue that this leads us to dividing people into smaller and smaller groups, which makes it difficult to draw conclusions or to design research studies. They say that whilst the idea that different factors

interact is indisputable, intersectionality leads people to make assumptions about people based on immutable characteristics, and that this is not how the theory was originally intended to be used.

Many aspects of a person's experience can affect their probability of developing mental health problems. However, the way in which this occurs is reflected in an individual's biology, and it is here that I will turn to next.

3.7 Biology

The importance of biology in mental health is indisputable. Everything that we think and do is reflected in our biology. Traditionally, the focus of attention in mental health has been on the brain, but there is a growing interest in how different parts of our brain and body interact (Palacios-Garcia and Parada, 2020).

This section will discuss different aspects of human biology and how they relate to mental health. These will include **heritability**, **neurotransmitters**, the **brain–gut axis**, and brain structure. There is some further discussion of **behavioural genetics** in Chapter 9.

Genes and heritability

It's common to see media reports claiming that mental health problems are down to our genes. In 2017, the Daily Mail told us that 80% of a person's risk of developing schizophrenia is genetic (Tanner, 2017). It's true that the heritability of being diagnosed with schizophrenia is usually estimated at about 80 (Avramopoulos, 2018). This is where the 80% figure comes from. Most mental health problems are **heritable** to some degree. What this really means is often misunderstood.

Heritability is a measure of variation between people. A high heritability means that much of the difference between people in a particular group can be explained by genetic differences. It doesn't mean that for any given individual, genes account for a particular percentage of a person's mental health difficulties. It also doesn't mean that the genes cause problems in brain development which directly cause mental health problems. Perhaps most counter-intuitively, a high heritability score does not imply that the environment is unimportant. In fact, the more equal an environment is, the more likely it is that heritability estimates will be high.

UNDERSTANDING THE TERMINOLOGY 3.1

Heritability

Imagine a group of people where everyone has enough to eat and therefore growth is not limited by nutrition. People will still differ in height, and these differences will largely be down to their genes. There is no other reason for a person to grow or not grow, except for childhood illness, accidents, or prematurity, which will affect only a few. Heritability will be high in this group, perhaps as high as .90 or more.

Now imagine a less equal group where some children are malnourished. In this group, heritability will be lower than

the first. This is because the malnourished children will not grow as tall as they would have done if they had had enough to eat. Being malnourished can disrupt growth. The unequal environment is an important source of variance between people.

This doesn't mean that the environment is more important for the second group than the first group. For both groups, the environment is an important factor, but for the first group it is not a source of difference between individuals.

This is easiest to visualise using the example of height, discussed in Box 3.1.

Even a relatively simply trait like height is affected by environment, and mental health problems are far more complex than height. The way that genes for complex traits work mean that the environment is always important. As Kathryn Paige Harden, behavioural geneticist and psychologist, explains in her book (Harden, 2021) this has the perhaps counter-intuitive consequence of meaning that interventions to improve the environment of disadvantaged groups can result in a rise in heritability. If a group (for example women) are barred from education due to discrimination and have few opportunities in life beyond marriage and motherhood, then their genes will make less difference to their life course. No matter what their genes, they aren't allowed to get an education, which means that the heritability of their educational achievement will be low. If women are allowed to access education, then educational achievement will become more heritable. Genetic differences become more important when the environment is more equal. One implication of this is that heritability estimates may well not generalise beyond the specific group being studied.

Current research indicates that genetic risk factors for mental health problems are made up of thousands of tiny genetic differences, all of which are present in the general population. These genetic differences are not mutations, or faulty genes, they are part of the normal range of genetic variation. Researchers add up all of the information across many different genes to create a single number—called the **polygenic index** or score. This polygenic index then is used to predict risk. These polygenic indices are, however, specific to

the population which was studied. Just because a polygenic index predicts a percentage of the likelihood of development of mental health problems in a group of white Swedish people, does not mean it would have the same effect in a population of Black Congolese individuals. As yet, almost all large-scale genetic studies are done with majority white populations from Europe or North America. This means that their usefulness is limited when thinking about a global population.

The actions of the many genes which make up a polygenic index are not well understood. It appears that many of the differences have several different actions—a gene which is associated with a diagnosis of schizophrenia may also be associated with doing well at school, for example. The quest to identify genetic influences in mental health is a fast-moving area of research and is discussed in more detail in Chapter 9.

Neurotransmitters

Neurotransmitters are biochemicals which transmit messages between cells in the brain by crossing the synapses. Many of the drugs used as anti-depressants and anti-psychotics work on these neurotransmitters, in particular the serotonin system (anti-depressants) and the **dopamine** system (anti-psychotics). Working backwards from this, it has been proposed that imbalances in neurotransmitters may cause problems in mental health—the 'chemical imbalance' theory. Many people are told this by their doctors and so it has become a common way of understanding mental health problems.

There are observable differences in the way neurotransmitters work in people with a diagnosis of mental health problems. Recent advances in brain imaging have enabled differences to be measured *in vivo* and have found, (for example) differences in synaptic functioning in 'schizophrenia patients' as compared to people with no history of symptoms of schizophrenia (Onwordi et al., 2020). Alterations in the neurotransmitters GABA and glutamate have been shown consistently in both those diagnosed with schizophrenia and mood disorders (Reddy-Thootkur, Kraguljac, and Lahti, 2020).

Findings of differences in the way that brains work often lead to claims that a particular trait is 'hard wired', meaning that it is just part of someone's neurological make up, rather than anything to do with environment. Critics say that this is misleading, as it ignores the ways in which brains change and adapt to the environment. They argue that in many cases, differences in the way that brains work could be attributed to antipsychotic drugs and do not pre-date a person's mental health problems. Anti-psychotic drugs themselves cause changes in neurotransmitters and most people who are given a diagnosis of schizophrenia in the UK or USA will be on these drugs for years.

It is clear that differences in neurotransmitters can be seen in those with mental health problems and that drugs act upon these pathways. It is less clear whether imbalances in these neurotransmitters are a cause rather than a consequence of these experiences.

Brain–gut axis

Sometimes when talking about the biology of mental health, the focus is on the brain as the location of emotions and thoughts, whilst ignoring the way in which our bodies and brains are interconnected. There is an increasing interest in research in the way in which other areas of the body communicate with the brain, in particular the brain–gut axis, a bidirectional communication network which allows the brain to influence intestinal activities as well as vice versa. The gastrointestinal tract hosts an abundance of microbes, and the way in which this microbiome links to wellbeing, cognition, and development is an increasing target of research interest (Rogers et al., 2016).

It has been proposed that this axis mediates the effect of both genetic and environmental factors on brain development and function. Much of this research is based on animal models, which have suggested a role for microbiota in anxiety, mood, cognition, and pain (Cryan and Dinan, 2012). In humans, this has led to hope that using prebiotic or probiotic dietary supplements might improve mental health, and there is some evidence that probiotics may reduce symptoms of depression, although the evidence for schizophrenia, stress, and anxiety is less clear (Zagorska et al., 2020).

The use of animal models for researching mental health problems is controversial, as it is not obvious whether a mouse being used to model depression can be said to experience the same thing as a human. In addition, using animal models inevitably focuses research away from social and psychological factors and onto basic biological mechanisms.

Brain structure

Brains can now be scanned using **functional magnetic resonance imaging (fMRI)**, meaning that, for the first time, it is possible to look at brains whilst they are working rather than only at post-mortem. This has led to a dramatic increase in our understanding of how brains function and develop over time. There is significant evidence for structural brain differences in those with serious mental health problems as compared to those with no history of difficulties. A meta-analysis including 2,028 individuals found that people with a diagnosis of schizophrenia had smaller hippocampus, amygdala, thalamus accumbens, and intracranial volumes, as well as larger pallidum and larger ventricle volumes (van Erp et al., 2015).

Experience will change brain structure and function, a process known as **neuroplasticity**, but brain function will also drive experience. Animal models suggest that there are sensitive periods for the development of distinct brain structures, meaning that the timing of a person's (and particularly a child's) experiences can be crucial when it comes to the long-term impact on development and mental health (Luby et al., 2020). Studies from the English-Romanian Adoptee study have shown that early childhood deprivation is associated with alterations in adult brain structure (Mackes et al., 2020). This does not mean that structural differences in the brain indicate that something is inevitable or entirely biologically determined. Environment and biology interact throughout development.

There are observable structural brain differences in children who experience early trauma (Bellis and Zisk, 2014). The result of this could be that these children may then demonstrate challenging behaviours, which will in turn influence their environment and how others treat them. If a child's behaviour is highly disruptive, for example, they may end up excluded from school, which will affect their education and development. In this way, brain structure can both drive experience and change in response to it. Of course, brain structure will also reflect psychological functioning, which acts as the mediating factor between biological difference and observed behaviour.

When it comes to people with severe mental health problems there is also the complicating factor of drugs. People who have a long involvement with mental health services have typically been on very strong, brain-altering drugs for years. There is evidence that long-term use of anti-psychotic drugs leads to changes in brain structure (Huhtaniska et al., 2017). Most studies of the effects of drugs used in mental health are short term and the long-term effects are not well understood.

Biology is clearly an important part of the picture when understanding mental health, with biological changes interacting with environmental events in highly complex cascading networks. Why then, do some people feel so strongly that we should not be spending so much time and money researching the biological causes of distress? Why does it matter?

It comes down to politics and priorities.

3.8 The politics of causation

How we understand the causes of distress is intensely political. If we believe that mental health problems are biological or located in the brain, this locates the problem with the individual. They are seen as ill and as requiring treatment. Funding will be channelled to genetic and neurobiological research, and drugs or other medical interventions will be seen as the most promising solution.

If, however, we understand mental health problems as being caused by wider social issues, mediated by biology and psychology, then the onus is on politicians and communities to address those social problems. Giving people drugs then seems like a less attractive long-term solution. It leads us to ask, would it not be better to address racial inequality rather than to deal with the consequences by admitting young Black men to hospital with psychosis? Focusing exclusively on a biological explanation can direct our attention away from injustice and power imbalances in the wider world.

Those who take this approach argue that we already know the most important social and societal factors which affect mental health. They suggest that rather than working on identifying the biomarkers, we should see these biological changes as mediators and our energies should be focused on changing the circumstances which put people at risk. We know, for example, that inequality, abuse, and poverty in childhood make people vulnerable, and so perhaps mental health programmes should be focused on this, rather than on identifying (and trying to change) biological and psychological factors.

Others strongly disagree, and feel that identifying biomarkers and genetic vulnerability is our best hope of helping those with mental health problems. They point out that when a person is in distress we need effective interventions, and they think that understanding what is happening on a biological level may help us to develop these. The latest research focuses on how biology and social factors work together and emphasises that they cannot be separated. Harden (Harden, 2021) argues that only by using genetically informed studies can we really understand how the environment affects us, as otherwise we may assume that environmental differences are causing something which is in fact mostly genetic.

Psychologists typically work at the individual psychological level, alongside psychiatrists who may be more biologically focused. This means that they hear about the details of a person's life and develop an appreciation of how mental health exists in context. However, they still are mainly reactive, addressing mental health problems as they arise. This is, after all, how the health system works. It is unusual for applied psychologists to be focused at the level of society. Organisations such as Psychologists for Social Change argue that psychology should be applied to policy and political action, seeking to change context rather than solely focusing on individuals.

Chapter Summary

- Causality is complex, and individual differences means that the effects of any one event may be very different for different people.

- Almost all causal influences in mental health, including biological factors, are probabilistic rather than deterministic.

- The main factors which have been identified as contributing to mental health problems are life experiences, social context, psychological factors, and biology.
- These factors interact with each other in a complex system.

- The way we understand the causes of mental health problems is political, as it determines where interventions and research are directed.

? QUESTIONS

1. How would you design a study to look at the effects of social interaction on depression? Describe your study design and justify why this is an appropriate choice.

2. What are the advantages and disadvantages of different study designs when looking at mental health? Which would you choose to investigate the impact of illegal drug use on mental health and how would you set the study up?

3. 'It has been proven that schizophrenia is 80% genetic'. True or false? Justify your response.

4. Does observing differences in the brains of people with mental health problems mean that their problems are caused by biology? Why or why not?

 ## FURTHER READING

Chambliss, D., and Schutt, R. (2019). *Making Sense of the Social World. Methods of Investigation*, Sixth Edition. Thousand Oaks, CA: Sage.

If you want to understand research design and the difficulties in establishing causality, then this is a thorough introduction.

Harden, K.P. (2021). *The Genetic Lottery: Why DNA Matters for Social Equality*. Princeton, NJ: Princeton University Press.

This highly readable book explores the interaction between genes and the environment, tackling issues of heritability, causality, and inequality head-on.

Linden, D. (2019). *The Biology of Psychological Disorders*. London: Red Globe Press.

Schaefer, J., Caspi, A., Belsky, D., Harrington, H., Houts, R., Horwood, L.J., Hussong, A., Ramrakha, S., Poulton, R., and Moffit, T. (2017). Enduring mental health: Prevalence and prediction. *Journal of Abnormal Psychology*, 126(2), 212–224. doi: 10.1037/abn0000232

This paper is from the longitudinal cohort Dunedin study and suggests that the majority of people do not experience 'enduring mental health' in the sense of never meeting criteria for a diagnosis.

Sonuga-Barke, E., Kennedy, M., Kumsta, R., Knights, N., Golm, D., Rutter, M., et al. (2017). Child-to-adult neurodevelopmental and mental health trajectories after early life deprivation: The young adult follow-up of the longitudinal English and Romanian Adoptees study. *The Lancet*, 389(10078), 1529–1548.

This is a follow-up study looking at the long-term outcomes of children adopted from Romania, when compared to English adoptees.

Vigen, T. (2015). *Spurious Correlations*. New York: Hachette Books.

This light-hearted book by a military intelligence analyst makes the point that we must never assume that correlation equals causation.

Wilkinson, R., and Pickett, K. (2018). *The Inner Level: How More Equal Societies Reduce Stress, Restore Sanity and Increase Everyone's Wellbeing*. London: Penguin.

This book, by two academics, argues that unequal societies are damaging mental health and that reducing inequality would be an effective way to improve wellbeing.

 **REFERENCES**

Astle, D.E., and Fletcher-Watson, S. (2020). Beyond the core-deficit hypothesis in developmental disorders. *Current Directions in Psychological Science*, 29(5), 431–437. doi:10.1177/0963721420925518

Avramopoulos, D. (2018). Recent advances in the genetics of schizophrenia. *Molecular Neuropsychiatry*, 4, 35–51.

Barnett, P., Mackay, E., Matthews, H., Gate, R., Greenwood, H., et al. (2019). Ethnic variations in compulsory detentions under the Mental Health Act: A systematic review and meta-analysis of international data. *The Lancet*, 6(4), 305–317.

Bellis, M., and Zisk, A. (2014). The biological effects of childhood trauma. *Child and Adolescent Psychiatric Clinics of North America*, 23, 185–222.

Brown, G.W., and Harris, T. (1978). *Social Origins of Depression: A Study of Psychiatric Disorder in Women.* London: Tavistock.

Caspi, A., Houts, R.M., Belsky, D.W., Goldman-Mellor, S.J., Harrington, H., Israel, S., Meier, M.H., Ramrakha, S., Shalev, I., Poulton, R., and Moffitt, T.E. (2014). The p Factor: One general psychopathology factor in the structure of psychiatric disorders? *Clinical Psychological Science: A Journal of the Association for Psychological Science*, 2(2), 119–137. doi:10.1177/2167702613497473

Cryan, J., and Dinan, T. (2012). Mind-altering microorganisms: The impact of the gut microbiota on brain and behaviour. *Nature Reviews Neuroscience*, 13, 701–712. doi:10.1038/nrn3346

Dagher, R., Bruckhein, H., Colpe, L., Edwards, E., and White, D. (2021). Perinatal depression: Challenges and opportunities. *Journal of Women's Health*, 30(2), 154–159. doi:10.1089/jwh.2020.8862

Felitti, V., Anda, R., Nordenberg, D., Edwards, V., Koss, M., Marks, J., et al. (1998). Relationship of childhood abuse and household dysfunction to many of the leading causes of death in adults: The Adverse Childhood Experiences (ACE) study. *American Journal of Preventative Medicine*, 14(4), 245–258.

Fried, E.I., and Robinaugh, D.J. (2020). Systems all the way down: Embracing complexity in mental health research. *BMC Medicine*, 18, 205.

Greenhalgh, T., Thorne, S., and Malterud, K. (2018). Time to challenge the spurious hierarchy of systematic over narrative reviews? *European Journal of Clinical Investigation*, 48(6), e12931. doi:10.1111/eci.12931

Harden, K.P. (2021). *The Genetic Lottery: Why DNA Matters for Social Equality.* Princeton, NJ: Princeton University Press.

Huhtaniska, S., Jääskeläinen, E., Hirvonen, N., Remes, J., Murray, G., et al. (2017). Long-term antipsychotic use and brain changes in schizophrenia—a systematic review and meta-analysis. *Human Psychopharmacology*, 32(2). doi:10.1002/hup.2574

Hughes, K., Bellis, M., Hardcastle, K., Sethi, D., Butchart, A., Mikton, C., Jones, L., and Dunne, M. (2017). The effect of multiple adverse childhood experiences on health: A systematic review and meta-analysis. *The Lancet Public Health*, 2(8), 356–366.

Hunt, M., Marx, R., Lipson, C., and Young, J. (2018). No more FOMO: Limiting social media decreases loneliness and depression. *Journal of Social and Clinical Psychology*, 37(10), 751. doi:10.1521/jscp.2018.37.10.751

Inyang, B., Gondal, F.J., Abah, G.A., Dhandapani, M.M., Manne, M., Khanna, M., … Mohammed, L. (2022). The role of childhood trauma in psychosis and schizophrenia: A systematic review. *Cureus*, 14(1), e21466. doi:10.7759/cureus.21466

Langellier, B.A., Yang, Y., Purtle, J., et al. (2019). Complex systems approaches to understand drivers of mental health and inform mental health policy: A systematic review. *Administration and Policy in Mental Health*, 46, 128–144. doi:10.1007/s10488-018-0887-5

Lieberman, A., Rogers, M., Graham, A., and Joiner, T. (2021). Examining correlates of suicidal ideation between those with and without psychosis in a psychiatric inpatient sample. *Journal of Affective Disorders*, 294, 245–260.

Linden, D. (2019). *The Biology of Psychological Disorders*. London: Red Globe Press.

Luby, J., Baram, T., Rogers, C., and Barch, D. (2020). Neurodevelopmental optimisation after early-life adversity: Cross-species studies to elucidate sensitive periods and brain mechanisms to inform early intervention. *Trends in Neurosciences*, 43(10), 744–751. doi:10.1016/j.tins.2020.08.001

Mackes, N.K., Golm, D., Sarkar, S., Kumsta, R., Rutter, M., Fairchild, G., Mehta, M.A., and Sonuga-Barke, E.J.S. on behalf of the ERA Young Adult Follow-up team (2020). Early childhood deprivation is associated with alterations in adult brain structure despite subsequent environmental enrichment. *Proceedings of the National Academy of Sciences*, 117(1), 641–649. doi:10.1073/pnas.1911264116

Marmot, M., Allen, J., Goldblatt, P., Boyce, T., McNeish, D., Grady, M., and Geddes, I. (2010). *Fair Society, Healthy Lives*. Strategic review of health inequalities in English post 2010. The Marmot Review report. Institute of Health Equity.

Masselink, M., Van Roekel, E., and Oldehinkel, A. (2018). Self-esteem in early adolescence as predictor of depressive symptoms in late adolescence and early adulthood: The mediating role of motivational and social factors. *Journal of Youth and Adolescence*, 47, 932–946. doi:10.1007/s10964-017-0727-z

Matheson, S.L., Shepherd, A.M., Pinchbeck, R.M., Laurens, K.R., and Carr, V.J. (2013). Childhood adversity in schizophrenia: A systematic meta-analysis. *Psychological Medicine*, 43(2), 225–238. doi:10.1017/S0033291712000785

Munafo, M., and Davey-Smith, G. (2018). Robust research needs many lines of evidence. *Nature*, 553(7689), 399–401. doi:10.1038/d41586-018-01023-3

OCEBM Levels of Evidence Working Group (2011). *The Oxford 2011 Levels of Evidence*. Oxford Centre for Evidence-Based Medicine. http://www.cebm.net/index.aspx?o=5653

Office for National Statistics (ONS) (2020a). *Child Sexual Abuse in England and Wales: Year Ending March 2019*. Updated January 2020. https://www.ons.gov.uk/peoplepopulationandcommunity/crimeandjustice/articles/childsexualabuseinengland andwales/yearendingmarch2019#characteristics-of-victims-of-child-sexual-abuse

Office For National Statistics (ONS) (2020b). *Statistical Bulletin: Coronavirus (COVID-19) Related Deaths by Ethnic Group, England and Wales: 2 March 2020 to 15 May 2020*. Released 19 June 2020. https://www. ons.gov.uk/peoplepopulationandcommunity/birthsdeathsandmarriages/deaths/articles/coronaviruscovid 19relateddeathsbyethnicgroupenglandandwales/2march2020to15may2020

Onwordi, E., Halff, E., Whitehurst, T., Mansur, A., Cotel, M., Wells, L., et al. (2020). Synaptic density marker SV2A is reduced in schizophrenia patients and unaffected by antipsychotics in rats. *Nature Communications*, 11, 246.

Patel, V., Burns, J., Dhingra, M., et al. (2018). Income inequality and depression: A systematic review and meta-analysis of the association and a scoping review of mechanisms. *World Psychiatry*, 17 (1), 76–89. doi:10.1002/wps.20492

Palacios-Garcia, I., and Parada, F. (2020). Measuring the brain-gut axis in psychological sciences: A necessary challenge. *Frontiers in Integrative Neuroscience*. doi:10.3389/fnint.2019.00073

Qassem, T., Bebbington, P., Spiers, N., McManus, S., Jenkins, R., and Dein, S. (2015). Prevalence of psychosis in black ethnic minorities in Britain: Analysis based on three national surveys. *Social Psychiatry and Psychiatric Epidemiology*, 50(7), 1057–1064. doi:10.1007/s00127-014-0960-7

Reddy-Thootkur, M., Kraguljac, N., and Lahti, A. (2020). The role of glutamate and GABA in cognitive dysfunction in schizophrenia and mood disorders—a systematic review of magnetic resonance spectroscopy studies. *Schizophrenia Research*, 249, 74–84. doi:10.1016/j.schres.2020.02.001

Rogers, G.B., Keating, D.J., Young, R.L., Wong, M.L., Licinio, J., and Wesselingh, S. (2016). From gut dysbiosis to altered brain function and mental illness: Mechanisms and pathways. *Molecular Psychiatry*, 21(6), 738–748. doi:10.1038/mp.2016.50

Sallis, H., Croft, J., Havdahl, A., Jones, H., Dunn, E., Davey Smith, G., ... Munafò, M. (2021). Genetic liability to schizophrenia is associated with exposure to traumatic events in childhood. *Psychological Medicine*, 51(11), 1814–1821. doi:10.1017/S0033291720000537

Schaefer, J., Caspi, A., Belsky, D., Harrington, H., Houts, R., Horwood, L.J., Hussong, A., Ramrakha, S., Poulton, R., and Moffit, T. (2017). Enduring mental health: Prevalence and prediction. *Journal of Abnormal Psychology*, 126(2), 212–224. doi:10.1037/abn0000232

Shakeshaft, A., Blakey, R., Kwong, A., Riglin, L., Smith, G., Stergiokouli, E., Tilling, K., and Thapar, A. (2023). Mental health before and during the COVID-19 pandemic in adults with neurodevelopmental disorder. *Journal of Psychiatric Research*, 159, 230–239. doi:10.1016/j.jpsychires.2023.01.029

Shean, G. (2014). Limitations of randomized control designs in psychotherapy research. *Advances in Psychiatry*, 2014, 561452. doi:10.1155/2014/561452

Sonuga-Barke, E., Kennedy, M., Kumsta, R., Knights, N., Golm, D., Rutter, M., et al. (2017). Child-to-adult neurodevelopmental and mental health trajectories after early life deprivation: The young adult follow-up of the longitudinal English and Romanian Adoptees study. *The Lancet*, 389(10078), 1529–1548.

Sweeney, A., Beresford, P., Faulkner, A., Nettle, M., and Rose, D. (2009). *This is Survivor Research*. Monmouth: PCCS Books.

Tanner, C. (2017). Seeds of schizophrenia are sown before birth: Almost 80% of a person's risk of developing the mental illness is genetic, reveals study. *Daily Mail* online. Retrieved 30 January 2020. https://www.dailymail.co.uk/health/article-4956030/Almost-80-schizophrenia-risk-genetics.html

Turkheimer, E. (2011). Commentary: Variation and causation in the environment and genome. *International Journal of Epidemiology*, 40(3), 598–601.

Van Erp, T., Hibar, D., Rasmussen, J., Glahn, D., et al. (2015). Subcortical brain volume abnormalities in 2028 individuals with schizophrenia and 2540 healthy controls via the ENIGMA consortium. *Molecular Psychiatry*, 21, 547–553.

VanderKruik, R., Barreix, M., Chou, D., Allen, T., Say, L., and Cohen, L. (2017). The global prevalence of postpartum psychosis: A systematic review. *BMC Psychiatry*, 17, 272. doi:10.1186/s12888-017-1427-7

Varese, F., Smeets, F., Drukker, M., Lieverse, R., Lataster, T., Viechtbauer, W., and Bentall, R.P. (2012). Childhood trauma increases the risk of psychosis: A meta-analysis of patient-control, prospective- and cross-sectional cohort studies. *Schizophrenia Bulletin*, 38(4), 661–671. doi:10.1093/schbul/sbs050

Vigen, T. (2015). *Spurious Correlations*. New York: Hachette Books.

Wallace, S., Nazroo, J., and Bécares, L. (2016). Cumulative effect of racial discrimination on the mental health of ethnic minorities in the United Kingdom. *American Journal of Public Health*, 106(7), 1294–1300. doi:10.2105/AJPH.2016.303121

Whisman, M., du Pont, A., and Butterworth, P. (2020). Longitudinal associations between rumination and depressive symptoms in a probability sample of adults. *Journal of Affective Disorders*, 260(1), 680–686.

Wilkinson, R., and Pickett, K. (2018). *The Inner Level: How More Equal Societies Reduce Stress, Restore Sanity and Increase Everyone's Wellbeing*. London: Penguin.

Zacher, H., and Rudolph, C. W. (2021). Individual differences and changes in subjective wellbeing during the early stages of the COVID-19 pandemic. *American Psychologist*, 76(1), 50–62. doi:10.1037/amp0000702

Zagorska, A., Marcinkowska, M., Jamrozik, M., Wisniowska, B., and Pasko, P. (2020). From probiotics to psychobiotics—the gut-brain axis in psychiatric disorders. *Beneficial Microbes*, 11(8), 717–732.

Chapter 4

Offering Explanations: Diagnosis, Formulation, and the Power Threat Meaning Framework

Learning objectives

When you have completed this chapter, you should be able to do the following:

4.1 Conceptualise one of the roles of a mental health practitioner as offering explanations for people's experiences and behaviour.

4.2 Explain how a psychiatric diagnosis is arrived at and how they differ to many diagnoses of physical health conditions.

4.3 Critically evaluate why alternatives to diagnosis may be necessary.

4.4 Outline what is meant by a psychological formulation and explain how they are used.

4.5 Describe the main assumptions underpinning the Power Threat Meaning Framework and explain how it differs from other frameworks.

4.6 Compare and contrast the three methods outlined in this chapter and give advantages and disadvantages of each.

Introduction

When a person (or their family) seeks help with their distress or unusual experiences, other people, including professionals, must respond. One of the ways in which they do this is to offer explanations or reasons as to why this person is feeling the way that they do. Not every professional will respond in the same way. The explanations they offer will be informed by the way that they understand emotional distress and unusual experiences and the theoretical models they use (see Chapter 2). This chapter will focus on the different types of explanations which professionals offer people within mental health services. You'll learn about the assumptions underpinning different systems. I will explain the advantages and disadvantages of each approach and will focus on three main alternatives: diagnosis, formulation, and the Power Threat Meaning Framework (PTMF).

CASE STUDY 4.1

Peter's Story

A few years ago, I was working in a neurodevelopmental clinic for children at a well-known teaching hospital. The waiting list was long, and some families had been waiting for almost two years. We offered each family an assessment. A clinical psychologist would do a structured diagnostic interview with the parents, whilst an assistant psychologist carried out a structured play-based assessment with the child. We would then discuss our results in a team, along with reviewing questionnaires completed by the child's school, their parents, and by the older children themselves, and we would come to a conclusion about a diagnosis. The possibilities were autism spectrum disorder (ASD), attention deficit hyperactivity disorder (ADHD), or to give no diagnosis.

I was confident in my ability to identify the relevant symptoms, I stuck closely to the diagnostic criteria, and would write my reports giving evidence for each criterion met. I would also discuss the child at length with the assistant psychologist and sometimes also with the consultant psychiatrist in charge of the team.

Peter was about seven. As he came into the room, he went straight to the corner to stand behind his mother's chair, quietly observing me. He didn't respond to any of my attempts to get to know him. His family was from eastern Europe. Peter attended the local primary school, where they were concerned about him because he hardly spoke and had no friends.

As I asked Peter's parents about his developmental history, they told me about how different he was from his siblings. He didn't interact with other children in the same way, and his play was repetitive. As I asked the series of questions which make up a diagnostic interview, it all seemed to be pointing towards a diagnosis of autism.

After a discussion with other members of the team and a review of the results of the diagnostic observations, interviews, and questionnaires, we had another meeting with Peter and his family. I explained that Peter met the criteria for a diagnosis of autism spectrum disorder. It is a lifelong diagnosis. I said that it was likely that he would not grow out of all his unusual behaviour although it would change over time, and that, given the problems he was having, he might need extra support at school or to attend a specialist school.

His father looked surprised. 'But', he said, 'the last doctor told us to stop worrying, that he wasn't autistic! Why are you telling me he is?'

My stomach dropped. I asked them to excuse me for a moment and went to talk to the team manager.

It turned out that due to an administrative error, Peter and his family had indeed been seen twice, three weeks apart, for the same assessment done by two different teams at the same hospital. Last time his family had been told that he was not autistic.

The family had assumed that the second appointment was for a follow-up, and had gone along with our questions, despite not knowing why we had called them in again.

It was a rude awakening for me. First, that a diagnostic process could be so unreliable within the same hospital that a child could be told that they didn't meet criteria for a diagnosis of autism and then three weeks later that they did. Second, that the family had such respect for the health system and the authority of health professionals that they had taken the day off work and school, turned up, and gone through an entire second assessment, despite having already been through the process. And third, that we were giving children diagnoses of neurodevelopmental disorders, telling their parents that their behaviour meant that there was something fundamentally different about them which would always be there, on the basis of something which was not reliable. How could we know that what we were telling them was true?

These children and families waiting for years to come to our clinic needed help, that was obvious. But (I asked myself) was the help that we were offering—a diagnosis—the most useful thing we could offer? What did that diagnosis mean to Peter and his family? What is the most helpful role for a psychologist in this situation?

Autism is classified as a 'neurodevelopmental disorder' rather than a 'mental health problem'. I've used Peter's example because neurodevelopmental diagnoses are often done more thoroughly than other diagnoses and they should therefore be particularly reliable. The process of assigning a diagnosis for most mental health problems is done more quickly and with fewer sources of information but is essentially the same process. A person's experience and behaviour are compared to a list of diagnostic criteria. Many of the issues which came up with Peter's diagnostic assessment apply across different diagnostic categories, and you may want to keep Peter in mind as you read the rest of this chapter.

4.1 Offering explanations

When a person presents to mental health services, their experiences and behaviour often seem inexplicable to them and to those around them. They sometimes arrive in crisis, having tried to harm themselves or having experiences which they cannot explain and find terrifying, such as hearing voices. When mental health professionals meet them, part of their role is to show them that they are not alone in their experiences, and to help them make sense of what is happening to them.

One way to do this is to sort people into groups through a diagnostic process. This is primarily a system of categorisation. Another approach, often used alongside diagnosis, is **formulation**. Formulation involves applying psychological theory to understanding an individual's problems, and is not concerned with assigning a person to a category. The **Power Threat Meaning Framework** (**PTMF**) is an alternative to systems of classification which starts with a different set of assumptions about mental distress to the diagnostic system. All of these systems set out to achieve different things and are based on different assumptions, which is why I am presenting all three.

4.2 Diagnosis

A psychiatric diagnosis is given when a person meets the diagnostic criteria set out in either DSM or ICD. For many people, being given a diagnosis is experienced as an explanation—rather in the same way as being given a diagnosis of COVID-19 following a PCR test explains symptoms such as a cough and fever. They will say that they finally know why they feel the way they do. However, psychiatric diagnoses are different in an important way to a diagnosis of COVID because there is no confirmatory test. The diagnosis is given based on symptoms alone. This means that a psychiatric diagnosis is descriptive rather than explanatory. It does not tell us *why* the person feels the way they do, but it gives a name to their experiences. The particular symptoms which make up each diagnostic category can and do change over time. I explained the way in which the psychiatric diagnosis system was developed and the assumptions on which it is based in Chapter 2.

Psychiatric diagnostic categories are constructed by humans, rather than existing in nature. One way to think about diagnostic categories could be as 'constellations' (Fletcher-Watson and Happé, 2019). To extend this metaphor, we look out at the stars, and we see patterns which we call constellations. The stars that make up these constellations are real, but there are also other ways to see patterns in the sky. The constellation is constructed by humans as a way to think about reality. In this metaphor, stars are the symptoms, whilst the constellations are the diagnoses we give. Psychiatric diagnoses are social constructs, based on real experiences and behaviour—but these social constructs then affect the way that we see ourselves and our experiences.

The mental health system is structured by psychiatric diagnosis. There are many good reasons why people want a diagnosis and why health professionals give them. Many people describe feeling relief when they are given a diagnosis and feel that it provides an explanation for their problems. It's sometimes difficult to get any help unless you first get a diagnosis and—in the USA in particular—a diagnosis is usually a prerequisite for insurance claims. Diagnoses are seen as a 'passport' to services. Diagnoses also give professionals a way to communicate with each other, and they make it possible for clinicians to find research that might be relevant to a person's treatment. Many people want to know why they are finding life so hard, and they believe that a diagnosis will explain their experiences. This will often be reinforced by a health professional who may sometimes tell them that now they have a diagnosis, the cause for their distress has been found. The diagnosis is presented as the answer. This is not actually the case, as you will know from Chapter 3.

Receiving a diagnosis gives people a way to find others who have gone through the same process and who may share similar experiences. There are support and self-help groups and websites for every psychiatric diagnosis, and many people say that the community they find is invaluable. In recent years there has been a move towards some people seeing their psychiatric diagnosis as part of their identity, meaning that when diagnostic criteria are changed (as happened in several cases in the transition from DSM-IV to DSM-5), people feel a loss and may continue to refer to themselves by the earlier term. Diagnostic categories have spread beyond mental health services and are prevalent on social media, with many people now identifying themselves in their online profile using a diagnosis.

When a diagnosis becomes an identity, there is often a move to redefine it in more positive terms and to stop using words such as 'disorder'. This can lead to tension between health professionals, who are using diagnostic manuals which focus on impairment and perceived deficits, and people with lived experience who focus on redefining their experiences in an affirmative way (Russell, 2020). There is then a question as to whether the diagnostic manuals and those with lived experience are describing the same thing at all, and the boundaries become even less well-defined as people start to self-diagnose. This is an issue which Ginny Russell, Steven Kapp, and colleagues have explored at length in the Exploring Diagnosis project at the University of Exeter which looked at the exponential rise in the diagnosis of autism since 1998 (Kapp, 2020).

Diagnostic categories are commonly used to group people for research exploring both causes and interventions for mental health problems. It is sometimes argued that without these categories, effective research would not be possible. Recently there has been a change in this, with influential medical scientists arguing that diagnostic categories are holding back our understanding, due to their lack of reliability and validity (Insel, 2013). Many researchers are now looking at the range of symptoms across the whole population, rather than comparing those with diagnoses and those without. It appears that this has more biological validity (Gillan et al., 2019), something which is supported by the behavioural genetics research.

There are also drawbacks to seeing mental distress and unusual behaviour through the lens of diagnosis, many of which can be hidden or longer term.

Drawbacks to diagnosis

Psychiatric diagnoses are different to those given in other areas of medicine, but the medical model encourages us to think about them as if they are the same. This has a number of disadvantages, not just for those who receive a diagnosis, but also for those who don't.

It sometimes seems that Western society offers only two explanations for unusual experiences and behaviour. You're either ill, or it's your fault. This 'brain or blame' dichotomy (Boyle, 2002) means that people see a diagnosis as a relief from self-blame and the blame of people around them. The diagnosis is seen as validation that their difficulties are not their fault, which can be extremely useful. However, this has the drawback of implying that the same behaviour in someone without a diagnosis *is* their fault, and that the diagnosis provides an explanation rather than simply a description. Anti-stigma campaigns frequently reinforce this

---

IN THE REAL WORLD 4.1

Early Diagnosis of Borderline Personality Disorder (BPD)

Borderline personality disorder is a controversial and gendered diagnosis, with 75% of diagnoses being given to women. Between 30% and 90% of people who meet criteria for BPD have a history of child abuse or trauma (Mainali, Rai, and Rutkofsky, 2020). The diagnostic features include a pervasive pattern of problems with interpersonal relationships and marked impulsivity, beginning by early adulthood. People who get diagnoses of BPD will often self-harm in some way, and will experience extremes of emotions, becoming very angry or distressed. In mental health services, people who have a diagnosis of BPD are often thought of as particularly complex and difficult to work with. It is one of the most stigmatised diagnoses. Once a diagnosis like this is on a medical record, it is extremely difficult to get it removed. People carry it with them for life.

Until recently, BPD has been a diagnosis of adulthood, with clinicians being reluctant to diagnose young people with such

a serious and stigmatised condition (Bozzatello et al., 2019). However, in 2020 the Royal College of Psychiatrists called for clinicians to be more ready to diagnose young people from the age of 14 with BPD (RCP, 2020). The argument is that this will enable them to access effective interventions earlier. This means that highly distressed teenagers who may be living in abusive situations will be given a diagnosis of a lifelong 'personality disorder'.

The idea from within the medical model is that early diagnosis will enable them to receive help, but receiving a diagnosis of BPD also has long-term consequences for how mental health staff view a person as well as how that person views themselves (Aviram et al., 2006). A diagnosis of 'personality disorder' contains within it the assumption that this is part of who the person is, and that the problem will never go away. The concern is that once someone has this diagnosis, their behaviour and distress will be seen as 'symptoms', and people will stop asking why they are behaving the way they do.

message, promoting the idea that a mental health problem is 'an illness like any other' (Malla et al., 2015) (and therefore you're not to blame that you feel this way). The catch with this is that there are only two options, and it inevitably pushes people towards seeing their difficulties in terms of illness—since the only other option is to feel that their problems are their own fault.

For physical illnesses early diagnosis is often crucial, as it means that treatments have more of a chance of working. Applying a medical model to mental health means that a similar assumption is often made—the earlier the diagnosis, the better. The potentially negative consequences of early diagnosis are rarely considered. These include stigma, hopelessness when a diagnosis does not hold the expectation of recovery, an assumption that a problem is now unlikely to change, and an assumption of the '**sick role**'.

The example in Box 4.2 illustrates how the medical model is applied with the diagnosis of Borderline Personality Disorder.

The assumption that diagnosis is necessary for effective intervention comes directly from the medical model. In physical health, diagnosis usually means that we have identified the cause of the problem and can therefore treat it. This is not the same for mental health, where diagnoses are descriptions which when used alone usually lack **explanatory** and often **predictive power**.

Without studies which look at the trajectory of those who are offered equal levels of help and support without being diagnosed as compared to those who are diagnosed, it is impossible to know if early diagnosis is *in itself* important. There is a presupposition that diagnosis is necessary for intervention (and in health systems based on insurance this may well be the case), but many psychologists in the UK work without diagnosing and plan their work based entirely on formulation instead. Some research studies indicate that in practice diagnoses are not necessary or sufficient to access services and plan treatment, and that clinicians work using broad clusters of difficulties instead (Allsopp and Kinderman, 2019).

As far back as the 1960s, sociologists began to observe the effects on individuals of the words used to describe them. Thomas Scheff (Scheff, 1966) argued that the label of 'mental illness' or disorder is given to people whose behaviour does not fit the social norms of a society and who are seen as deviant. He wrote that the process of receiving this label leads to a set of responses from society which are usually negative, since 'mental illness' is stigmatised. These responses may compel a person to take on the role of an ill or disordered person, and they internalise this identity.

Labelling theory states that assigning someone with a label or diagnosis is not a neutral act. It will affect how people behave towards that person, and also how they see themselves and consequently behave (Tannenbaum, 1938). This theory suggests that when children are given diagnoses very young, this will have effects on their self-concept and development, as well as the way in which the people around them treat them.

Think back to Peter. One of the reasons that Peter's parents had brought him to the clinic is because his school had said that they could not provide extra help unless he had a diagnosis. Peter will be the same child, with the same needs, whether he gets a diagnosis or not. Yet if the diagnostic report says he is autistic, he will be eligible for help that he was not eligible for before. This puts a pressure on professionals, who know that getting a diagnosis can mean the difference between a child being left to struggle alone or getting funding for a learning support assistant. It puts pressure on parents too, who come knowing that if the answer is 'no diagnosis' then they are left without an explanation for their child's unusual behaviour and that others may blame them for it.

The diagnosis may have other consequences. When he gets a diagnosis, Peter may start to think of himself as someone who is qualitatively different from other people, and those around him may treat him this way too. This might be something that he likes, but equally he might prefer not to be thought of as different to others, and to emphasise the ways in which he is similar. Because he is a child, he is not able to choose for himself whether he wants a diagnosis or not. We don't know how this might affect his life and the way he sees himself, and while we do not acknowledge the many consequences of diagnosis, both positive and negative, we are unlikely to find out.

The business of diagnosis

Diagnoses are big business. There are private clinics all over the UK where you can get a psychiatric diagnosis, often paying several thousand pounds for an assessment and report. When a person has a diagnosis, they may be able to get extra time in exams, extra help at school, access extra funding, or adjustments may be made at work. This means that those who have the capacity to pay are more likely to get this extra help, which can drive social disparities and inequality. This can be particularly stark for children, where the waiting list for diagnosis on the NHS is often years long.

Diagnoses are sometimes presented in the press as the answer to a lifetime of difficulties. In a recent article in *The Guardian* newspaper, Jason Wilson wrote how 'being diagnosed with ADHD in my 40s has given me something quite magical' (Wilson, 2020). For Wilson, a diagnosis of ADHD explained his lifelong problems with distractibility and self-organisation. He summarises the process as 'a quiz, a name, a drug'. He did a quiz about symptoms of ADHD, went to the doctor to get a diagnosis, and was given Adderall, a prescription amphetamine.

It's taken for granted in this account that the diagnosis has explanatory power. Wilson writes confidently about insufficient dopamine and his 'peculiar neurology', although this is not tested at any point in the diagnostic process. The article describes an entirely medicalised approach to his difficulties. It is a doctor who gives the diagnosis, although there are no medical tests involved, and then psychoactive drugs are offered as treatment. Articles like this will contribute to the public understanding of what ADHD (or other diagnoses) actually are, leading to more people seeing their difficulties with life in those medicalised terms which will in turn lead to more people seeking diagnosis. This then can lead to a widening of the diagnostic criteria.

The process by which a population becomes more aware of the psychiatric model of mental health (leading to an increase in diagnosis) is described by Ethan Watters in his book *Crazy Like Us*. This book tracks the way in which Western ideas about mental health have been exported to countries such as Hong Kong, Sri Lanka, and Japan. This can happen through awareness campaigns (often funded by pharmaceutical companies) but also through well-intentioned efforts on the part of charities and overseas agencies to provide mental health support to those in need (Watters, 2010). When this happens, new markets are created for pharmaceutical companies and traditional (usually non-medical) ways of understanding mental health problems can come to be seen as out-dated and old-fashioned.

People are clearly different from each other. Some of these differences cause problems in everyday life. These differences will be reflected in their brains.

Conceptualising this as a disorder or illness, however, is something which has only really happened on a large scale since the publication of DSM-III in 1980.

This redefining of behaviour as a disorder has obvious advantages for the pharmaceutical industry. There is a profit motive in convincing more people that they are ill and expanding diagnostic boundaries, something which is called *disease-mongering* (Kaczmarek, 2021). Pharmaceutical companies support awareness campaigns which support a very particular sort of awareness. These campaigns repeatedly link particular experiences with a diagnosis, followed by treatment and relief (Moynihan and Cassels, 2005). This does not only happen with mental distress—physical ill-health is subject to the same process. Diagnoses themselves are promoted to people as a solution to their problems, but because there is no obvious product being sold, this is not considered to be advertising. This may be particularly important in the UK, since—unlike in the USA—direct marketing of drugs to consumers is not allowed. Articles describing a diagnosis as a solution to life's problems actively promote that diagnosis to people who previously did not think about themselves in this way, thus creating a new market for pharmaceutical drugs. This process also happens on social media where diagnoses are sometimes described by social influencers as a way for people to accept themselves and to find others like them. In this way, medicalised understandings of human experiences can quickly spread.

4.3 Why look for alternatives to diagnosis?

The effects of the diagnostic system are complex and this way of thinking is entrenched in mental health services. Despite this, concerns have grown to the extent that in the last ten years several different alternative frameworks have been proposed. Two of these—HiToP and rDoC—are only used in research rather than in applied psychology, and they are discussed in Chapter 9. Clinical and counselling psychologists have long used formulation as an alternative or in addition to diagnosis and it is seen as a key part of their professional skillset. Formulation usually takes an individualised approach, using a quasi-scientific method to generate hypotheses.

Alternatives to diagnosis come from a wide range of philosophical standpoints and differ greatly from each other. Some believe that mental health problems should still be conceptualised primarily as biomedical disorders, but assert that manuals such as DSM have got the structure of the classification system wrong (Insel et al., 2010). Others start with a different set of assumptions altogether. The Power Threat Meaning Framework argues that we need a paradigm shift in how we think about mental health, and proposes an alternative to classification systems.

4.4 Formulation

Formulation is regarded as one of the key skills of a clinical psychologist (BPS, 2011). A formulation can be defined as 'a hypothesis about a person's difficulties which draws from psychological theory' (Johnstone and Dallos, 2014).

Formulations are developed collaboratively between a psychologist and the person they are working with. A formulation will contain hypotheses or 'best guesses' about why a person is feeling and acting the way they do, and interventions are planned on the basis of these hypotheses. Formulation seeks to understand an individual's difficulties in the context of their life, in contrast with diagnosis which seeks to group people together on the basis of their difficulties.

There are many different approaches to formulation. Figure 4.1 shows the frequently used 'Five Ps' structure (e.g., Macneil et al., 2012). This starts with a person's experiences at the centre—labelled **presenting problems**. These are more specific than a diagnosis and describe the reason why a person is seeking help. They could include low mood, worrying, hearing voices, or a difficulty sleeping. These could also include

problems in the person's life, for example conflict with family members, or not being able to get a job.

Around this are four boxes, each of which add to our understanding of what is happening.

- **Predisposing factors** are the things which have made it more likely that this person has these problems. These include experiences such as racism, discrimination, poverty, and deprivation. They will include adverse childhood experiences. They also include biological factors, perhaps if the person has a disability or has had a severe illness.

- **Protective factors** are the things that give a person resilience and help them cope. These could include supportive family members, skills or a job that keeps a person going. They could also include personal qualities such as determination, or a strong faith.

- **Precipitating factors** are the things which have happened just before the problems arose. These might include the loss of a job, a bereavement, a serious illness, or stressful life events.

- **Perpetuating factors** would perhaps be easier to understand if they had called them 'Maintaining factors' but the Four Ps and One M structure doesn't sound as good. These are the things which keep the person stuck and mean that they can't solve their problems themselves. They could include substance misuse, family conflict, avoidance, and financial hardship.

Formulations are by their very nature individualised and flexible, and subject to constant revaluation. In the text box you see an example of the Five Ps approach as applied to Vincent.

The formulation helps the psychologist think about the role that alcohol plays in Vincent's life. She sees that cutting down on alcohol will be particularly difficult when his whole life revolves around it. Her intervention might start with helping Vincent find meaningful things to do outside the hostel, and meeting people whose lives do not revolve around alcohol. Cutting down on drinking could come later, when his social life isn't entirely focused on drinking, and she might also look at helping him find a dry hostel, if his aim is to stop drinking entirely.

If Vincent seeks a diagnosis, he could receive one of Alcohol Use Disorder. This could sit alongside this formulation. This would not explain the nuances of the role that alcohol plays in his life, although it

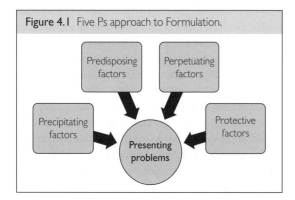

Figure 4.1 Five Ps approach to Formulation.

Predisposing factors

Perpetuating factors

Precipitating factors

Protective factors

Presenting problems

CASE STUDY 4.2

Vincent: Formulation with the 5 Ps

Vincent had always enjoyed a drink at the pub in the evenings, but after he lost his job he started to drink throughout the day. Vincent found that drinking stopped him from worrying about finding a new job and his evenings at the pub were the only time he met people. He split up with his girlfriend after he got into a fight when drunk. Vincent started spending more money than he could afford on alcohol and stopped keeping up with his rent. Vincent was evicted from his flat and ended up in a homeless hostel. He was referred to mental health services, where he met a psychologist. Her formulation is below.

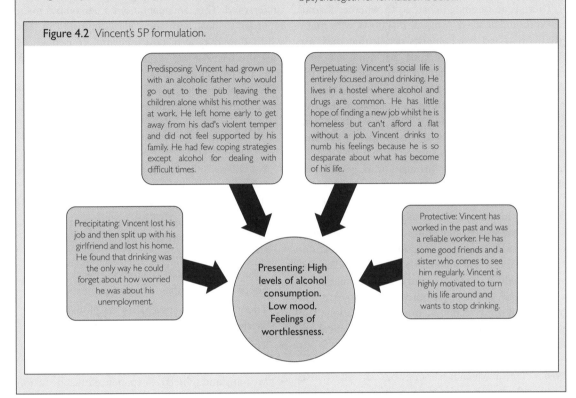

Figure 4.2 Vincent's 5P formulation.

might enable him to be referred to an alcohol service. A psychological formulation seeks to explain a person's individual experiences and can offer an alternative to the 'brain or blame' dichotomy. They offer a structure which explains a person's problems as an understandable reaction to their life events and circumstances.

Psychological theory is inherent to formulation. The theoretical stance of the psychologist will make an enormous difference to the meanings that they offer to a person. The cultural perspective of the psychologist and the service user will also make a difference. A psychologist in the UK, for example, is likely to be sceptical about explanations which include supernatural influences, although if they are preferred by a service user they could still be included in a formulation.

Drawbacks to formulation

As you can see, formulations are highly individualised. They generate hypotheses and suggest ways of intervening, but the formulation a person is offered is highly influenced by the background training of the psychologist they are seeing. Two different psychologists may come up with different formulations for the same person and will then offer different interventions. This gets to the heart of whether we think in terms of individual differences or group categories, and whether we think that everyone with similar difficulties should be offered the same intervention.

Formulations are not a way to group people or classify their experiences. They are instead hypotheses about why a person is having their difficulties. These hypotheses are used to plan intervention, and then can be revised if this intervention does not help. They are highly individualised, which makes them difficult to test empirically on a group level. Formulations can be constantly revised when new evidence arises, meaning that it doesn't really make sense to test them for reliability—consistency over time or between psychologists is not necessarily part of what makes a formulation useful.

There is an ongoing debate as to whether formulation should be used alongside diagnosis, with many psychiatrists and psychologists saying that they use the two together. Others argue that using diagnosis fundamentally undermines the formulation, since the diagnosis introduces medical concepts whilst the formulation explains something in psychological terms (Johnstone and Dallos, 2014). They argue that essentially clients are then offered two competing explanations, with the diagnosis suggested that they have a 'mental disorder' and the formulation suggesting that their difficulties make sense given their experiences. In practice, many services insist on at least a 'working diagnosis' (meaning an informally given diagnosis) and so psychologists are often obliged to give some indication of possible diagnosis alongside their formulation.

Formulations are inherently a non-standardised approach which can make them harder to evaluate on a group level. Multiple formulations can co-exist and in fact, uniformity is not an aim of formulation. The worth of a specific formulation lies in its practical use for the individual concerned.

In the final part of this chapter, I will discuss the Power Threat Meaning Framework, an alternative to classification systems developed by clinical psychologists and service users. I am including this here because it is an unusual example of an over-arching framework developed by those in the health service rather than a research institute, deliberately conceptualised as an alternative to medicalised ways of thinking about mental health. It is an attempt to devise a non-pathologising framework for understanding mental health, avoiding concepts such as disorder, dysfunction, and abnormality entirely.

4.5 The Power Threat Meaning Framework

The Power Threat Meaning Framework (Johnstone and Boyle, 2018) co-produced by a core team of psychologists and service users, sets out an approach to human distress which is non-pathologising, and acknowledges the central role of power and oppression in people's lives. As such, it is a framework for all human experience, not just that of those deemed to have mental health problems.

Their core assumption is that behaviours and experiences which are commonly labelled as symptoms have a function and meaning, and this needs to be understood. They are adaptations a person has made in order to deal with their life circumstances, and whilst they may also have unhelpful consequences, they also have (or had) a purpose within the environment the person was (or is) in.

Some of the main underlying assumptions which differ from other approaches are summarised below:

- All behaviour exists on a continuum; 'abnormal' is on a continuum with 'normal'.

- We will never be able to make precise cause–effect links between someone's life circumstances and the impact this has on them.

- Experiences and expressions of emotional distress are enabled and mediated by, rather than caused by, bodies and biology.

- Humans exist in a social context and are inseparable from their different contexts.

- There is no 'global psychiatry' or 'global psychology' which applies to everyone.

- Theories about mental distress, both in terms of explaining and intervening, are not value-free.

- Meaning and subjective experience must be taken seriously.

The PTMF starts with the assumption that humans are social beings with core needs, and that anything which prevents these needs being met may be experienced as a threat. It suggests that the negative operation of power in people's lives leads to them experiencing threat, which they then ascribe meaning to. Power is defined widely, including societal inequalities and oppression as well as individual power wielded over others. It also includes ideological power—the pressure to think, feel, and lead our lives in certain ways, often filtered through language use and social norms and expectations. A central aim is to restore the link between personal distress and social injustice of all kinds.

They suggest starting with four questions in order to understand someone's narrative.

Table 4.1 The Power Threat Meaning Framework

Function	Behaviour and Experiences
Regulating overwhelming feelings	E.g. by dissociation, self-injury, bingeing and purging, carrying out rituals, 'high' mood, low mood, hearing voices, use of alcohol and drugs, compulsive activity of various kinds, overeating
Protection from physical danger	E.g. by hypervigilance, insomnia, flashbacks, nightmares, fight/flight/freeze, suspicious thoughts, isolation, aggression
Maintaining a sense of control	E.g. by self-starvation, rituals, violence, dominance in relationships
Seeking attachments	E.g. by idealisation, appeasement, seeking care and emotional responses, use of sexuality
Protection against attachment loss, hurt, and abandonment	E.g. by rejection of others, distrust, seeking care and emotional responses, submission, self-blame, hoarding, self-silencing, self-punishment
Preserving identify, self-image, and self-esteem	E.g. by grandiosity, unusual beliefs, feeling entitled, perfectionism, striving, dominance, hostility, aggression
Preserving a place within the social group	E.g. by striving, competitiveness, appeasement, self-silencing, self-blame
Meeting emotional needs/self-soothing	E.g. by rocking, self-harm, skin-picking, bingeing, alcohol use, over-eating, compulsive sexuality
Communication about distress, elicit care	E.g. by self-injury, unusual beliefs, voice-hearing, self-starvation
Finding meaning and purpose	E.g. by unusual beliefs, overwork, high moods

Adapted from Johnstone and Boyle, 2018.

- What happened to you? (How is Power operating in your life?)
- How did it affect you? (What kind of Threats does this pose?)
- What sense did you make of it? (What is the Meaning of these situations and experiences to you?)
- What did you have to do to survive? (What kinds of Threat Response are you using?)

(From Johnstone and Boyle, 2018).

Threat Responses are the ways in which people behave in order to protect themselves, on an emotional and social as well as a physical level. These include the behaviours and experiences defined as symptoms in a biomedical model.

The PTMF groups behaviours and experiences by function, rather than by disorder. Table 4.1 illustrates this and comes from the framework. Experiences such as flashbacks, nightmares, and insomnia, often experienced after a traumatic event, can be seen as a threat response which protects a person from physical danger.

This shift in meaning has a significant implication, because seeing 'symptoms' as a functional response to threat is incompatible with seeing them as

pathological or disordered. If flashbacks are a meaningful response to threat, then it makes no sense to be looking for the biological correlate of a flashback with the aim of blocking the process. The process is not at fault—it is working as it is supposed to. The only way forward is to make sure the person is safe from physical threat, and if they still feel unsafe, to find ways to help them actually feel safe again.

This could involve forms of psychological therapy, but also should involve thinking about a person's life, and whether they really are safe. It is surprising how many people present to mental health services saying they feel unsafe, who, when asked, reveal that they live in the same house as their partner who regularly attacks them, or in the same street as the parent who abused them as a child.

The PTMF proposes that instead of concentrating on symptoms and constellations of symptoms, it makes more sense to focus on patterns of threat response. The authors describe general patterns which have titles such as 'Surviving rejection, entrapment, and invalidation' or 'Surviving social exclusion, shame, and coercive power'. These general patterns can be used to support the construction of personal stories, showing that people are not alone in their reactions and struggles. In this way, the PTMF shifts the perspective from disorder to survival, and therefore puts resilience at the centre of the framework rather than deficiencies.

The PTMF was published by the British Psychological Society in 2018 as an optional framework. It has attracted widespread interest in the UK and a number of other countries, and has also been met with intense criticism. Questioning a biomedical approach to mental health is often reacted to as if it were a threat. Those who do so are either accused of not taking mental health problems seriously, or of blaming people for their problems, which brings us straight back to the brain or blame dichotomy.

Drawbacks to the PTMF

The PTMF has been criticised as being inaccessible (the full document is over 400 pages long), and for not providing enough detail about how its ideas might be translated into practice in the real world. Some critics have argued that the patterns described in the PTMF are too much like diagnostic categories, and therefore suffer from some of the same problems, in particular a lack of reliability and validity.

Others argue that the PTMF is ideologically driven and that it is based on empirically untestable claims. The PTMF is a radical change from what has gone before, starting as it does with power and functional responses to circumstances rather than symptoms, and this may be hard for services to implement practically.

4.6 Comparative approaches

What do these differences mean in practice? Case study 4.3 presents one person, Elinor, and briefly describes several different ways of thinking about the same individual.

Elinor is highly anxious. She goes to her GP who refers her on to the local mental health service. What happens next will depend on who she sees. Case study 4.3, in the text box shows five different ways of understanding Elinor's problems; diagnosis, three different types of formulation, and then finally the PTMF. Each approach will lead to a different suggestion as to what intervention is most appropriate.

4.7 Reliability, validity, and utility

Comparing these different approaches is hard, precisely because they are so different. Three concepts to consider when evaluating systems are:

1. how reliable the systems are (**reliability**);
2. whether they reflect something in the real world (**validity**); and
3. how useful the concepts are (**utility**).

The importance of these different aspects will vary depending on what the system is hoping to achieve.

Reliability

Reliability is a measure of how confident we can be that a repeated measurement will give us the same result. For psychiatric diagnosis, this means how sure we are that if a person goes to several different clinicians, they will receive the same diagnosis each time. When I assessed Peter and got a different result, the problem was a lack of reliability.

The detailed symptom lists of DSM and ICD are an attempt to improve reliability, and there are specialised diagnostic interviews available which clinicians can attend extra training to use. In order to assess reliability, field trials are conducted for diagnostic manuals before they are released (Clarke et al., 2013). The trials for DSM-5 found significantly lower levels of reliability than had been found for DSM-IV and this led to some intense criticism of DSM-5 and furious discussion between psychiatrists, some of whom felt that DSM-5 should not be allowed to go ahead at all (Frances, 2012).

Formulation is often criticised as lacking reliability, because formulation can vary across psychologists and across different time points. Others argue that reliability is not necessarily an aim of formulation—a formulation is open to constant re-evaluation as new information emerges and as the situation changes. Formulation can also vary between psychologists at the same time point, depending on what information they deem to be most relevant and their theoretical perspective.

Validity

If a category is valid then it reflects something useful in the real world. A valid diagnosis will be accurate, meaningful, and useful. There are several different types of validity to take into account in mental

CASE STUDY 4.3

Formulating and explaining Elinor's distress

Diagnosis	Elinor's doctor says that she is suffering from generalised anxiety disorder. She has symptoms such as a racing heart, an inability to relax, difficulty sleeping, feeling constantly 'on edge', and irritability. Her score on the GAD-7[1] is 17, indicating a severe level of anxiety. She should be offered a diagnosis and medication considered if she doesn't improve.
Cognitive-behavioural formulation	Elinor sees a cognitive therapist, who suggests after assessment that she has a core belief that she is not good enough, formed by her early experiences when she really struggled to learn to read at school and the teacher told her mother it was because she was lazy. When something minor goes wrong, she has a tendency to catastrophise, with automatic thoughts such as 'I will never get anything right' and 'Things will never get any better'. Elinor hates the physical feeling of anxiety and has started to avoid taking on challenging projects at work in order not to feel those feelings. She has a range of other behaviours which she uses to help her feel safer including taking her lucky stone everywhere with her and calling her mother ten times a day. These reinforce her sense that she can't cope alone and isn't good enough. Therapy could focus on challenging Elinor's dysfunctional thinking patterns and use behavioural exposure to reduce avoidance and challenge her safety-seeking behaviours.
Systemic formulation	The family therapist who she sees next quickly discovers that Elinor grew up in a family where doing well at school mattered. Her elder sister did very well, and Elinor's role in the family was the less clever one. Elinor's parents were strict and quite emotionally detached but when she was very anxious, her mother would cuddle her and tell her that none of it matters and she didn't need to do her homework. As an adult, Elinor has found a partner who pays her special attention when she is anxious and who encourages her not to push herself and so the pattern continues. Elinor calls her mother several times a day and her mother will reassure her. Elinor's anxiety plays a role in her family system, getting Elinor comfort and also meaning her mother and partner can play a caring role, which makes them feel good about themselves. Her therapy could focus on shifting the dynamic between Elinor and other family members, and on changing the feedback loops which maintain Elinor's anxiety.
Trauma-informed formulation	Elinor's trauma therapist sees Elinor's anxiety as rooted in her traumatic experiences. Elinor has several experiences which she experienced as traumatic during childhood, all of which sensitised her and made her more likely to go into flight/fight/freeze mode as an adult. In a school assembly when she was six she had to read a poem, but was so nervous that she wet herself in front of the whole school and was mocked by the other children. She was bullied by her peers and felt trapped in the playground with them. Her feelings of anxiety now are a sign of her survival response being triggered in response to situations which remind her of these traumatic experiences. Her therapy could focus on processing the traumatic memories using a trauma-focused therapy.
Power Threat Meaning Framework	Elinor's PTMF-informed therapist starts from the assumption that Elinor's distress has a function, and should be seen in context. She asks what had happened to her and how this affected her. Elinor said that as a child she knew that teachers and her parents (who had power over her) thought that she should be able to do things which she found extremely difficult. This made her feel unsafe and as if her acceptance by others depended on her performing in a certain way (a threat). The sense she made of this was to conclude that she was not good enough as she was and that others would reject her if she didn't achieve. In order to survive, Elinor learnt to seek reassurance from others, but was constantly anxious in case they let her down. Elinor's therapist helped her to explore the ways in which she felt she was failing to live up to expectations and whether these were realistic. Elinor was spending many hours a day online, and believed that she was failing to look, feel, and achieve as she should. Elinor and her therapist explored her own values and messages, and Elinor started to see how she had been persuaded by all sorts of wider messages to feel bad about herself. Elinor stopped seeing herself as suffering from an anxiety disorder, and instead saw herself as doing her best in difficult circumstances.

[1] GAD-7. The 7-item Generalised Anxiety Disorder Scale.

health, in particular predictive validity (does it enable us to predict outcomes?), face validity (on the face of it, does it seem accurate?), descriptive validity (does it accurately describe what is being observed?), and construct validity (does it correlate with other measures which we think are assessing the same thing?).

Assessing whether psychiatric diagnoses have construct validity is difficult, due to the lack of agreement on what a 'mental disorder' is. There are no biological markers against which to compare. Many people get multiple diagnoses and the boundaries between the different categories are often blurred. However, psychiatric diagnoses do have face validity for many, and are used in the health service to decide which service a person should access and what treatment they should be offered.

Validity for formulation and alternative frameworks could be thought about in terms of descriptive validity and whether it 'rings true' for the client. Does it seem to explain their problems in a way which makes sense for them?

Utility

Even if a system does not have high validity or reliability, it may still have utility (Jablensky, 2016). Utility refers to the usefulness of a concept in the real world. A diagnosis has utility, for example, if it enables a person to access support which they could not have otherwise accessed. Utility is often what matters to clients seeking help, and they may use diagnoses to explain their experiences to others or to find others with similar experiences.

Utility is dependent on what we hope to achieve through the system and who is using it. The new dimensional systems described in Chapter 9 have utility for researchers, but currently not for clinicians. A formulation has utility if it enables the clinician to plan and carry out an effective intervention. An aim of the PTMF is to de-pathologise experiences of emotional distress and to emphasise the functional nature

of many 'symptoms', and so if it achieves this, it could be said to have a particular type of utility.

Chapter Summary

- One of the ways in which psychologists intervene is to offer people explanations for their mental health problems. Three different ways in which this happens are diagnosis, formulation, and the PTMF.
- Diagnoses have practical applications within the health system and fulfil an important role for many people.
- Psychiatric diagnoses are descriptions but are often talked about as if they were explanations and are experienced as such by service users.
- Formulation is a collaborative way to make sense of a person's problems and to plan interventions, using psychological theory to form hypotheses.
- Formulation is individualised and highly influenced by the theoretical stance of the psychologist, which some see as a drawback.
- The Power Threat Meaning Framework conceptualises the experiences usually classified as symptoms as functional responses to the threats in people's lives.
- The PTMF aims to be non-pathologising and to move emphatically away from a model of disorder. It provides the tools for people to construct or co-construct non-diagnostic narratives.

? QUESTIONS

1. Without a diagnosis, we would have no way of knowing how best to help people experiencing mental health problems. Discuss.

2. What is disease-mongering? Do you think this is something which psychologists need to be aware of? Why or why not?

3. Do an internet search for articles and awareness campaigns about a particular diagnosis (e.g. ADHD, social anxiety, autism or schizophrenia) in the mainstream press. How is that diagnosis talked about? How is this likely to affect the public perception of that diagnosis?

4. What is formulation? How is it used and what are the advantages and disadvantages of this approach? Illustrate with an example using the Five Ps framework.

5. What makes the Power Threat Meaning Framework different to classification systems? Is it just another set of alternative diagnoses or is it fundamentally different?

FURTHER READING

American Psychiatric Association (2013). *Diagnostic and Statistical Manual of Mental Disorders: Fifth Edition*. Arlington, VA: American Psychiatric Association.

The American 'Bible' of diagnoses.

Bentall, R. (2008). *Doctoring the Mind: Why Psychiatric Treatments Fail.* London: Allen Lane.

Boyle, M., and Johnstone, L. (2020). *A Straight Talking Introduction to the Power Threat Meaning Framework.* Monmouth: PCCS Books.

A brief introduction to the PTMF written in plain English. For those who are interested, the framework itself and supporting documents can be found on the British Psychological Society website. https://www.bps.org.uk/power-threat-meaning-framework

Frances, A. (2014). *Saving Normal: An Insider's Revolt against Out-of-Control Psychiatric Diagnosis, DSM-5, Big Pharma, and the Medicalization of Ordinary Life.* New York: William Morrow Books.

Insel, T. (2013). *Transforming Diagnosis.* Blog post, National Institute of Mental Health. https://psychrights.org/2013/130429NIMHTransformingDiagnosis.htm

Kinderman, P. (2019). *A Manifesto for Mental Health: Why We Need a Revolution in Mental Health Care.* Cham, Switzerland: Palgrave Macmillan.

Johnstone, L., and Dallos, R. (eds) (2014). *Formulation in Psychology and Psychotherapy,* Second Edition. London, UK: Routledge.

Very thorough introduction to formulation, covering formulation from different theoretical standpoints.

Johnstone, L. (2022). *A Straight Talking Introduction to Psychiatric Diagnosis,* Second Edition. Monmouth: PCCS Books.

Another in this series written in plain English, designed to be accessible for service users, which takes a critical approach to diagnosis.

Schwarz, A. (2016). *ADHD Nation: The Disorder, the Drugs, the Inside Story.* Boston, MA: Little, Brown.

This book by an investigative journalist gives a detailed account of the development of the diagnosis of ADHD and how pharmaceutical companies have marketed this diagnosis to the general public.

Russell, G. (2020). *The Rise of Autism: Risk and Resistance in the Age of Diagnosis.* London: Routledge.

Thoughtful analysis of changing patterns of diagnosis over time and what this means, using autism as a case study.

World Health Organization (2019). *International Statistical Classification of Diseases and Related Health Problems,* Eleventh Edition. Geneva: WHO. https://icd.who.int/

ICD-11, the WHO diagnostical manual which includes physical diseases as well as mental health problems.

REFERENCES

Allsopp, K., and Kinderman, P. (2019). The use of diagnoses in mental health service eligibility and exclusion criteria. *Journal of Mental Health*, 30(1), 97–103. doi:10.1080/09638237.2019.1677875.

Aviram, R., Brodsky, B., and Stanley, B. (2006). Borderline personality disorder, stigma, and treatment implication. *Harvard Review of Psychiatry*, 14(5), 249–256.

Bentall, R. (2008). *Doctoring the Mind: Why Psychiatric Treatments Fail*. London: Allen Lane.

Bozzatello, P., Bellion, S., Bosia, M., and Rocca, P. (2019). Early detection and outcome in borderline personality disorder. *Frontiers in Psychiatry*, 10, 710. doi:10.3389/fpsyt.2019.00710

Boyle, M. (2002). *Schizophrenia: A Scientific Delusion?*, Second Edition. London: Routledge.

BPS (British Psychological Society, Division of Clinical Psychology) (2011). Good Practice Guidelines on the use of psychological formulation. https://explore.bps.org.uk/content/report-guideline/bpsrep.2011.rep100

Clarke, D., Narrow, W., Regier, D., Kuramoto, S., Kupfer, D., Kuhl, E., Greiner, L., and Kraemer, H. (2013). DSM-5 field trials in the United States and Canada, Part 1: Study design, sampling strategy, implementation and analystic approaches. *American Journal of Psychiatry*, 170(1), 43–58.

Fletcher-Watson, S., and Happé, F. (2019). *Autism: A New Introduction to Psychological Theory and Current Debate*. London: Routledge.

Frances, A. (2012). Two fallacies invalidate the DSM-5 field trials. *Psychiatric Times*, 10 January 2012. Retrieved 28 February 2020.

Frances, A. (2014). *Saving Normal: An Insider's Revolt against Out-of-Control Psychiatric Diagnosis, DSM-5, Big Pharma, and the Medicalization of Ordinary Life*. New York: William Morrow Books

Fletcher-Watson, S., and Happé, F. (2019). *Autism: A New Introduction to Psychological Theory and Current Debate*. Abingdon: Routledge.

Gillan, C.M., Kalanthroff, E., Evans, M., et al. (2019). Comparison of the association between goal-directed planning and self-reported compulsivity vs obsessive-compulsive disorder diagnosis. *JAMA Psychiatry*, 77(1), 77–85. doi:10.1001/jamapsychiatry.2019.2998

Insel, T., Cuthbert, B., Garvey, M., Heinssen, R., Pine, D.S., Quinn, K., Sanislow, C., and Wang, P. (2010). Research Domain Criteria (rDoC): Toward a new classification framework for research on mental disorders. *Am J Psychiatry*, 167(7), 748–51.

Jablensky, A. (2016). Psychiatric classifications: Validity and utility. *World Psychiatry*, 15(1), 26–31.

Johnstone, L., and Boyle, M., with Cromby, J., Dillon, J., Harper, D., Kinderman, P., Longden, E., Pilgrim, D., and Read, J. (2018). *The Power Threat Meaning Framework*. Leicester: British Psychological Society. Available at https://www.bps.org.uk/power-threat-meaning-framework

Johnstone, L., and Dallos, R. (eds) (2014). *Formulation in Psychology and Psychotherapy*, Second Edition. London, UK: Routledge.

Kaczmarek, E. (2021). Promoting diseases to promote drugs: The role of the pharmaceutical industry in fostering good and bad medicalization. *British Journal of Clinical Pharmacology*, 88(1), 34–39. doi:10.1111/bcp.14835

Kapp, S. (ed.) (2020). *Autistic Community and the Neurodiversity Movement: Stories from the Frontline*. Singapore: Palgrave Macmillan.

Kinderman, P. (2019). *A Manifesto for Mental Health: Why We Need a Revolution in Mental Health Care*. Cham, Switzerland: Palgrave Macmillan.

Macneil, C.A., Hasty, M.K., Conus, P., and Berk, M. (2012). Is diagnosis enough to guide interventions in mental health? Using case formulation in clinical practice. *BMC Medicine*, 10, 111. doi:10.1186/1741-7015-10-111

Mainali, P., Rai, T., and Rutkofsky, I.H. (2020). From child abuse to developing borderline personality disorder into adulthood: Exploring the neuromorphological and epigenetic pathway. *Cureus*, 12(7), e9474. doi:10.7759/cureus.9474

Malla, A., Joober, R., and Garcia, A. (2015). Editorial: 'Mental illness is like any other medical illness': A critical examination of the statement and its impact on patient care and society. *Journal of Psychiatry and Neuroscience*, 40(3), 147–150. doi:10.1503/jpn.150099

Moynihan, R., and Cassels, A. (2005). *Selling Sickness: How the World's Biggest Pharmaceutical Companies are Turning Us All into Patients.* Sydney: Allen & Unwin.

Royal College of Psychiatrists (2020). *Services for People Diagnosable with Personality Disorder.* Position Statement, January 2020.

Russell, G. (2020). *The Rise of Autism: Risk and Resistance in the Age of Diagnosis.* London: Routledge.

Scheff, T. (1966). *Being Mentally Ill: A Sociological Theory.* Chicago: Aldine Publishing Company.

Tannenbaum, F. (1938). *Crime and Community.* New York: Columbia University Press.

Watters, E. (2010). *Crazy Like Us: The Globalization of the Western Mind.* London: Robinson.

Wilson, J. (2020). A New Life: Being diagnosed with ADHD in my 40s has given me something quite magical. *The Guardian.* Retrieved 15 January 2020. https://www.theguardian.com/society/commentisfree/2020/jan/15/a-new-life-being-diagnosed-with-adhd-in-my-40s-has-given-me-something-quite-magical

Chapter 5
Mental Health Across the Lifespan

Learning objectives

When you have completed this chapter, you should be able to do the following:

5.1 Explain why considering interactions between a person and their environment are important in mental health.

5.2 Use the example of the COVID-19 pandemic to illustrate how events have differential impacts on different people.

5.3 Describe the concept of 'developmental tasks' and why this is relevant to mental health.

5.4 Give examples of how a person's stage of life can impact their mental health and show how there can be specific challenges at different times. Explain the concept of 'malignant social psychology'.

Introduction

The circumstances of a person's life and the culture in which they live will affect their experiences and how society interprets their difficulties. This chapter encourages you to think about culture, context, and stages of life, and how these things interact with an individual's experiences.

This chapter will start with using the example of the COVID-19 pandemic to demonstrate how environmental events interact with individual characteristics. I will then discuss changes over the lifespan, using the concept of 'developmental tasks' as another example of how each person interacts with the world around them and how this varies over time. I will focus specifically on four periods of life, showing how individual differences and development combine with life events and expectations and how mental health problems may be expressed differently. These periods are childhood, adolescence, the perinatal period, and older adulthood, and I have chosen them because they are life stages which are often missing from more general discussions of mental health, and times when there is particular reason to think about the interaction between biological, psychological, and societal factors.

CASE STUDY 5.1

Lisa's Story

Lisa had a hard start in life. Her family was poor, and couldn't always afford food and clothing. At primary school, Lisa felt constantly ashamed of her dirty school uniform and was worried that she would get in trouble and her father would hit her. Teachers noticed Lisa's difficulties in concentrating in class and sent her for an assessment. She was diagnosed with dyslexia and ADHD.

As Lisa grew older, she started skipping school. She hung out at the amusement arcade with older boys. When she was with them she felt good about herself, and they gave her money so that she could afford to buy nice clothes. However, as time went on they expected her to shoplift for them as they said she owed them. She got in trouble with the police. She started self-harming. She was referred to children and adolescent mental health services (called CAMHS in the UK) and was offered cognitive behaviour therapy for depression.

When Lisa was 18, her father died. Lisa had to get a job to support her mother and younger siblings. The money she could earn was never quite enough and Lisa stopped eating so that her little sisters could eat. Over time Lisa found she liked the feeling of losing weight and found it increasingly difficult to eat. She was admitted to hospital after collapsing at work, and the hospital diagnosed her with anorexia.

For the next twenty years, Lisa struggled with her eating, and was admitted to hospital on several occasions. Despite this she met a partner and had two children, and did her best to be a good mother to them. She worked in a clothes shop and did well there, being promoted to manager. Her children had enough to eat and clean clothes.

When Lisa's children left home Lisa decided to study to be a counsellor, to help girls like she had been. It took years of studying in the evenings and at weekends. She felt strange sometimes when compared to the other trainees. They were mostly younger than her and no one else had had the experience of growing up in poverty. She felt this gave her a connection to the people she worked with; her life wasn't that different to theirs and she had struggled too. Her eating improved and she felt happy.

Just as Lisa was about to start working as a counsellor for a local charity, her husband had a stroke. He needed full time care and Lisa was the only one who could do it. She gave up her job and stayed at home. They were reliant on benefits. Money was tight. Lisa started to feel very low and stopped eating. She started to develop memory and concentration problems, forgetting to turn off the stove or leaving the front door open. After a visit Lisa's daughter rang the GP as she was worried that Lisa had early-onset dementia.

The case study in Box 5.1 describes the course of a person's life, and how their experiences change as they move through the lifespan. As you read it, ask yourself: What is gained (or lost) by seeing Lisa's problems in the context of her whole life? Does understanding Lisa's history make any difference to what help she might need?

5.1 Interactions and complexity

Part of the medical model is the assumption that diagnostic categories are universally applicable because they are indicative of an underlying disorder. From this perspective, culture can affect how someone expresses their distress, but the underlying issue is the same. For example, some cultures might be more likely to report headaches as symptoms of panic attacks, whilst others describe difficulty breathing (APA, 2013), but the medical model would see both of these as indicative of the same underlying 'disorder'. This has the advantage of simplicity; cultural differences can be accounted for with some minor changes.

For other situations, it has been clear that there are some constellations of symptoms which do not have analogies in other cultures. For example, *Hwa-byung* is a Korean **culture-bound syndrome** whereby people express their suppressed emotions physically, with symptoms including vomiting blood and heart problems (Paniagua, 2018). For this, a new diagnostic category is necessary, which is considered to apply only in Korea. Critics say that the diagnostic manuals rest upon a narrow understanding of culture, with some people seen as culturally 'other' whilst others are not (Bredström, 2019). They ask why some cultures (usually non-Western) have 'culture-bound syndromes' whilst other diagnostic categories are viewed as culture-free.

Inevitably, taking a different perspective on mental health increases complexity. One approach which has gained popularity in recent years is to look at mental health as a **complex system**, with interconnecting psychological, biological. and social elements (Fried, 2021). In a complex system, cultural beliefs and behaviours interact with other elements in an interdependent way. This perspective proposes that that in order to understand mental health, we must integrate the different levels rather than thinking about them (or researching them) in isolation.

This chapter will encourage you to think about how a person's biological and psychological characteristics interact with their environment and the expectations of the world around them. There is a growing interest in the interactions between a person and their environment, and the differential effect of environment on development (Belsky and Pluess, 2013). There are a variety of ways in which genes can affect the environment, and Scarr and McCartney (1983) propose three ways in which this happens in development: passive, evocative, and active.

How does this happen? Imagine two babies, living next door to each other and born on the same day. The environment those babies come home to will already be related to their genotypes, as long as it is provided by their genetically related parents. This effect is known as a **passive interaction** because it requires no input from the baby. Then let's say that one baby is difficult to soothe and frequently cries. Their parents will do their best to calm them, perhaps by rocking them or carrying them everywhere in a sling. They constantly entertain them. The baby next door, in contrast, is placid and rarely cries. Their parents can leave them in their cot or sitting in the bouncy chair for hours. The two babies are not only temperamentally different, but they now have very different life experiences. This is an **evocative interaction**; the babies have elicited different responses from the people around them. As the babies get older, they will shape their environment by choosing what they do and with whom they spend their time. One child may spend hours reading alone, whilst the other spends their time playing football with other children in the park. This is an **active interaction**—different people choose different environments. These three mechanisms mean that even what appears to be a very similar environment can have different effects on different individuals.

5.2 A pandemic of mental health problems?

Starting from early 2020, the COVID-19 global pandemic had a major impact on the lives of billions of people. Lockdown confined them to their homes. Schools and workplaces closed, and people were urged to stay away from others at all times. The rhetoric was that 'we are all in this together'. But it didn't affect everyone in the same way.

Many people were highly distressed. Levels of anxiety, low mood, and frustration rose (Wu et al., 2021). Domestic violence increased (Piquero et al., 2021). Others spent their time baking sourdough bread and joining online choirs and weren't distressed at all. Soon there were media articles about the 'mental health pandemic' which was predicted to follow the virus. Studies showed an increase in suicidal thinking during the first weeks of lockdown, particularly among those with pre-existing mental health conditions, although they also found that anxiety and depression symptoms did not increase in this time (O'Connor et al., 2021).

The term 'mental health pandemic' defines an emotional reaction to the pandemic as another health problem—a disorder or disease. For some people that might feel appropriate and describes their experiences well, but others might ask what a 'mentally healthy' response to this situation would look like, and whether it is plausible that humans should be able to adapt to any change of circumstance, including a global pandemic and virtual house arrest, without experiencing emotional distress and suffering. Some researchers emphasised the heterogeneity of people's response to the COVID-19 pandemic, arguing that focusing on prevalence scores for the population at a whole obscured the different ways in which people respond, with the majority of the population being resilient and showing minimal or no change in their mental health (Shevlin et al., 2023).

It is self-evident that people's experience of the COVID-19 pandemic will differ according to their context, culture, and life stage. A small child who is happy to be with their parents in their house and garden will have a very different experience to an 8-year-old who can no longer play with her friends or attend school. Young adults who must leave university and return to their childhood home may struggle with the loss of independence and lack of clarity about the future job market and their prospects. An office worker who can continue to earn a living from home will have a different experience to a hospitality worker who loses their job and income, and both will have a completely different experience to healthcare workers who face the threat of the virus on a daily basis. People from ethnic minorities were told that they were at higher risk of catching the virus and were consequently more anxious, as well as often being angry about the inequalities which the virus exposed. Older adults are more likely to have other health conditions which they may be unable to get treated, whilst some may feel cared for by their community and encouraged by an increased sense of neighbourliness. A person's characteristics and circumstances affect how they experience the same major global event. Rather than being a leveller, inequalities that already existed are exacerbated.

Events in people's lives interact with their individual characteristics, resulting in some people experiencing extreme distress which may then be defined as a mental health problem. Others are able to be more resilient, and the reasons for the difference will be multifactorial.

5.3 Life expectations and developmental tasks

From the moment that a child is born, they are subject to a set of changing expectations. Successfully navigating these developmental expectations is part of how society defines someone as mentally healthy. These have been termed '**developmental tasks**' (Kellam and Rebok, 1992). Whilst some milestones—such as learning to walk and talk—are more or less

the same universally, others are cultural expectations rather than simply development.

We tend to think of development as something which only happens to children, but developmental tasks cover the whole lifespan. Each decade of life brings new challenges—and new ways to fall short. The age at which children are expected to sleep independently, the age that they go to school, and when a young adult is expected to leave home or get married all vary greatly in different countries and at different time periods.

Critics note that inherent (but often unspoken) in many models of human development is the assumption that there is such a thing as *natural optimal human development,* resulting in an individual who is resilient, autonomous, pro-social, in touch with their emotions, physically healthy, and long-lived (Belsky and Pluess, 2013). These models are culturally bound, and what is considered to be optimal emotional development (and culturally appropriate behaviour) will vary. Until quite recently in the UK the cultural concept of the 'stiff upper lip' meant that for men to show emotions was considered a sign of weakness, whilst recent cultural changes have meant that expressing emotions in public is now often considered a sign of strength.

Bearing this in mind, Table 5.1 outlines some of the developmental tasks which define different life stages in western culture. This list does not imply that everyone must do these things nor that this represents some sort of ideal life pathway. Note how different (and specific) the problems of each life stage are.

How a person meets the challenges of each stage will affect their emotional wellbeing and mental health, and their life stage and culture will affect

Table 5.1 Major life changes and developmental tasks across the lifespan

Major life changes and developmental tasks	Life stages	Difficulties which may be defined as mental health (or neurodevelopmental) problems
Being born		Skills not acquired in the expected timescale, often defined as 'developmental milestones not met'
Learning to crawl and walk		
Acquiring language	Infancy and toddlerhood	Problems with feeding and sleeping
Toilet training		
Sleep independence		Difficulties with emotion regulation
Learning to control behaviour		Lack of compliance with adult expectations for behaviour

(Continued)

Table 5.1 Major life changes and developmental tasks across the lifespan (continued)

Major life changes and developmental tasks	Life stages	Difficulties which may be defined as mental health (or neurodevelopmental) problems
Starting education	Childhood	Difficulties forming relationships with peers
Learning to read and write		Difficulties in acquiring academic skills at the same pace as peers
Developing social skills		Problems with controlling behaviour and emotions
Learning skills for managing at school		Difficulties with organisation and self-management
Learning to organise self	Adolescence	Eating problems
Learning independent living skills		Risk-taking, including drug and alcohol use
Developing identity		Self-harm and suicidal thoughts
Gaining qualifications		Difficulties in managing emotions
Developing sexuality		Distress about gendered or sexed roles and expectations
		Difficulties with peer group
Choosing a possible career path		Conflict with parents
		Sexually risky behaviour
		Hearing voices and other unusual experiences
Successfully separating from family and leaving home	Early adulthood	Problems 'launching'
		'Quarter-life crisis'
Acquiring skills or higher education		Difficulties in living independently
Finding a job		Difficulties in complying with demands of workplace
Finding a partner		
Becoming financially independent		Difficulties with establishing adult relationships
Managing fertility	Perinatal period	Birth trauma
Pregnancy		Distress after miscarriage and fertility problems
Becoming a parent		Adjustment to role of parent
Parenting	Adulthood	Problems with balancing demands of work and caring
Holding onto a job		
Moving between jobs		Difficulties of parenting
Career progression		Disillusionment with work
Becoming financially secure		Work-place bullying
		Lack of life satisfaction
		'Mid-life crisis'
		Losing a job/redundancy
Providing care for ill parents		Relationship difficulties
Becoming a grandparent		Work pressures
Retirement	Older adulthood	Memory problems
Coping with illness or disability		Loss of identity
Coping with death of spouse		Loneliness
Coping with death of peers		Chronic and acute health problems
Dying		Facing the end of life

Adapted from Kellam and Rebok, 1992

how they express their feelings. This can be viewed as a series of disorders—as in the case of Lisa—or it could be viewed as more of a life trajectory, with distress being expressed in different ways at different life stages. A formulation-based approach would be more likely to see it as a trajectory, whilst a diagnostic approach is more likely to be sequential. The effect on a person will be as a result of biological, psychological, and socio-cultural factors interacting, and how professionals respond will be a function of the model they are working within.

5.4 Life stages

Different life stages bring challenges on a biological, psychological, and social level. When people have adequate resources and can cope with the demands put upon them, there is no problem. When they cannot, difficulties arise, and they may develop mental health problems. The following case examples will help illustrate some of the different ways in which people present to mental health services at different times in their life—and how much their life stage is an integral part of the difficulties they are experiencing.

Mental health in childhood

Abbas is ten, and his school has asked for a referral to a neurodevelopmental clinic. When you read the case study in Box 5.2, ask yourself what Abbas needs and what his behaviour is telling us. Warning, this case study includes domestic abuse.

Abbas's life has been punctuated by his father's erratic behaviour and violence. He now struggles to concentrate and sleep. He can't meet the

expectations of his school. The adults in Abbas's life are keen for him to get a diagnosis of ADHD; they see it as a way he can access support. This might help Abbas get the help he needs. At the same time, focusing on ADHD may mean that Abbas's history and the ongoing instability in Abbas's life will not be seen as an important part of the picture. Abbas will have been defined as having a neurodevelopmental disorder, which locates the problem in him. He may be given medication. This might help him concentrate more at school.

As an alternative, a formulation-based approach might be useful, perhaps thinking about ways in which Abbas could feel safer and helping his mother to make plans for establishing a stable future. A systemic intervention could look at how Abbas's school manages his behaviour, and to see if any changes could be made there in order to help him. He might benefit from someone to talk to about what is going on at home, or a quiet place to go at the end of the day. He also might be helped by practical interventions such as a Breakfast Club, meaning that he does not come to school hungry.

Children who present to mental health services differ from adults in an important way. Most children do not bring themselves to services. They are brought because other people are concerned about them, and what happens then can have consequences for the rest of their lives. Some of the diagnoses given in childhood, such as autism spectrum disorders, are defined as neurodevelopmental disabilities and the diagnosis is for life. These diagnoses can be very useful and without them, many children cannot get the help they need. However, critics point out that they can also narrow the way in which families and professionals think about behaviour, as in the case of Abbas. They

---

CASE STUDY 5.2

Abbas

Abbas is failing at school, largely because he can't sit still and focus on his lessons. He is constantly jumpy and irritable, and his mother says he can't sleep at night. He has poor impulse control and has hit other children in the playground.

When Abbas meets the psychologist, she goes through a structured interview and observes Abbas at school. His teachers fill in questionnaires. Abbas meets the criteria for a diagnosis of ADHD. After the assessment, the psychologist starts chatting

to Abbas' mother, Sara. Sara explains that until six months ago, they were living with Abbas's father who was violent towards her and Abbas. She left with Abbas, and they were now living in temporary accommodation. Abbas had spent his childhood in fear of his father's violence, and did not believe that they were now safe. At the same time, Abbas was angry with his mother for leaving. Each Saturday, Abbas sees his father who tells him that it was all his mother's fault that they are no longer together. They are struggling to get by financially. Abbas often goes to school without having eaten breakfast.

locate the reason for the problem in the child, rather than in their environment, and children may be given these lifelong diagnoses without their consent or even knowledge.

Childhood is a time of biological and psychological immaturity, meaning that children often express themselves in very different ways to adults. Deciding what level of difficulty merits intervention is complicated with children, no matter how the decision is made. With children, this often means looking at behaviour. This brings the problem of deciding at what age a particular behaviour is still developmentally appropriate. Emotional outbursts, bed-wetting, hitting other people, resistance to change, and high anxiety on separating from a parent are all typical behaviours in the very young, and cultures differ as to by what age they think a child should have outgrown them.

Once referred to mental health services, children's problems may be described in a range of different ways. Below are the main groups of diagnoses which children may receive in the health service. Critics of the psychiatric system point out that failing to comply with adult cultural expectations regarding compliance, behaviour, and academic progress is inherent in many of these descriptions. They also point out that, in childhood in particular, taking account of context is important, because children do not have the power to change their environment. For this reason, many child psychologists work with families rather than individuals.

Common diagnoses given to children include

- **Emotional disorders**. These describe problems with mood or worrying, such as depression and anxiety. Children can also be diagnosed with more serious problems such as bipolar disorder or schizophrenia.
- **Hyperactivity disorders**. These describe children who have difficulty in paying attention, concentrating, and who are more active than usual. These children frequently have trouble at school and are given a diagnosis of attention deficit/hyperactivity disorder (ADHD).
- **Behavioural disorders**. These describe children whose behaviour is anti-social, or who refuse to cooperate with adults. They can be diagnosed with conduct disorder, or oppositional defiant disorder.

- **Autism spectrum disorders (ASD)**. These are now sometimes called autism spectrum conditions, in order to avoid use of the word 'disorder'. In order to meet diagnostic criteria for autism, a child must have difficulties in social communication and have a restricted and repetitive pattern of behaviour, interests, or activities. These difficulties must be evident early on and significantly impact their functioning.
- **Specific learning disorders**. These include problems in learning to read, learning to write, speaking, and mathematics.

Many children are affected by genetic disorders (e.g., **Trisomy 21**, or **Down Syndrome**) which lead to intellectual disabilities and developmental problems. These are not diagnosed using diagnostic manuals. This is because they can be diagnosed with certainty using genetic tests.

Many children's mental health services **work systemically**. This means that they will formulate the child's problems in the context of their family, and will work with the family as well as the child in order to try to change the situation. They may also work with school to try and resolve problems there. When a child is very distressed, it will affect everyone in the family and so siblings may also sometimes be involved. Some support for children is delivered through schools, and educational psychologists specialise in working with and through schools.

Adolescence

The way in which distress is expressed changes as children go through puberty. Adolescence is a particularly vulnerable time, with rapid physical and neurological development happening alongside increased pressure and more independence. Many young people who have managed well throughout childhood start to show signs of distress as they get older. They express this distress in more extreme ways, with self-harm and suicidal thinking becoming more common (Gillies et al., 2018). The case study of Maisie illustrates some of the issues which often start in adolescence, and illustrates how different these issues can be to those demonstrated by younger children.

Adolescents are managing significant changes in their brains and bodies at the same time as increased stress and pressure in their environment. They start

CASE STUDY 5.3

Maisie

Maisie was fourteen when she was referred to see a psychologist. She had enjoyed primary school but had found secondary school increasingly challenging, finding it hard to make and keep friends. She had become anxious about the future, breaking down in tears when she heard stories about climate change on the news. She would stay up all night worrying and then would go to school exhausted in the mornings. Recently she started to self-harm with razor blades. She found that it relieved her feelings for a while. When her mother saw the cuts

they had a fight and Maisie stormed out the house and did not come back for hours. She then sent her dad a text saying that she wanted to kill herself. When she came back she had clearly been drinking. They had a row and Maisie told her parents that that they needed to wake up and realise just how bad things were in the world, and that their generation had let hers down.

Maisie's parents didn't know what to do. Maisie did not think that her problems were psychological, and felt that it was appropriate to be very concerned about the future, given what she read in the news. She was not keen to talk to the psychologist.

to have access to alcohol and drugs, and many take exams, the results of which can affect their whole life course. Many serious mental health problems start for the first time in adolescence. It is a time of vulnerability as well as a time of increasing capability and independence.

Recent studies using MRI scans show that the brain continues to develop for much longer than was previously understood. Whilst the volume of the brain does not change much from the age of 8 or 9 onwards, the structural changes during adolescence are significant. Neuroscientists now see adolescence as a period which extends from around age 10 to age 24. During this period, young people's brains become more sensitive to rewards (particularly social rewards), whilst their capacity for self-control develops more slowly and steadily over the whole time period. This is called the dual systems model of adolescent brain development. This combination could account for the risk-taking behaviour often associated with adolescence (Blakemore, 2018).

Sarah-Jayne Blakemore, a cognitive neuroscientist and professor of psychology, argues that our education system is not informed by neuroscience, relying as it does on high-stakes exams relatively early on in adolescence. These exams are taken at an age when the capacity for self-control is still developing and when the level of brain development varies greatly between young people. She suggests that late adolescence could be a window of opportunity for educational development which can be easily missed. By this point in their lives, young people have already been assessed several times using high-stakes exams, and many will have given up on education altogether. There is also the question of the impact of high levels of pressure to

perform at a time when young people's brains appear to be more sensitive to rewards. Large, cross-cultural surveys have shown that around two-thirds of 15–16 year-olds in countries that are a part of the **Organisation for Economic Co-operation and Development (OECD)** report feeling stressed about school (OECD, 2017). Stress (a term which is often used in quite a non-specific way) has been found to increase the risk of problems in many other aspects of the life of adolescents, including physical health, mental health, and use of drugs and alcohol (Pascoe et al., 2020).

There is reason to be concerned about the vulnerability of adolescents. Late adolescence or early adulthood is the most common time for experiences such as hearing voices and unusual beliefs to begin. Large-scale population-based studies find that about 75% of people who hear voices or have unusual beliefs start before the age of 40, with half starting before the age of 26 (McGrath et al., 2016). Eating problems, suicidal thinking, and problems with drugs and alcohol often start in adolescence. The prevalence of young people diagnosed with a mental health problem rises with age, with a UK survey finding that 16.9% of 17–19 year-olds met criteria for a diagnosis of mental disorder (NHS Digital, 2018). This could be due to the biological changes going on at this time but it could also be the result of difficulties associated with becoming independent and the pressures placed on this age group.

It can be particularly hard for older adolescents to access appropriate mental health support, something else which might contribute to their vulnerability. Child and adolescent services usually end on a person's eighteenth birthday, and adult services are organised in a very different way. They have higher expectations in terms of personal responsibility for attending appointments, and are less likely to involve families or work systemically. Since this often coincides with young people leaving education, it can feel like familiar institutions are no longer there for support. Given that recent neuroscientific findings would indicate that adolescence as a period of brain development continues until the mid-20s, it may be unrealistic and unhelpful for many to expect an adult level of responsibility at age 18.

Perinatal/transition to parenthood

Moving now through adulthood, the **perinatal period** is the time before and after birth. Becoming a parent can make demands on a person's psychological and social resources in a way which they have never faced before. Media coverage focuses on the joys of becoming parents, leaving many feeling like failures when they find it harder than they expected. It is a time when new parents are emotionally vulnerable, and they may not be able to access the family and community support which traditionally would have helped the transition into this new stage of life. The case study 5.4 illustrates some of the issues which can arise.

Svetlana's experience is not uncommon. After childbirth, around 1–2% of women report experiences which fit diagnostic criteria for post-traumatic stress disorder. Factors which contribute to this include obstetrical emergencies, lack of support during birth, and complications with the baby (Andersen et al., 2012).

Low mood and anxiety when parenting a new baby is a common reaction, with depression in the first year after birth or during pregnancy often being diagnosed as peri-natal depression (Dagher et al., 2021). Whilst this diagnosis was first applied to women and was thought to be related to hormonal changes, men are now also being diagnosed with post-natal depression (Ramchandani et al., 2008). A small minority of women develop very severe mental health problems for the first time after childbirth. This is sometimes called postpartum psychosis, and can involve women having very distressing experiences where they lose touch with reality (Sit et al., 2006).

There is evidence that perinatal depression may have long-lasting effects on children. The large-scale cohort studies which I discussed in Chapter 3 are able to look at the associations between parental mental health around the time of birth and the outcomes many years later for the children. A study using data from the Avon Longitudinal Study of Parents and Children found that levels of depression reported by parents when their baby was eight weeks old predicted lower academic performance in those children at aged 16 (Psychogiou, Russell and Owens, 2020). Of course, these studies cannot show causation, only correlation, and the authors of this paper suggest that this relationship is mediated by the quality of the interactions between mothers and children throughout childhood, among other factors.

Perinatal depression can be addressed in various ways. An individual might be offered psychological therapy or drugs. If they have PTSD, then trauma-focused therapy might be offered. A psychologist might try to set up community groups for parents with new babies, to improve social connections and to reduce the degree of loneliness and isolation experienced by many in the first year of parenthood.

CASE STUDY 5.4

Svetlana

Svetlana was a high achiever. She had done well at school, gone to university, and now had a professional job she enjoyed. She had got pregnant easily and had been delighted, planning to spend her maternity leave in art galleries and taking long walks with friends. She planned a water birth and hoped to avoid drugs. It all started to go wrong when she hadn't gone into labour in time and had to be induced. The induction took several days and ended with an emergency caesarean where she was rushed to theatre because the baby was in distress. She had thought he was going to die. Then, when he was born, she couldn't breast feed and he was inconsolable. When Svetlana came to perinatal mental health services, she described herself as broken. She said her body was a wreck, her emotions were in ruins, and her life was over. It was all she could do to get through the day, and she dragged herself from morning to evening. She had constant flashbacks to the birth and woke every thirty minutes to check that her baby was breathing. She had intrusive thoughts that her baby would be better off without her and talked about giving him up for adoption. Her partner couldn't understand what had gone wrong—the baby was healthy, the birth had been difficult but had ended well, and he was overjoyed to be a father. But for Svetlana, her sense of control over her life had been taken away. Before she had seen herself as someone who could succeed at anything, now she felt like she could hardly make it through the day.

Later life

Moving now to the other end of the lifespan, later life is usually considered to begin around the age of 65–70, when most people retire from full-time paid employment. This period of life is sometimes divided into the 'third age' which usually includes those up to the age of about 85, and the fourth age, by which time the physical problems associated with ageing are often significant.

There are some specific issues which arise in later life. In addition to retirement, later life is a time when many experience bereavement, physical health problems, or dementia. **Dementia** is an umbrella term for a group of progressive conditions which affect the brain, leading to memory loss and cognitive decline. Dementia becomes more likely with age, being relatively rare in people under 65. In those over 85, between a quarter and a third are affected by some level of dementia.

Inequalities have a cumulative effect over time. By the time people reach later life, the differences in health between the wealthiest and poorest in society are highly significant. In fact, length of life itself is strongly associated with wealth and social status, with the gap in life expectancy between the most deprived areas of the UK and the wealthiest areas being over twenty years, even when those regions are located only a few kilometres away from each other (Marmot, 2015). This goes for mental health as well. Older people with low **socioeconomic status (SES)** are at a much higher risk of reporting depression than are those of a high SES (Zenebe et al., 2021).

Different age cohorts have shared experiences which shape how they deal with challenges in their life. The generation who grew up during and immediately after World War 2 share formative experiences of food rationing, bombing, and family separation. The so-called 'Windrush generation' share experiences of coming to the UK from the Caribbean in order to start a new life and of being met by a very different and sometimes hostile and racist culture. Cultural differences can also exist between different age cohorts, with social attitudes changing dramatically in the course of a couple of generations. All of these things can affect how a person will respond to and understand emotional distress.

CASE STUDY 5.5

Winifred

Winifred was 78 when she told her GP that she was feeling very tired and wondered if she needed iron supplements. Her husband had died three years before and Winifred was spending a lot of time alone. When the GP asked, Winifred described frequently crying during the day, although she said this was just her being silly. She had no energy and was having trouble sleeping.

The GP had known Winifred for a long time. She knew that Winifred had a strong circle of friends in the area who she saw when she went out walking her dog. She also knew that Winifred had a daughter who lived close by and whose children she saw regularly. She was an active member of the local church. Until recently, Winifred had seemed to be thriving and active. She asked what had changed.

Winifred described having had a frightening experience when she had almost fallen at home. She had caught herself in time but had been worrying ever since that it might happen again. She felt that she was going into decline and that there was nothing to look forward to. She had stopped walking the dog, looking after her grandchildren, or meeting up with her friends. Consequently, the dog was unhappy and making a mess at home, which made things worse.

The GP said she didn't think that iron levels were the problem, although she arranged for some blood tests to make sure. She referred Winifred to an occupational therapist, to see if Winifred's home needed any adaptation to make it easier for her to get around safely. She asked Winifred if she would like to be put in contact with local befrienders who could come and walk the dog with her. She suggested that Winifred kept her mobile phone close by so that she could call for help if she needed it. And she suggested that Winifred tried doing some of her usual activities for a few weeks and then came back to see her. If at that point she wasn't any better, they could consider a referral to the practice counsellor. The GP therefore offered a social and a psychological intervention, for a problem which Winifred had assumed was physical.

Winifred left feeling more optimistic, took the dog out that afternoon, and met one of her friends. She arranged to see her daughter. It didn't happen overnight, but as Winifred started to do more meaningful activities, she gradually started to feel that life might be worth living. Her energy increased and she felt less tired. She decided to wear a pendant in case of falls, something she had always refused to do before. This improved her confidence at home, and her sleep was better.

This means that for older people, understanding the factors which influence their mental health requires us to think about the whole of their lives, as well as what is going on for them now. The case study of Winifred illustrates how thinking about the context of a person's life may mean considering the environmental and physical health factors, as well as directly addressing their emotional experiences. Cultural reasons also mean that some people will describe their distress in physical terms, as Winifred does.

Winifred's GP has a hypothesis that her tiredness is not physical, and so she has chosen to focus on what Winifred is doing in her life, rather than directly on her symptoms of distress or her tiredness. She's helped in this by her long relationship with and knowledge of Winifred. The GP is hoping that Winifred can start to do more, and then will feel better. Her low mood and withdrawal make sense because of her fear of falling and because she is no longer doing any of the things which made her life worthwhile. A more medical approach might have been to prescribe her sleeping pills to improve her sleep, or to give her antidepressants. In Winifred's case, all the different factors interact and so by changing one thing, other changes can start to happen, with the result that her mental health improves.

Much discussion of ageing focuses on the perceived increase of problems as people age. This is called the 'deficit model', one in which older adults are seen as a burden on society. Research has tended to focus on sickness, poverty, isolation, and demoralisation in older people (Atchley, 1982). Contrary to common opinion, the majority of older adults remain fit and able to care for themselves into later life. There is very little focus in Western society on the positive attributes of ageing. Instead, ageing is portrayed in negative terms, something which contributes to the ageism which many older people report experiencing (Chasteen et al., 2021).

Dementia

Dementia affects millions of people, most of them over the age of 65. There are over 850,000 people living with dementia in the UK, and 45,000 of these are under the age of 65. In dementia, **neurones** are damaged meaning that the brain functions less effectively. It is a **progressive** disease.

There are over 200 different subtypes of dementia. The most common are Alzheimer's disease, vascular dementia, dementia with Lewy bodies, frontotemporal dementia, and mixed dementia.

The neurological damage associated with dementia is the result of biological processes. Changes can be seen in the brain of many people with dementia at post-mortem. Diagnosis usually involves a referral to a memory clinic where the person will often be asked to complete a set of cognitive tests. They will then be asked back later to complete the same tests, in order to look for a decline in performance.

Dementia is an interesting case because it has a clear biological cause, and is therefore sometimes considered not to be a mental health problem at all. Out of all the problems discussed in this book, dementia is perhaps the one which most unequivocally fits the description of a 'brain disorder'.

You may be thinking that this means that surely for dementia, the biomedical model is the most appropriate way to approach people's experiences. The biomedical model sees dementia as a chronic illness which will lead to irrevocable decline, meaning that the person will become progressively less capable and more in need of care. Treatment focuses on ways to stop this decline, usually with drugs. This is the dominant way in which dementia is understood in Western culture.

However, even here there are drawbacks. A diagnosis of dementia tends to frame everything that a person does as a 'symptom' and puts their difficulties and deficits at the centre of their life. This can mean that people around them focus on trying to treat or minimise the symptoms, for example by constantly reminding them of where they are and what year it is. This can be very distressing and confusing for people. An alternative would be not to remind them unless it was necessary, and instead to focus on helping them feel safe and cared for. The focus on symptoms directs attention away from the person and their individual experiences.

Malignant social psychology

Working in the 1990s, Tom Kitwood, a clinical psychologist, suggested that a 'malignant social psychology' played a part in the decline of people with dementia. This referred to the environment around a person, which Kitwood argued contributes to their poor quality of life. Kitwood described how people with dementia are '**depersonalised**', often being ignored, mistreated, and dismissed, and proposed that this magnified their losses and contributed to their decline (Kitwood, 1997, Kitwood and Bredin, 1992). He suggested an alternative of 'person-centred care', where the person is cared for as an individual, responding to their actual needs rather than following set criteria. This idea changed the focus of care for many people with dementia.

It is now recognised that the experience of dementia is a complex interaction between multiple factors, including a person's life history, their health, personality, and the environment around them, alongside neurological impairment (Bruens, 2013). This has opened the door to other ways of thinking about dementia. These recognise how the social environment affects experiences and quality of life. Interventions have been developed which focus on respecting personhood and nurturing relationships (Milne, 2020).

Chapter Summary

- Each stage of life presents different challenges. What we perceive as 'good mental health' differs for different age groups.
- Seeing a person's emotional reactions and wellbeing in the context of their environment

and their individual characteristics may help us to understand their distress and behaviour.

- Many developmental models implicitly assume that there is a natural optimal pathway of development which, if followed, results in a psychologically and physically healthy human being.
- Culture plays a part in our experiences and assumptions throughout life, which will impact what we see as good or poor mental health.
- All types of inequality, discrimination, and poverty have a cumulative effect over life, meaning that by later life the effects of inequality can result in differences in life expectancy of around twenty years.
- Even for problems which have an identified physical cause, such as dementia, the environment influences how dementia affects a person's life.
- The experience of dementia has multiple influences and the social context can dramatically improve the life experiences of people with dementia.

? QUESTIONS

1. How do world events such as the COVID-19 pandemic interact with individual characteristics to (potentially) result in mental health problems? Is there any such thing as a common experience?

2. Why are developmental tasks relevant to mental health? How does life stage make a difference to mental health?

3. What difference does it make to consider the whole of someone's life when seeking to understand their mental health, as opposed to focusing on their current symptoms?

4. Why are culture and context important in mental health? Give examples of how this plays out in reality.

5. Dementia is a biological problem which should be treated biologically. Do you agree?

FURTHER READING

Blakemore, S.-J. (2018). *Inventing Ourselves: The Secret Life of the Teenage Brain*. London: Black Swan.

Sarah-Jayne Blakemore is a professor of psychology and cognitive neuroscience who specialises in adolescence. In this book she explains how new insights into brain development in adolescence help us to understand adolescent behaviour and vulnerabilities.

Caspi, A., Houts, R.M., Ambler, A., et al. (2020). Longitudinal assessments of mental health disorders and comorbidities across 4 decades among participants in the Dunedin Birth Cohort Study. *JAMA Network Open*, 3(4), e203221. doi:10.1001/jamanetworkopen.2020.3221

This paper from the Dunedin study describes how their participants met diagnostic criteria for different mental health problems at different times in their lives, and cautions against an overreliance on diagnosis in both clinical work and research.

Kitwood, T. (1997). *Dementia Reconsidered: The Person Comes First*. Buckingham: Open University Press.

Tom Kitwood proposes a person-centred approach to caring for people with dementia.

Marmot, M. (2015). *Status Syndrome: How Your Place on the Social Gradient Directly Affects Your Health*. London: Bloomsbury Paperbacks.

Michael Marmot is a professor of social epidemiology who writes about how society affects health. In this book he argues that inequality affects everyone across the social gradient, not just those at the bottom.

O'Connor, R., Wetherall, K., Cleare, S., McClelland, H., Melson, A., Niedzwiedz, C., … Robb, K. (2021). Mental health and well-being during the COVID-19 pandemic: Longitudinal analyses of adults in the UK COVID-19 Mental Health and Wellbeing study. *The British Journal of Psychiatry*, 218(6), 326–333. doi: 10.1192/bjp.2020.212

This is a large-scale survey study of the first six weeks of lockdown due to the COVID-19 pandemic. The authors use subgroup analysis to look at how different groups were affected in different ways by the pandemic.

 ## REFERENCES

American Psychiatric Association (2013). Cultural Concepts in DSM-5. https://www.psychiatry.org/File%20Library/Psychiatrists/Practice/DSM/APA_DSM_Cultural-Concepts-in-DSM-5.pdf

Andersen, L.B., Melvaer, L.B., Videbech, P., Lamont, R.F., and Joergensen, J.S. (2012). Risk factors for developing post-traumatic stress disorder following childbirth: A systematic review. *Acta Obstetrica Gynecologica Scandinavica*, 91, 1261–1272.

Atchley, R.C. (1982). The aging self. *Psychotherapy: Theory, Research & Practice*, 19(4), 388–396. doi: 10.1037/h0088450

Belsky, J., and Pluess, M. (2013). Beyond risk, resilience, and dysregulation: Phenotypic plasticity and human development. *Development and Psychopathology*, 25, 1243–1261. doi: 10.1017/S095457941300059X

Blakemore, S.-J. (2018). *Inventing Ourselves: The Secret Life of the Teenage Brain*. London: Black Swan.

Bredström, A. (2019). Culture and context in mental health diagnosing: Scrutinizing the DSM-5 revision. *Journal of Medical Humanities*, 40, 347–363. doi: 10.1007/s10912-017-9501-1

Bruens, M.T. (2013). Dementia: Beyond structures of medicalisation and cultural neglect. In J. Baars, J. Dohmen, A. Grenier, and C. Phillipson (eds), *Ageing, Meaning and Social Structure*. Bristol: Policy Press, pp. 81–96.

Chasteen, A.L., Horhota, M., and Crumley-Branyon, J.J. (2021). Overlooked and underestimated: Experiences of ageism in young, middle-aged, and older adults. *The Journals of Gerontology: Series B*, 76(7), 1323–1328. doi: 10.1093/geronb/gbaa043

Criado-Perez, C. (2019). *Invisible Women: Exposing Data Bias in a World Designed for Men*. London: Chatto & Windus.

Dagher, R., Bruckheim, H., Colpe, L., Edwards, E., and White, D. (2021). Perinatal depression: Challenges and opportunities. *Journal of Women's Health*, 30(2), 154–159. doi: 10.1089/jwh.2020.8862

Fried, E.I. (2021). Studying mental disorders as systems, not syndromes. PsyArXiv Preprints. doi: 10.31234/osf.io/k4mhv

Gillies, D., Christou, M., Dixon, A., Featherston, O., Rapti, I., et al. (2018). Prevalence and characteristics of self-harm in adolescents: Meta-analyses of community-based studies 1990–2015. *Journal of the American Academy of Child & Adolescent Psychiatry*, 57(10), 733–741.

Kellam, S.G., and Rebok, G.W. (1992). Building developmental and etiological theory through epidemiologically based preventive intervention trials. In J. McCord and R.E. Tremblay, (eds), *Preventing Antisocial Behavior: Interventions from Birth Through Adolescence*. New York: Guilford Press, pp. 162–195.

Kitwood, T., and Bredin, K. (1992). Towards a theory of dementia case, personhood and well-being. *Ageing and Society*, 12(3), 269–287.

Kitwood, T. (1997). *Dementia Reconsidered: The Person Comes First*. Buckingham: Open University Press.

Marmot, M. (2015). *Status Syndrome: How Your Place on the Social Gradient Directly Affects Your Health*. London: Bloomsbury Paperbacks.

McGrath, J.J., Saha, S., Al-Hamzawi, A.O., Alonso, J., Andrade, L., Borges, G., Bromet, E.J., Oakley Browne, M., Bruffaerts, R., Caldas de Almeida, J.M., Fayyad, J., Florescu, S., de Girolamo, G., Gureje, O., Hu, C., de Jonge, P., Kovess-Masfety, V., Lepine, J.P., Lim, C.C., Navarro-Mateu, F., … Kessler, R. C. (2016). Age of onset and lifetime projected risk of psychotic experiences: Cross-national data from the world mental health survey. *Schizophrenia Bulletin*, 42(4), 933–941. doi:10.1093/schbul/sbw011

Milne, A. (2020). *Mental Health in Later Life: Taking a Life Course Approach*. Bristol: Bristol University Press.

NHS Digital (2018). Mental health of children and young people in England. https://digital.nhs.uk/data-and-information/publications/statistical/mental-health-of-children-and-young-people-in-england/2017/2017#summary

O'Connor, R., Wetherall, K., Cleare, S., McClelland, H., Melson, A., Niedzwiedz, C., … Robb, K. (2021). Mental health and well-being during the COVID-19 pandemic: Longitudinal analyses of adults in the UK COVID-19 Mental Health & Wellbeing study. *The British Journal of Psychiatry*, 218(6), 326–333. doi:10.1192/bjp.2020.212

OECD (2017). *PISA 2015 Results (Volume III)*. Paris, France: OECD.

Paniagua, F.A. (2018). ICD-10 versus DSM-5 on cultural issues. *SAGE Open*, 8(1). doi:10.1177/2158244018756165

Pascoe, M.C., Hetrick, S.E., and Parker, A.G. (2020). The impact of stress on students in secondary school and higher education. *International Journal of Adolescence and Youth*, 25(1), 104–112. Doi:10.1080/02673843.2019.1596823

Piquero, A.R., Jennings, W.G., Jemison, E., Kaukinen, C., and Knaul, F.M. (2021). Evidence from a systematic review and meta-analysis: Domestic violence during the COVID-19 pandemic. *Journal of Criminal Justice*, 74, 101806. doi:10.1016/j.jcrimjus.2021.101806

Psychogiou, L., Russell, G., and Owens, M. (2020). Parents' postnatal depressive symptoms and their children's academic attainment at 16 years: Pathways of risk transmission. *British Journal of Psychology*, 111(1), 1–16. doi:10.1111/bjop.12378

Ramchandani, P.G., O'Connor, T.G., Evans, J., Heron, J., Murray, L., and Stein, A. (2008). The effects of pre- and postnatal depression in fathers: A natural experiment comparing the effects of exposure to depression on offspring. *Journal of Child Psychology and Psychiatry*, 49(10), 1069–1078. doi:10.1111/j.1469-7610.2008.02000.x. PMID: 19017023; PMCID: PMC2737608.

Scarr, S., and McCartney, K. (1983). How people make their own environments: A theory of genotype → environment effects. *Child Development*, 54(2), 424–435.

Shevlin, M., Butter, S., McBride, O., Murphy, J., Gibson-Miller, J., Hartman, T., … Bentall, R. (2023). Refuting the myth of a 'tsunami' of mental ill-health in populations affected by COVID-19: Evidence that response to the pandemic is heterogeneous, not homogeneous. *Psychological Medicine*, 53(2), 429–437. doi:10.1017/S0033291721001665

Sit, D., Rothschild, A.J., and Wisner, K.L. (2006). A review of postpartum psychosis. *Journal of Women's Health*, 15(4), 352–368. doi:10.1089/jwh.2006.15.352. PMID: 16724884; PMCID: PMC3109493.

Wu, T., Jia, X., Shi, H., Niu, J., Yin, X., Xie, J., and Wang, X. (2021). Prevalence of mental health problems during the COVID-19 pandemic: A systematic review and meta-analysis. *Journal of Affective Disorders*, 281, 91–98.

Zenebe, Y., Akele, B., W/Selassie, M., and Necho, M. (2021). Prevalence and determinants of depression among old age: A systematic review and meta-analysis. *Annals of General Psychiatry*, 20(1), 55. doi:10.1186/s12991-021-00375-x. PMID: 34922595; PMCID: PMC8684627.

Chapter 6
Interventions

Learning objectives

When you have completed this chapter, you should be able to do the following:

6.1 Critically discuss the language used in this area.

6.2 Explain the difference between first- and second-order interventions.

6.3 Critically evaluate the ways in which using a hierarchy of evidence to decide on interventions can affect what is available.

6.4 Use an ecological model to illustrate different levels of intervention.

6.5 Describe the main individual interventions offered to those with mental health problems, and give a detailed example of how CBT looks in practice.

6.6 Explain how family level interventions differ to individual interventions.

6.7 Give examples of interventions on a community level.

6.8 Discuss what a structural level intervention might look like.

Introduction

In earlier chapters I have talked about how we understand distress and unusual behaviour, what might be the causes of such experiences, and the different models which we use to try to make sense of people's experiences. I've discussed the biomedical model of mental health on which the mental health system is founded and introduced alternatives. In this chapter I'm going to get down to some practicalities. For the point of all this is surely to work out how psychologists can help those in distress, and how we can reduce suffering.

You may think that it's obvious how this is done; better mental health care and shorter waiting lists. That's what many people say when asked how to improve mental health. However, even if we accept that mental health is best approached as a healthcare problem, improving mental health services will only get us so far. This is because healthcare is about resolving problems which have already arisen. To improve the overall level of wellbeing in the population, we need to do more than treat health problems—we must address the factors that are causing the problems in the first place.

Ibrahim's Story

Ibrahim was desperate. He felt low and anxious, was constantly worrying about his future and his children, and he didn't know where to turn. His job as a healthcare assistant left him struggling to put enough food on the table, let alone pay the bills and the rent. His family lived far away and expected him to send them money to help out. As he was walking past the station on his way to work one day, he saw a poster.'Don't suffer alone. We're here to help', it said, with a picture of a melancholy man holding a mobile phone.

Ibrahim thought about it. He did need help and so he rang the number. He discovered that the help they were offering was to listen to him talk about his problems. When he said he was still feeling terrible they suggested that he should go to his GP.

Ibrahim went to the GP and was offered an anti-depressant. He was referred to the psychological therapies service and after waiting for several months was offered cognitive therapy for depression. He went along each week and learnt to challenge his negative thoughts, but he still felt desperately worried.'I do want help' he thought to himself,'When I have enough money to pay the rent each month, then I think I will feel better. Who will help me with that?'.

To understand why, think of lung cancer. No matter how good the treatment for lung cancer becomes, public health campaigns aimed at educating people about the risks of smoking, banning smoking in public places, and increasing the price of cigarettes will be more effective in improving overall health than treating those who already have lung cancer.

The same applies to mental health. Without addressing the factors which cause people's difficulties, there will be an endless flow of more people needing help, whilst services struggle to keep up with demand.

In this chapter I start by discussing the different ways in which change can happen. I'll introduce the different levels on which an intervention might occur and give some examples of each.

What defines an effective intervention? As you read Ibrahim's story, ask yourself what the most useful intervention would be.

In Chapter 5 I introduced the idea of a complex systems approach to mental health. This would suggest that many approaches to mental health intervention are too simplistic, focusing as they do on one level of analysis. Advocates suggest that using a systems model would mean looking at the interrelationships between different factors, and planning a combination of responses, including those on the individual level, as well as looking at the broader social context (Atkinson et al., 2020). These interrelationships are something to bear in mind as you read this chapter—each intervention will have unexpected and often unmeasured impacts on other elements of the problem.

6.1 Treatment or intervention?

Most textbooks focus solely on the interventions used within the mental health care system. These are typically called **treatments**. Treatments are drugs and therapies used to try and improve people's mental state—or in other words, to treat their mental health problem.

Treatment is a word which evokes the medical model. When applied to mental health, it directs our attention towards individual interventions. Treatment cannot include wider changes to society or communities which improve the mental health and wellbeing of the people living in them.

Cast your mind back to the Afghan refugee camp from Chapter 1. It's probable that the most dramatic improvement in the mental health of these refugees would come if they were granted leave to remain, helped to find places to live outside the camp, and were able to earn money to support themselves. That type of change wouldn't be thought of as a 'treatment' and isn't within the remit of mental health care. The sorts of treatment available within mental health services will be drugs or psychotherapy, neither of which can solve the problem of being incarcerated indefinitely in a refugee camp.

If we want to understand the complexity of the psychology of mental health then we must include changes which work on the level of community or society as well as those that focus on the individual. That is why this chapter is about interventions, rather than treatment.

6.2 First- and second-order interventions

There are two different ways of bringing about change. First order focuses on an individual in order to try to fix a problem. Second order focuses on systems and structures in order to change the interaction between a person and their environment (Waszlawick et al., 2011).

The example in the Box 6.2 below illustrates the difference between these two approaches.

Psychologist A is working in a paradigm of first-order change. Her working hypothesis is that there is a problem with these children which, if properly identified, can be treated or managed.

Psychologist B is hoping to change the problem through second-order change. Her working hypothesis is that there is a problem with how the school system is operating. She hopes to change this, thus changing the experience of the children within it. Second-order interventions often focus on factors which are known to cause distress, such as inequality, discrimination, and bullying.

In the chapter which follows, the individual level interventions are likely to be first order, whilst the community or system level interventions are second

---

CASE STUDY 6.2

First- and Second-Order Interventions

A school was having difficulties with several children. They were fighting with other children and hostile to the teachers. They were not achieving academically. The school called in two psychologists and asked them to work out what was wrong.

Psychologist A got down to work. She made appointments for all the children, called their parents in and observed the children in class. She gave the children cognitive tests and diagnostic interviews. Quite quickly she identified that several of the children fit the criteria for conduct disorder, whilst others fit the criteria for intellectual disabilities. She wrote reports and recommendations for the children's parents and teachers, including new strategies to manage behaviour and a system of rewards and punishments based on things the children value. She thought that some of the children needed more support and started the process of applying for education and health care plans (EHCP) for them.

Psychologist B spent a few days in the school, talking to the children, teachers, and observing what was going on. She observed the school's 'zero-tolerance' behaviour strategy which meant that children who did things such as shouting out in class or rocking on their chair were written up on the board immediately, something which the children found shameful. Those who came to school in incomplete uniform or forgot their homework were sent to see the headteacher.

Many children were being written up and being sent to see the headteacher and for some children, particularly those from visible minorities, this was happening nearly every day. She asked the children about their experience of school, and they told her that they felt that no one was interested in them except when they did something wrong, and they felt like everyone thought they were bad.

At this point, the school was asking Psychologist B what she was spending all her time on. They were hoping for a concrete outcome and were wondering where her reports were. Psychologist B collected the children's stories, and ran a workshop with the teachers, asking them to consider the zero-tolerance behaviour strategy from the viewpoint of some of the children. The teachers were shocked, dismayed, and initially defensive. They were proud of their behaviour policy. Over the course of several meetings they started to think about other ways in which they might manage behaviour in the school without shaming and singling out children in the same way. They also thought about ways to give children more positive attention and set up optional 'nurture groups' during the lunch break where children could drop in, play games, and chat with a member of staff if they wanted. Ultimately the school changed to a more relational approach to behaviour. They thought about how the structures of their school targeted particular children, the impact on these children, and what they needed to do to change this. The experience of the children at school changed, and their behaviour improved.

order. The focus in the health system is typically on first-order interventions.

6.3 Evidence-based interventions

Research evidence is an important part of how health professionals decide which interventions to offer. Institutions such as The National Institute for Health and Care Excellence (NICE) regularly release guidelines which tell clinicians which interventions they should be using, based on their evaluation of the evidence base. They use a hierarchy of evidence, which I introduced in Chapter 3. This was developed for **evidence-based medicine.**

The hierarchy of evidence favours certain types of interventions. These are first-order, short-term and standardised, with clear outcome measures and end points. It is easy to design a randomised control study to test the **efficacy** of a drug on reducing symptoms of depression over a couple of months. Randomised controlled trials to test the effects of a long-term community intervention designed to promote community cohesion are practically impossible.

Using the principles of evidence-based medicine in mental health means that some interventions are prioritised over others. This is often because they are easier to evaluate using the methods which were developed for evidence-based medicine. These methods have been transferred to mental health, frequently without acknowledgement of the differences. Typically, these are individual-level treatments which use symptom questionnaires as their outcome measure. Many interventions can never be evaluated using randomised control trials, and unless other types of research are valued, interventions on a community or systemic level will never make the grade.

Problems with the evidence base

Evaluating scientific evidence is not as simple as searching for research studies on a data base. Research can always be interpreted in multiple ways, and frequently the way in which a study is designed will reflect the bias of the researchers and the results that they hoped to find. Publication bias means that studies which show a positive result are more likely to be published—and once they are published, they are more likely to be cited, meaning that the bias accumulates and studies with negative findings effectively disappear (de Vries

et al., 2018). In addition, the reliance on diagnostic categories may limit the conclusions we can draw from much research, given how heterogenous these groups are and the lack of reliability of the categories.

Research into drug treatments for mental health problems have come under fire due to accusations of bias. Most of the research is carried out by the pharmaceutical companies who sell the drugs. They therefore have a strong interest in showing that their drugs work, and that they work better than the drugs produced by other companies. Unsurprisingly, this is generally what their research studies show (Melander et al., 2003).

There is some evidence that pharmaceutical companies use various practices in order to make their products seem more effective than they actually are. One common approach is to conduct several trials of a drug, and then to only publish those which show the benefits of the drug (Kirsch, 2009). Those trials which do not show the preferred results simply disappear. An NHS systematic review in 2010 found that about 50% of clinical trials were never published, meaning that drawing firm conclusions from the published research is problematic.

This problem of disappearing studies is recognised to be such a problem that the European Union now requires all clinical trials to be registered before participants are recruited. In theory this means that all trials can be tracked. The results of this have been mixed, with one study finding that only 46% of the trials on the world's largest clinical trials register had reported any results (Ross et al., 2009).

The evidence base for psychological therapies shares many of the same problems, and in the last ten years psychology has been in the grip of a 'replication crisis', where it has become clear that the results of many studies do not replicate when repeated by other researchers (see Wiggins and Christopherson, 2019). Psychotherapy studies are not exempt from this. Findings about the efficacy of therapy are highly inconsistent. Studies of psychological therapies tend to be carried out by those who are convinced of the usefulness of a therapy, often by those who developed the intervention and whose livelihood may be reliant on it (Cristea, 2015). Research which does not show a positive benefit is less likely to be written up and published (something known as the 'back of the filing cabinet' problem). Even with meta-analyses, there is evidence that the allegiance of the authors makes a difference to the results, with meta-analyses conducted in a very similar timeframe finding strik-ingly different results for the comparative merits of psychodynamic psychotherapy and CBT (Hengartner, 2018). In addition, there are methodological problems with evaluating psychological therapies, since a psy-chological therapy cannot be effectively 'blinded' to therapist and client, meaning that expectations may play a part in the results.

Evaluating community-based interventions bring another set of methodological issues. Interventions are highly varied, making them hard to compare or review systematically. Community involvement is often a key part of these interventions which further complicates research—if members of a community are involved in planning and implementing an inter-vention, it may not be desirable or possible to replicate the same programme elsewhere. Again, those who do the research are usually invested in the success of the programme, making the risk of bias high.

Structural interventions are usually evaluated on a population level, meaning that they must rely on ques-tionnaires and on large-scale changes. These types of interventions typically have complex aims, targeting factors such as economic instability, discrimination, lack of resources, and limited access to education and healthcare. Results may only be evident in the long term and will be complicated by multiple fac-tors and unpredictable events (such as the COVID-19 pandemic). The research into public health policies, particularly mental health, is not generally of a high quality (Thomson et al., 2018).

6.4 Levels of intervention

In the next part of this chapter I will discuss the differ-ent types of intervention, starting with the individual and moving outwards. **Community psychologists** call this an 'ecological model'. Figure 6.1 illustrates the different levels of analysis in an ecological model.

6.5 Individual-level interventions

On an individual level, the most common interven-tions are drugs or psychotherapy.

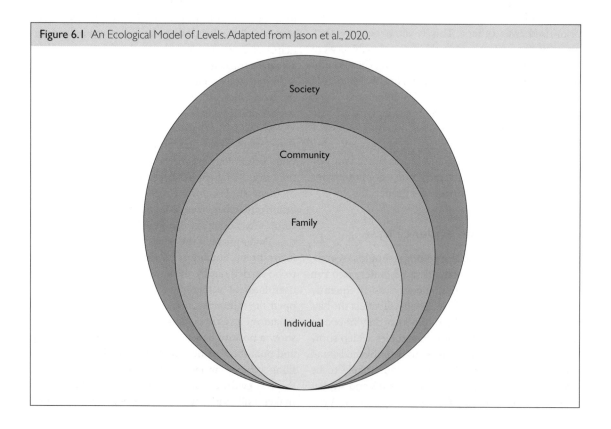

Figure 6.1 An Ecological Model of Levels. Adapted from Jason et al., 2020.

Society

Community

Family

Individual

Drugs

Drugs are far and away the most common intervention offered to people with mental health problems. The Adult Psychiatric Morbidity Survey in 2014 found that of the 12% of the population who were receiving an intervention for their mental health problems, 10% were receiving drugs and only 3% were receiving psychological therapy, with 1.3% receiving both drugs and psychological therapy (McManus et al., 2014). Figures from Public Health England show that, in 2017–2018, 17% of the adult population in England were prescribed anti-depressants (Public Health England, 2019). This was an increase from the year before.

Drugs prescribed for mental health problems fall into broad categories. Anti-depressants include drugs such as citalopram, sertraline, and mirtazapine. Anti-psychotic drugs include the 'first generation' drugs such as haloperidol and chlorpromazine, and the second generation, used more since the 1990s. These include risperidone, quetiapine and olanzapine. Lithium is used as a mood stabiliser for those with manic episodes, and other drugs used as mood stabilisers include benzodiazepines and anticonvulsants.

The molecular mechanisms by how these drugs work are quite well understood. They alter the balance of neurotransmitters in the brain, either by directly targeting the neurotransmitter or by targeting receptors on the synapses. Anti-psychotics generally target the dopamine pathway, whilst anti-depressants target the monoamine neurotransmitters serotonin, norepinephrine, and dopamine. Early anti-depressants were monoamine oxidase inhibitors (MAOI), inhibiting the enzyme which breaks down monoamine neurotransmitters and resulting in higher levels of those neurotransmitters. They were followed by the tricyclics, which inhibited the synaptic uptake of norepinephrine and serotonin. Both these classes of drugs had unpleasant side effects and are infrequently used today. Since the 1980s the most commonly prescribed anti-depressants are selective serotonin reuptake inhibitors (SSRIs), drugs which selectively block the reuptake of serotonin. These include drugs such as fluoxetine and citalopram. All of the drugs used as anti-depressants increase the amount of one or several monoamines available in the brain through different mechanisms.

A major controversy in recent years has been the question of whether anti-depressant drugs are effective beyond what we would expect from a placebo effect. Psychologist Irving Kirsch carried out meta-analyses which included unpublished studies, and which showed that whilst people respond to anti-depressant drugs, they also respond strongly to placebos (Kirsch, 2009). Others argue that many of the studies he included were badly done and included too many people who didn't qualify for a depression diagnosis (Kramer, 2016). Kirsch fought back, arguing that the research showed psychotherapy and physical exercise had the same benefits as anti-depressants without the side effects (Kirsch, 2019). A separate metanalysis and systematic review of anti-depressants for those diagnosed with major depressive disorder found that they were more effective in adults than placebo (Cipriani et al., 2018). However, other researchers argue that methodological limitations are underestimated in this review and that the mean difference reported on the 17-item Hamilton depression scale was less than two points (Munkholm et al., 2019). The debate on this is ongoing.

Another recent area of controversy has been withdrawal effects from anti-depressants. For years, people were told by their doctors that there were no severe withdrawal effects from anti-depressants and any symptoms upon stopping taking them were due to a relapse of depression. It took doctors speaking openly about their own experiences trying to come off anti-depressants for it to be acknowledged by the NHS and the Royal College of Psychiatrists that some people have severe withdrawal effects from anti-depressants, and that this was not something which was addressed in the clinical trials (Horowitz and Wilcock, 2022).

One of the things that contributes to the complexity of this discussion (which applies to a whole range of different interventions, not just anti-depressants) is the heterogeneity present—both in the people who receive an intervention and of their responses to that intervention. This is even more of a problem when you consider that anti-depressants are prescribed to many people by their GPs without a formal diagnosis of depression and so the people who take these drugs in real life are likely to be much more varied than those in the research studies.

Anti-psychotics act in a different way, decreasing the receptivity of the brain to dopamine. They do this by binding to dopamine receptors in synapses in the brain, meaning that the dopamine itself cannot do so and thereby preventing the neurones from firing. First-generation anti-psychotic drugs have severe side effects which are known as extrapyramidal side effects, including muscle tremors, a shuffling gait, and dribbling.

Long-term use of these drugs sometimes results in an irreversible syndrome known as tardive dyskinesia, involving repetitive and involuntary muscle movements. Second-generation anti-psychotics have fewer side effects and are now more widely used.

Anti-psychotic drugs target mostly what are called the 'positive symptoms' of psychosis. These are symptoms such as hallucinations, delusions, and mania. 'Negative symptoms' are used to describe behaviours which reflect a reduced engagement with life, including social withdrawal, loss of pleasure, and apathy. In general, these symptoms do not respond well to anti-psychotic drugs (Correll and Schooler, 2020). Meta-analyses of the acute use of anti-psychotics find that they have a significant effect on symptom reduction and quality of life over and above placebo (Haddad and Correll, 2018), being more likely to work for people experiencing their first episode of psychosis. Responses to these drugs are heterogenous, with some people finding them less helpful, particularly those who have had several episodes. In addition, survivor-led movements such as the Hearing Voices Network argue that learning to live with positive symptoms may be more helpful for some people than trying to suppress them with drugs. Side effects continue to be a problem, among them weight gain and increased risk of diabetes.

It appears that high prescribing levels of drugs have not led to a dramatic improvement in mental health recovery rates, particularly in the longer term. There is some evidence that those who are put on and stay on medication for first episode psychosis actually have worse outcomes that those who stop taking medication (Wunderink et al., 2013) and that those who take medication for major depressive disorder may have poorer long-term outcomes (Vittengl, 2017).

Theories which follow clinical practice

The use of both anti-depressants and anti-psychotics to alleviate symptoms led to new theories of what causes these symptoms in the first place. In both cases, use of the drugs (which target these neurotransmitters) pre-date the theories.

The dopamine hypothesis of schizophrenia holds that an excess of dopamine is the problem, whilst the serotonin hypothesis of depression suggests that a lack of serotonin is the core issue. These theories have become extremely widespread. People are often told by their doctors that they feel the way they do because of a problem with the chemical levels in their

brain and that the drugs will correct this—or 'restore the balance of dopamine with other chemicals in the brain' as Rethink Mental Illness put it on their website (Rethink Mental Illness, 2020). Television and print adverts directed at consumers in the United States tell people that depression is due to a low level of serotonin, which the drugs correct (France et al., 2007). This belief may have unintended side effects, such as reducing people's willingness to try non-pharmacological interventions. As France et al. (2007) put it, 'Psychotherapy can alleviate depression; therefore (using the above logic) a deficiency of psychotherapy causes depression (of course, we are unaware of any serious assertions to this effect)'. A systematic review of the evidence has found that there is no evidence for an association between serotonin and depression (Moncrieff et al., 2022).

The evidence does show that psychiatric drugs can cause a change in a person's mental state, and this can be helpful in some cases (notwithstanding the controversies about placebos). However, the leap to a chemical imbalance theory is not supported by the evidence. Alcohol, recreational drugs, and caffeine can also cause a change in mental state, and some suggest that it would be more realistic to think about psychiatric drugs in a similar way (Moncrieff, 2018). This approach suggests that drugs can be useful in altering a person's mental state, but this does not have to mean that they are correcting a disease-state or healing a disordered brain.

Psychological therapy

Psychological therapy (or talking therapy) is what most people think psychologists and psychiatrists spend their time doing. Many psychologists do indeed spend their time offering different types of therapy to people in distress.

There is a confusing array of different types of psychological therapies. In the UK at the time of writing the most popular are cognitive behaviour therapy, **counselling** or humanistic psychotherapy, psychoanalytic psychotherapy, and family or systemic therapy. This varies between countries and also over time.

All psychological therapies share elements in common, and there is evidence that these common factors may be the mechanisms responsible for many of the benefits of psychological therapy. These include a **therapeutic relationship** between the therapist and client, the creation of expectations of recovery or improvement, and the encouragement of health-promoting behaviour (Wampold, 2015).

In this section I will describe some common psychological therapies. I'll spend most time on cognitive behaviour therapy, using a case example to demonstrate. I've chosen to do this for CBT since it has the largest evidence base, is widely used, and is frequently referred to as the 'gold standard' in psychological therapy (David, Cristea, and Hofmann, 2018). CBT has received large amounts of government funding and has been made available to many people across the UK as part of the 'Improving Access to Psychological Therapies (IAPT)' programme.

Cognitive behaviour therapy

Cognitive Behaviour Therapy (CBT) conceptualises a person's mental health problems as being due to their thoughts about what is happening to them. It was started by Aaron Beck (1921–2021), a psychiatrist, and has been developed further by many psychologists and psychiatrists.

The central principle in CBT is that it is not a person's life *in itself* that causes distress, it is the way that the person interprets and thinks about their life. Therefore, goes the logic, if we could change how a person perceives their experiences (and what they do about it), then we could reduce their distress. The mechanism of change is through helping people change their thoughts and behaviours. A very popular CBT self-help book sums it up as 'Change How You Feel by Changing the Way You Think' (Greenberger and Padesky, 2015).

CBT sessions follow a structure laid down by the therapist. Many CBT **protocols** have been **manualised**, and for this reason, as well as the focus on symptom reduction, it lends itself well to research trials. It is the psychotherapy on which most research trials have been done. CBT protocols are often diagnosis-specific although several **transdiagnostic** models are currently in development.

The extended case example in Box 6.3 illustrates how CBT works for one person describing symptoms of depression, Nadja.

Nadja's case is an example of how CBT can work for someone with a common mental health problem. CBT often focuses on the here and now, and prioritises making observable changes to people's lives.

As CBT has developed, it has expanded to include other techniques, some of which are quite different from CBT in its original form. These include mindfulness, a form of Buddhist meditation which has been secularised and integrated into cognitive therapy group programmes, called Mindfulness Based Cognitive Therapy (MBCT) (Segal, Williams, and Teasdale, 2018). Acceptance and Commitment Therapy (ACT)

CASE STUDY 6.3

Cognitive Behavioural Therapy

Nadja was referred to a psychologist for CBT by her GP. She was feeling low in mood and had no energy.

Therapy began with what is called a **cognitive conceptualisation** which is a type of formulation (see Chapter 4). Nadja and the therapist followed a template like the one in Figure 6.2. They identified some formative early experiences and discussed how these led Nadja to form beliefs about herself. Nadja said that she felt that bullying at school and her dad leaving the family home when she was eight had had a negative impact on her when growing up. Her mother was sometimes critical although she was also loving, and she had had a close relationship with her grandparents.

Nadja and her therapist identified 'core beliefs' which Nadja had formed as result of her experiences. These are beliefs which are deeply held and expressed in absolute terms. For Nadja, these were around not being good enough and being unlovable.

These core beliefs led Nadja to form 'underlying assumptions' which guided her behaviour in the world. Nadja believed that she must try terribly hard in order to prevent other people discovering that she was not good enough, and that friends were bound to let her down.

Then Nadja and her therapist focused on a specific trigger which had happened in the week before. A friend had been very late to a meeting at the local cinema. Nadja had started to feel very low and overwhelmed, and after fifteen minutes she left and went home. Nadja identified her 'automatic thoughts'— thoughts which popped into her head such as 'Of course she's not coming, who'd want to meet a loser like me?' and 'I'm so stupid for ever thinking that she'd want to meet me, I should have known better'.

Nadja and her therapist filled in the sheet below (Figure 6.2). Nadja took that home.

(Continued)

CASE STUDY 6.3 (continued)

Figure 6.2 Nadja's cognitive conceptualisation. Adapted from Fennell, 2016.

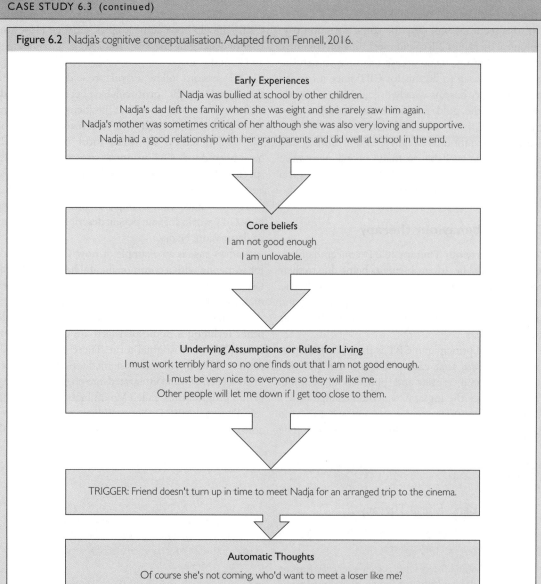

Early Experiences
Nadja was bullied at school by other children.
Nadja's dad left the family when she was eight and she rarely saw him again.
Nadja's mother was sometimes critical of her although she was also very loving and supportive.
Nadja had a good relationship with her grandparents and did well at school in the end.

Core beliefs
I am not good enough
I am unlovable.

Underlying Assumptions or Rules for Living
I must work terribly hard so no one finds out that I am not good enough.
I must be very nice to everyone so they will like me.
Other people will let me down if I get too close to them.

TRIGGER: Friend doesn't turn up in time to meet Nadja for an arranged trip to the cinema.

Automatic Thoughts
Of course she's not coming, who'd want to meet a loser like me?
It's my fault for even thinking she'd want to come, I should have known better.
I'm so stupid for arranging this.

The next stage was to identify how Nadja's thoughts, feelings, physiology, and behaviour interacted when she was in a trigger situation. When Nadja was waiting for her friend and experiencing negative thoughts, she started to feel very low and sad. Her limbs started to feel heavy and she felt lethargic and tired. She wanted to get away.

By the time her friend arrived 20 minutes later, it was too late. Nadja had gone. She went home and went straight to bed, where she lay and cried all afternoon. As she lay in bed, she had more thoughts about how useless she was, and how pointless her life was. This made her mood worse, she felt more tired, and she felt even less inclined to get out of bed. The longer she stayed in bed, the more negative she felt about herself. In this way, Nadja's thoughts, feelings, physiological reactions, and behaviour formed a vicious cycle, as is shown in Figure 6.3 below.

Figure 6.3 A cognitive model of how thoughts, feeling, behaviour, and physiology interact. Adapted from Greenberger and Padesky, 2015.

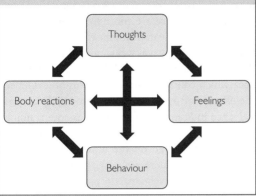

Nadja's therapy focused on helping her break those cycles. She filled in thought diaries during the week, and together she and the therapist practiced challenging her negative thoughts. They collected evidence for and against the thoughts she had had outside the cinema. When she gathered all her courage and asked her friend why she was late, she discovered that it was because the bus had been diverted and her phone had run out of battery so she couldn't text Nadja. This was evidence against Nadja's thoughts about her friend not wanting to see her. Other evidence was that the friend continued to make plans to meet up with her.

Nadja and her therapist planned 'behavioural experiments' where Nadja experimented with behaving differently to see what would happen. The next time she found herself overwhelmed with negative thoughts, instead of leaving and going home to bed she tried to challenge her thinking and find an alternative thought, meaning she gave the outing another chance. She tried contacting other friends who she had been avoiding and they responded well. She found that after this she started to gradually feel better.

Nadja was given questionnaires throughout her therapy rating her symptoms of depression and anxiety, and after 12 sessions she was feeling happier. She was doing more activities and felt more optimistic about the future. She was discharged.

(Hayes et al., 2009) is another therapy which focuses on accepting negative thoughts and feelings rather than challenging them. These therapies are called 'third-wave CBT'.

CBT has attracted far more research and government funding than other psychological therapies. There are many meta-analyses showing its efficacy for a wide range of problems (e.g., Feng et al., 2020, Hofmann et al., 2012). However, it has also come under criticism for being overly symptom-focused, and for addressing problems on a superficial level. CBT often requires homework between sessions, and gives people written tasks to complete, which can make it harder to access for people who struggle with literacy. The founding principle of CBT—that it is our interpretation of events, rather than events themselves, which cause distress—has been criticised as dismissing the reality of many people's lives and reinforcing the medical model (Dalal, 2019).

Humanistic psychotherapy

Humanistic psychotherapy is based on the work of Carl Rogers and Abraham Maslow and takes quite a different approach from CBT. There is now a group of psychotherapies which comes under this heading, including emotion-focused therapy, person-centred therapy, gestalt therapy, and expressive psychotherapy. They share certain core features, including an emphasis on an empathic and authentic therapeutic relationship and a goal of self-awareness and personal growth, and are generally not directive or advisory (Elliott et al., 2020).

Humanistic psychotherapies are based on the principle that all people have the capacity to move towards psychological growth and fulfilment. They see a non-judgemental relationship with a therapist as the catalyst for this change. They are not focused on diagnosis and symptom reduction. Each session will usually start with what the individual brings to therapy, and the therapist does not impose a structure. The therapist focuses on creating a space of 'unconditional positive regard' where the person can talk without fear of censure or judgement. The mechanism for change is therefore assumed to be the sense that the person has of being accepted unconditionally, which will—according to the theory—enable them to move towards self-actualisation and healing.

Humanistic psychotherapies have lagged behind other psychotherapies in terms of developing an evidence base. Since humanistic psychotherapy does not focus on diagnoses or symptom reduction, collecting an evidence base is not as straightforward as using the same questionnaires used to assess outcomes in CBT.

Success in humanistic psychotherapy will be defined individually by each person, and many people who seek this type of help may not have a diagnosable 'disorder'. Each person's experience will be different, making it again difficult to compare the results with other psychotherapies. This lack of research is now being addressed, with a recent meta-analysis finding that humanistic-existential psychotherapies are effective for a wide range of problems, including depression, interpersonal difficulties, chronic medical conditions, and psychosis (Elliot et al., 2020).

Psychoanalytic psychotherapy

Psychoanalytic psychotherapy was originally based on the theories of Sigmund Freud (1856–1939), but has been influenced and developed by other prominent psychotherapists such as Melanie Klein (1882–1960) and Carl Jung (1875–1961). Psychoanalytic therapy is traditionally long term and intensive, with therapists and clients meeting for several years, sometimes several times a week. Psychoanalytic theory suggests that everyone has unresolved unconscious conflicts from their childhood which they could benefit from exploring through therapy.

The therapeutic relationship is central to psychoanalytic psychotherapy. It is considered to be the place in which the unconscious will reveals itself, as the client will re-enact relational and emotional patterns from their childhood. The therapist uses the relationship in the therapy, including reflecting on their own experiences and emotions during the therapy session. Central to this type of therapy is the idea that the struggles that the client has outside the therapy room will be brought into the relationship with the therapist.

Psychoanalytic psychotherapists will refer to transference and counter transference. Transference is when a client unconsciously redirects feelings that they have about an important person in their lives (usually their parent) onto the therapist. A person may experience rage, love, frustration, and attraction towards their therapist. According to psychoanalytic theory, this is due to unresolved conflicts with figures from their childhood. Freud saw the recognition and exploration of the transference as one of the most important tasks of psychotherapy.

Countertransference is what the therapist feels towards the client. Exploring the countertransference gives the therapist insight into their client and the feelings that they elicit in others. Symptom reduction is not necessarily the aim in psychoanalytic psychotherapy, which focuses more on understanding unconscious patterns.

The theories of psychoanalysis have been modified for use in shorter-term therapies (often called psychodynamic) and these are more frequently used in the health service. Research into the efficacy of psychoanalytic psychotherapy was weak until quite recently, with the French government publishing a study in February 2004 which concluded that there was no evidence for the efficacy of psychoanalysis (particularly controversial since in France psychoanalysis is core training for psychologists; Gonon and Keller, 2020). Findings such as this have spurred on the development of an evidence base, and there are now several meta-analyses of the effects of psychoanalytic psychotherapy, leading Gonon and Kelly to claim that it is 'at least as effective as other active treatments'. Recent meta-analyses have indicated that adding short-term psychodynamic psychotherapy to drug treatment has more of an effect than drugs alone (Driessen et al., 2020).

6.6 Family-level interventions

Family therapy moves away from the individual and sees a person's problems in the context of the people who surround them. This is usually their family, although this can include anyone who is consistently present in their life.

Rather than seeing an individual as disordered, a family therapist will ask what function that person's problems have within the family, and how the responses of other people in the family are maintaining the problem. The therapist will then help families to make changes in how they relate to each other. The assumption is that by changing the group dynamics, a client's problems can start to change.

Therapists will use different techniques to help families communicate with each other. The therapist will look out for dynamics in the family, such as noticing who takes on the role of making decisions, who usually gets upset first when things go wrong, who is seen as the problem member of the family, and who is the person who calms everyone down. They might ask members of a family to imagine what would happen if the problem ceased to exist overnight, or to try exercises where they take on different roles.

There are different schools of family therapy, but they share a focus on addressing problems at the level of the whole family rather than on an individual level (Nichols and Schwartz, 2009). Family therapy is most frequently used for children and adolescents, although many couples therapists are trained in family therapy.

Family interventions have been shown to be particularly effective when a family member has psychosis, with the evidence showing that they can significantly reduce relapse and hospital readmission rates (Claxton, Onwumere, and Fornells-Ambrojo, 2017). There is also evidence that using couples therapy is effective for depression, with a recent Cochrane meta-analysis finding that couples therapy and individual therapy had similar effects on depressive symptoms, and was more effective at alleviating couples' distress (Barbato and D'Avanzo, 2020).

Other interventions aim to improve the life and psychological wellbeing of family members but are not therapy. Programmes such as Surestart in the UK and Headstart in the US aimed to support families early on in children's lives. They did this through a combination of different approaches, including befrienders, local children's centres, family support workers, and affordable nurseries.

Interventions do not always have to be either one or the other. Addressing different levels at the same time may improve the chances that someone will benefit from the intervention. Combining drug treatment with psychological therapy appears to be significantly more effective than offering drugs alone (Cuijpers et al., 2014). If someone is very distressed, drugs may enable them to function well enough to engage in psychological therapy.

Psychological therapies are not without their detractors. They do not work for everyone, with studies consistently finding that between 5% and 10% of people may actually get worse after therapy. It can also be argued that they reinforce an individualised perspective on mental health (rather like the medical model), putting the onus on the person themselves to change, rather than looking at the context around them. Some argue that mental health services, including psychological therapies, are themselves part of a 'mental health industry'. This industry is seen as promoting a Western model of wellbeing, whilst failing to recognise how culturally specific these models are and the damage which can be done by encouraging people to see their emotions as symptoms of mental dysfunction (Timimi, 2021) The CBT model, in particular, is seen by some as a reflection of the American dream, teaching people that they alone are responsible for their feelings

and their destiny, and promoting individualistic values over community-focused ones (Dalal, 2019).

6.7 Community-level interventions

Frequently, whole communities are affected by conflict, trauma, or natural disasters.

Political oppression affects whole countries, social classes, and ethnic groups. Racism and sexism negatively affect the life experience of large sectors of many societies. The legacies of colonialism and slavery continue to affect the lives of people today.

Intervening on a community level means trying to improve aspects of how a community functions, which will then change the experience and lives of the people living there. Community psychologists may support people who are trying to make a positive change in their community, or they may organise community projects alongside local people. These projects are unlikely to be focused on symptom reduction but will instead take a **strengths approach**, building resilience and wellness rather than focusing on deficits. Rashid and McGrath (2020) suggested that a strengths approach to the COVID-19 pandemic would focus on taking pragmatic and purposeful actions driven by character strengths such as creativity, curiosity, and kindness. They argue that this will increase a sense of self-confidence and self-efficacy and move the focus from the fear and stress caused by a pandemic.

One example of a large-scale community intervention is a Truth and Reconciliation Commission (TRC). These are forums created in the aftermath of major conflicts with the aim of helping a community come back together. Their aim is to promote social transformation and to allow people to move on with their lives following significant community trauma. They have been used in South Africa following apartheid (Truth and Reconciliation Commission, n.d.), El Salvador after their twelve-year civil war, and in Canada as an attempt to help people heal from the damage done to First Nations people by residential schools.

Most community-level interventions are not as ambitious as a TRC. Community interventions can include courses in English for immigrant families, or befriending schemes where volunteers are paired with vulnerable members of the community. In Chapter 7, a community psychologist describes how she used Forum Theatre to work with communities on issues such as domestic violence. During the COVID-19 crisis in 2020, thousands of mutual aid groups were set up across the UK to support local people who might need help. Organisations such as these promote community cohesion as well as providing practical support. There is evidence that community interventions ranging from school-wide CBT programmes to child abuse prevention programmes with parents can be effective, affecting mental health, interpersonal relationships, and social determinants of health (Castillo et al., 2019).

Running an effective community level intervention is not straightforward, and many of the best community interventions come from local people organising themselves rather than professionals intervening. Community-level interventions are usually open to whoever wants to participate (inclusion often being part of the philosophy of a community approach). This can mean that the people who are the most vulnerable or excluded from society do not join. Some community-level interventions try to target vulnerable groups, but this can then lead to participation being stigmatised and people refusing to come. It can be hard to measure the effects of community-level interventions, which are often co-created with members of the community and therefore may be different each time they are used. Community psychologists may use measures such as qualitative interviews with people, the number of people who attend, and the interest that people show in order to evaluate their interventions.

6.8 Structural-level interventions

Inequality, conflict, and poverty cause distress for millions of people. This distress can be defined as a mental health problem, which means that it is seen as a problem to be addressed on an individual level. Those who argue for structural interventions say that building societies which are more peaceful and **equitable** would be the most effective way of improving wellbeing over the whole population.

Policies such as large-scale public housing provision, accessible and affordable healthcare, land reform, and wealth sharing programmes reduce inequality, which has been shown to improve the mental health of the population as a whole (Wilkinson and Pickett, 2018). This is evidence based but moves into the scope of public health, rather than healthcare.

Structural interventions require fundamental shifts in society and commitment by governments. They are expensive to implement, and it takes years to see the impact. When addressing structural problems such as institutional racism, long-term commitment to change is necessary. When mental health is seen as an illness, a problem of disordered individuals, this removes motivation for politicians to address the problems in society which underlie the extreme distress experienced by millions of people.

Chapter Summary

- Interventions into mental health can happen on several levels.

- First-order interventions prioritise change in the individual, whilst second-order interventions include measures taken to change the interaction between a person and their environment.

- Both are necessary if the aim is to improve the overall mental health of a population. Individual interventions may also enable people to interact in a different way with their environment, resulting in positive change.

- When we see mental health as an individual problem, then interventions or treatments are focused on those individuals. These include drugs and psychological therapies.

- When we see mental health in context, then interventions take place at a family, community, and even country level. Seeing mental health as a complex system would lead us to develop combinations of interventions which take account of interactions as well as the individual elements.

- Interventions which improve mental health can include many programmes and organisations which do not explicitly focus on mental health, but which increase community cohesion or reduce inequality.

- All of these interventions can exist together, and will interact with each other.

- Community or systemic interventions may not be possible without the availability of individual interventions for those who need them.

QUESTIONS

1. What are some of the issues with the evidence base for assessing mental health interventions?

2. All mental health interventions should be evidence-based. Do you agree? Why or why not?

3. How do anti-depressants and anti-psychotics work? What does this imply for how we understand depression and psychosis?

4. What are some of the problems in using the evidence base to evaluate the effectiveness of psychological therapies and therefore plan services? Choose several potential issues and discuss how these might affect the usefulness of the evidence available (e.g. researcher allegiance, publication bias, problems with diagnostic categories, choice of outcome measure).

5. The best way to invest in mental health is to train more psychiatrists and psychologists. Do you agree? Why or why not?

FURTHER READING

Fennell, M. (2016). *Overcoming Low Self Esteem. A Self-Help Guide using Cognitive Behavioural Techniques*, Second Edition. London: Robinson.

This self-help book by a psychologist uses cognitive behaviour techniques and is a great introduction if you are interested in understanding more about how CBT works.

Kirsch, I. (2009). *The Emperor's New Drugs: Exploding the Antidepressant Myth*. Rochester, UK: Vintage Digital.

This book by a psychologist argues that the chemical imbalance theory of depression is wrong and that anti-depressants are powerful and active placebos, rather than drugs which directly treat depression.

Kramer, P. (2016). *Ordinarily Well: The Case for Antidepressants*. New York: Farrar, Straus & Giroux.

Peter Kramer is a psychiatrist who writes here about anti-depressant use, the positive effects they can have, and the beneficial ways in which he has seen his patients respond to them.

Moncrieff, J. (2020). *A Straight Talking Introduction to Psychiatric Drugs: The Truth About How They Work and How to Come Off Them*. Monmouth: PCCS Books.

Joanna Moncrieff is a psychiatrist who is often critical of the way in which psychiatric drugs are used, arguing that they do not treat or cure an illness and can in fact cause damage.

Wilkinson, R., and Pickett, K. (2018). *The Inner Level: How More Equal Societies Reduce Stress, Restore Sanity and Improve Everyone's Wellbeing*. London: Penguin.

This book by two academics outlines the research on how inequality causes damage to mental health and argues for structural changes to society in order to improve mental health and wellbeing.

REFERENCES

Atkinson, J., Song, Y., Merikangas, K., et al. (2020). The science of complex systems is needed to ameliorate the impacts of COVID-19 on mental health. *Frontiers in Psychiatry*, 11. doi:10.3389/fpsyt.2020.606035

Barbato, A., and D'Avanzo, B. (2020). The findings of a Cochrane meta-analysis of couple therapy in adult depression: Implications for research and clinical practice. *Family Process*, 59(2), 361–375.

Castillo, E.G., Ijadi-Maghsoodi, R., Shadravan, S., et al. (2019). Community interventions to promote mental health and social equity. *Current Psychiatry Reports*, 21, 35. doi: 10.1007/s11920-019-1017-0

Cipriani, A., Furukawa, T.A., Salanti, G., Chaimani, A., Atkinson, L.Z., Ogawa, Y., Leucht, S., Ruhe, H.G., Turner, E.H., Higgins, J.P.T., Egger, M., Takeshima, N., Hayasaka, Y., Imai, H., Shinohara, K., Tajika, A., Ioannidis, J.P.A., and Geddes, J.R. (2018). Comparative efficacy and acceptability of 21 antidepressant drugs for the acute treatment of adults with major depressive disorder: A systematic review and network meta-analysis. *FOCUS: The Journal of Lifelong Learning in Psychiatry*, 16(4), 420–429.

Claxton, M., Onwumere, J., and Fornells-Ambrojo, M. (2017). Do family interventions improve outcomes in early psychosis? A systematic review and meta-analysis. *Frontiers in Psychology*, 8, 371. doi: 10.3389/fpsyg.2017.00371

Correll, C.U., and Schooler, N.R. (2020). Negative symptoms in schizophrenia: A review and clinical guide for recognition, assessment, and treatment. *Neuropsychiatric Disease and Treatment*, 16, 519–534. doi: 10.2147/NDT.S225643

Cristea, I. (2015). Researcher Allegiance: The Achilles' heel of psychotherapy trials. *The Mental Elf*. Retrieved 2 December 2021. https://www.nationalelfservice.net/treatment/psychotherapy/researcher-allegiance-the-achilles-heel-of-psychotherapy-trials/

Cuijpers, P., Sijbrandij, M., Koole, S.L., Andersson, G., Beekman, A.T., and Reynolds, C. F., 3rd (2014). Adding psychotherapy to antidepressant medication in depression and anxiety disorders: a meta-analysis. *World Psychiatry: Official Journal of the World Psychiatric Association*, 13(1), 56–67. doi: 10.1002/wps.20089

Dalal, F. (2019). *The Cognitive Behavioural Tsunami: Managerialism, Politics and the Corruptions of Science*. London, Routledge.

David, D., Cristea, I., and Hofmann, S. (2018). Why cognitive behavioural therapy is the current gold standard of psychotherapy. *Frontiers in Psychiatry*, 9, 4. doi: 10.3389/fpsyt.2018.00004

De Vries, Y., Roest, A., De Jonge, P., Cuijpers, P., Munafò, M., and Bastiaansen, J. (2018). The cumulative effect of reporting and citation biases on the apparent efficacy of treatments: The case of depression. *Psychological Medicine*, 48(15), 2453–2455. doi: 10.1017/S0033291718001873

Driessen, E., Dekker, J.J., Peen, J., Van, H.L., Maina, G., Rosso, G., ... Cuijpers, P. (2020). The efficacy of adding short-term psychodynamic psychotherapy to antidepressants in the treatment of depression: A systematic review and meta-analysis of individual participant data. *Clinical Psychology Review*, 80, 101886.

Elliott, R., Watson, J.C., Timulak, L., and Sharbanee, J. (2020). Research on humanistic-experiential psychotherapies: Updated review. In M. Barkham, W. Lutz, and L.G. Castonguay (eds), *Bergin and Garfield's Handbook of Psychotherapy and Behavior Change*. New York: John Wiley & Sons, Chapter 13.

Feng, G., Han, M., Li, X., Geng, L., and Miao, Y. (2020). The clinical effectiveness of cognitive behavioral therapy for patients with insomnia and depression: A systematic review and meta-analysis. *Evidence-Based Complementary and Alternative Medicine*, 2020, 8071821. doi: 10.1155/2020/8071821

Fennell, M. (2016). *Overcoming Low Self Esteem: A Self-Help Guide using Cognitive Behavioural Techniques*, Second Edition. London: Robinson.

France, C.M., Lysaker, P.H., and Robinson, R.P. (2007). The 'chemical imbalance' explanation for depression: Origins, lay endorsement, and clinical implications. *Professional Psychology: Research and Practice*, 38(4), 411.

Gonon, F., and Keller, P.H. (2020). Efficacy of psychodynamic therapies: A systematic review of the recent literature. *L'encephale*, 47(1), 49–57. doi: 10.1016/j.encep.2020.04.020. [In French.]

Greenberger, D., and Padesky, C.A. (2015). *Mind Over Mood: Change How You Feel by Changing the Way You Think*. New York: Guilford Press.

Haddad, P.M., and Correll, C.U. (2018). The acute efficacy of antipsychotics in schizophrenia: A review of recent meta-analyses. *Therapeutic Advances in Psychopharmacology*, 8(11), 303–318.

Hayes, S.C., Strosahl, K.D., and Wilson, K.G. (2009). *Acceptance and Commitment Therapy*. Washington, DC: American Psychological Association.

Hengartner, M. (2018). Raising awareness for the replication crisis in clinical psychology by focusing on inconsistencies in psychotherapy research: How much can we rely on published findings from efficacy trials? *Frontiers in Psychology*, 9. doi:10.3389/fpsyg.2018.0025

Hofmann, S., Asnanni, A., Vonk, I., Sawyer, A., and Fang, A. (2012). The efficacy of cognitive behavioural therapy: A review of meta-analyses. *Cognitive Therapy Research*, 36, 427–440.

Horowitz, M., and Wilcock, M. (2022). Newer generation antidepressants and withdrawal effects: Reconsidering the role of antidepressants and helping patients to stop. *Drug and Therapeutics Bulletin*, 60, 7–12.

Jason, L.A., Glantsman, O., O'Brien, J.F., and Ramian, K.N. (2020). Introduction to community psychology. In R. Biswas-Diener and E. Diener (eds), *Psychology,* Noba textbook series. Champaign, IL: DEF Publishers.

Kirsch, I. (2009). *The Emperor's New Drugs: Exploding the Antidepressant Myth*. Rochester, UK: Vintage Digital.

Kirsch, I. (2019). Placebo effect in the treatment of depression and anxiety. *Frontiers in Psychiatry*, 10, 407. doi:10.3389/fpsyt.2019.00407

Kramer, P. (2016). *Ordinarily Well: The Case for Antidepressants*. New York: Farrar, Straus & Giroux.

McManus, S., Bebbington, P., Jenkins, R., and Brugha, T. (eds) (2014). *Mental Health and Wellbeing in England: Adult Psychiatric Morbidity Survey 2014*. Leeds: NHS Digital.

Melander, H., Ahlqvist-Rastad, J., Meijer, G., and Beermann, B. (2003). Evidence b(i)ased medicine—Selective reporting from studies sponsored by pharmaceutical industry: Review of studies in new drug applications. *BMJ*, 326(7400), 1171–1173.

Moncrieff, J. (2018). Against the stream: Antidepressants are not antidepressants—An alternative approach to drug action and implications for the use of antidepressants. *BJPsych Bulletin*, 42(1), 42–44.

Moncrieff, J., Cooper, R.E., Stockmann, T., et al. (2022). The serotonin theory of depression: A systematic umbrella review of the evidence. *Molecular Psychiatry*, 28, 3243–3256. doi:10.1038/s41380-022-01661-0

Moncrieff, J. (2020). *A Straight Talking Introduction to Psychiatric Drugs: The Truth About How They Work and How to Come Off Them*. Monmouth: PCCS Books.

Munkholm, K., Paludan-Müller, A.S., and Boesen, K. (2019). Considering the methodological limitations in the evidence base of antidepressants for depression: A reanalysis of a network meta-analysis. *BMJ Open*, 9, e024886. doi:10.1136/bmjopen-2018-024886

Nichols. M., and Schwartz, R.C. (2012). *Family Therapy: Concepts and Methods,* International Edition. Hoboken, NJ: Pearson.

Public Health England (2019). *Research and Analysis. Prescribed Medicines Review: Summary*. https://www.gov.uk/government/publications/prescribed-medicines-review-report/prescribed-medicines-review-summary

Rashid, T., and McGrath, R. (2020). Strengths-based actions to enhance wellbeing in the time of COVID-19. *International Journal of Wellbeing*, 10(4). doi:10.5502/ijw.v10i4.1441

Rethink Mental Illness (2020). *About Antipsychotics*. Retrieved 29 May 2020. https://www.rethink.org/advice-and-information/living-with-mental-illness/medications/antipsychotics/?gclid=CjwKCAjw5cL2BRASEiwAENqAPITvfGdvFE0dkKFqhFenC14JqUSAs-gLrxS3bp6VHy1ZE1zOVRTqOxoCX4kQAvD_BwE

Ross, J.S., Mulvey, G.K., Hines, E.M., et al. (2009). Trial publication after registration in ClinicalTrials.Gov: A cross sectional analysis. *PLoS Medicine,* 8, 6.

Segal, Z.V., Williams, M., and Teasdale, J. (2018). *Mindfulness-based Cognitive Therapy for Depression*. New York: Guilford Publications.

Thomson, K., Hillier-Brown, F., Todd, A., McNamara, C., Huijts, T., and Bambra, C. (2018). The effects of public health policies on health inequalities in high-income countries: an umbrella review. *BMC Public Health*, 18(1), 1–21.

Timimi, S. (2021). *Insane Medicine: How the Mental Health Industry Creates Damaging Treatment Traps and How You can Escape Them.* Independently Published.

Truth and Reconciliation Commission (n.d.) www.justice.gov.za

Vittengl, J.R. (2017). Poorer long-term outcomes among persons with major depressive disorder treated with medication. *Psychotherapy and Psychosomatics*, 86, 302–304.

Wampold, B. (2015). How important are the common factors in psychotherapy? An update. *World Psychiatry*, 1493, 270–277.

Waszlawick, P., Weakland, J., and Fisch, R. (2011). *Change: Principles of Problem Formation and Problem Resolution,* Reprint Edition. New York: Norton & Company.

Wilkinson, R., and Pickett, K. (2018). *The Inner Level: How More Equal Societies Reduce Stress, Restore Sanity and Improve Everyone's Wellbeing.* London: Penguin.

Wiggins, B.J., and Christopherson, C.D. (2019). The replication crisis in psychology: An overview for theoretical and philosophical psychology. *Journal of Theoretical and Philosophical Psychology*, 39(4), 202–217. doi:10.1037/teo0000137

Wunderink, L., et al. (2013). Recovery in remitted first episode psychosis at 7 years of follow-up of an early dose reduction/discontinuation or maintenance treatment strategy: Long-term follow up of a 2-year randomised clinical trial. *JAMA Psychiatry*, 70(9), 913–920. doi:10.1001/jamapsychiatry.2013.19

Chapter 7
The Experience of Mental Health

Learning objectives

When you have completed this chapter, you should be able to do the following:

7.1 Give examples of how service users and professionals understand the causes of mental health problems.

7.2 Compare and contrast experiences of being offered a diagnosis or using a diagnosis in the mental health system.

7.3 Appreciate the different ways in which people experience mental health interventions.

7.4 Compare the different ways in which professionals offer help, both inside and outside the mental health system.

7.5 Give examples of some ways in which people describe how their lives improved and what they think made a difference.

7.6 Explain some ways in which the mental health system could evolve in the future.

Introduction

So far in this book I have taken the perspective of the professional, observing from the outside. I have described distress, but you have not heard the voices of those who have actually had these experiences, nor the voices of those who work with them. This chapter is different. I have brought together first-person accounts, mostly obtained through interviews directly with the individuals concerned, but sometimes taken from written sources. These accounts are sometimes called 'experts by experience' although this term is often used to refer to service users only, whilst this chapter also includes the lived experience of professionals. The people in this chapter are real. They are service users, psychologists, community activists, and psychiatrists. They talk about their lives and professional experiences in the first person. You may find some of them distressing. Inevitably, when hearing personal stories, the full spectrum of experience is not covered. I have tried to find a range of voices from different ethnicities, ages, sex, professional backgrounds, and perspectives, but inevitably many are missing. This does not mean that they are less important. This is a disadvantage of using accounts of lived experience in this way. An advantage is the depth of each story, and the way in which the stories enable us to reflect on the human impact of the problems discussed in the rest of the book.

At the start of this chapter I have listed all the contributors with a brief description of each so that you can refer back to this as you read. We have used the real names of those who have already publicly talked about their experiences, otherwise we have anonymised their accounts.

The people who participated in this chapter have all given informed consent for their stories to be used. I interviewed all the people personally except where we have used text which was already published. They checked and edited the transcripts of the interviews. We have used pseudonyms for those whose stories were not already in the public domain to protect their anonymity.

Their accounts illustrate many of the concepts covered earlier in this book—you'll read accounts of stigma, about the meaning people attribute to their experiences, and how this has helped them (or not). They all understand their difficulties in different ways. Some have found medication helped them whilst others feel ambivalent about its effects. Psychological therapy hasn't always been useful either, with some talking about meeting many therapists before finding one who can help.

A recent development in mental health has been an attempt to actively involve service users in developing and carrying out research. This has been driven by service users (such as Peter Beresford, who is included below) and by a recognition that many interventions have been experienced by service users as 'done to' them rather than 'done with' them. Other approaches are taken by grass-roots organisations such as Healing Justice London, who aim to provide what they call a 'safe space for healing' for marginalised people, and whose approach is very different to that of the mental health service.

Putting the voices of service users first means listening to their experiences and to what they think needs to change. Of course, a problem with this is that different people think that different things are necessary and in some cases service users and professionals may directly disagree about what should be done. Each person's experience is highly individual. Some want research to be focused on societal response and stigma, whilst others would like better drugs or psychotherapies. Others want quicker diagnoses and more access to psychiatrists. As you will see in even this small sample, people have very different ideas

about what has helped them and what they would like in the future.

Contributors

Peter Beresford is Visiting Professor at the University of East Anglia and Emeritus Professor of citizen participation at the University of Essex and of social policy at Brunel University London. His work has focused on citizen participation and user-led research. He used mental health services himself for eleven years and is co-chair of Shaping Our Lives, the national user-led organisation. His recent book *A Straight Talking Introduction to Emotional Wellbeing: from Mental Illness to Mad Studies* (PCCS) discusses some of the same issues as this chapter.

Chris Coombs describes himself as a suicide-attempt survivor who has dealt with depression and anxiety for more than a decade. He has cerebral palsy. The quotes here are reproduced with permission from his chapter in *Drop The Disorder: Challenging the Culture of Psychiatric Diagnosis*.

Y.E. is a psychiatrist in the NHS who for the last few years has predominantly worked in children and adolescent mental health services. She has a specialist interest in trauma and has undergone extra training in trauma-focused therapies.

Y.H. is a creative bubbly entrepreneur who currently lives in Croydon. He is studying business at a university. He describes himself as a second-generation immigrant. His parents moved to the UK from Nigeria before he was born. He has been admitted to hospital several times after breakdowns in his mental health.

Josiah Hartley is the author (with Amanda Prowse) of *The Boy Between: A Mother and Son's Journey from a World Gone Grey*. The quotes here from him are from this book and are reproduced with permission. He developed serious depression at the age of nineteen.

Farzana Khan is the co-founder of Healing Justice London (HJL). She describes HJL as working at the intersection of healing, health, and anti-oppression and liberation practice. They work with marginalised communities, predominantly those who are racially marginalised. Their aim is to create capacity for transformation.

O.N. is a consultant clinical psychologist working in an NHS psychosis team in London. He took an unconventional route into clinical psychology, having started off as a research scientist in immunology. He describes himself as in a minority in many ways, being male in a mostly female profession, Black in a mostly white profession, and having come in as an older trainee with a scientific background.

H.N. is a clinical psychologist who works with people who have been trafficked and with victims of torture. She works in several jobs, including an NHS specialist team, the voluntary sector, and writing reports for court proceedings.

Heather Hunt is a retired clinical and community psychologist now in the North of England. She has worked in NHS posts with an early intervention and prevention brief, taking public health and feminist approaches. After leaving the NHS she has worked with a National Park engaging inner city children with the natural world and sustainable futures.

Fran Stalley is an expert by experience in complex trauma who has lived experience of childhood abuse. She feels her trauma is rooted in the abuse she experienced in childhood from both her parents. She has experience of seeking help both inside and outside the NHS. She has published a book called *Childhood Trauma Recovery: The Email Conversations with My Therapist That Helped Me Overcome Childhood PTSD* with her therapist. She feels that receiving genuine, practical support in addition to therapy has made all the difference to her being able to rebuild her life. She is hopeful about the future and is getting her life back on track.

Sami Timimi is a consultant psychiatrist originally from Iran who works in the NHS in Lincolnshire. He is the author of several books challenging the medical model. He describes himself as writing from a critical psychiatry perspective.

7.1 Causes of distress

In Chapter 3 I discussed why people develop mental health problems and how this is studied. This section addresses the same question by asking individuals why they think they developed mental health problems, or why they think the people they work with develop mental health problems. The people here all explain

their distress as rooted in their life experiences, something which research shows is a common way for people to make sense of mental health problems (Read, 2020).

Fran Stalley sees a direct relationship between her childhood experiences and her mental health problems as an adult. Fran believes that her experiences led to the formation of beliefs about her worth as a person and the way she thought about other people. She therefore describes her problems as psychological, but caused by events.

> **❝** I was sexually, physically, and emotionally abused by my dad and psychologically abused and neglected by my mum. My mum was the ringleader of the abuse and her abuse caused me the most psychological damage. It left me feeling that I was worthless. I was also bullied at school that meant I wasn't safe anywhere. My mum knew I was being bullied but she didn't do anything about it. Even when somebody called me names right in front of her. I was the youngest child, the third one which they didn't want. My mum kind of let that slip when I was a teenager, and it explained to me how she had been with me.
>
> I think growing up I learnt that other people are not safe for me to be around. It's hard to develop friendships and relationships with people if I never felt safe. As an adult, I never knew how to handle the ups and downs of human relationships and so was always breaking off friendships at the first miscommunication. This meant I never had any social support or anyone to turn to for help when I was struggling, which was most of the time. **❞**

Peter Beresford focuses on the social pressure he felt of growing up with secrecy as well as in living in poverty as an adult.

> **❝** My life started with secrecy. I grew up in a single parent family because my father died when I was very young. My mother was Jewish, so I identify as Jewish. My mother had a very difficult life. For her being Jewish was a secret, although she grew up in a working class, orthodox Jewish home. And it was meant to be a secret for us too.
>
> I think it's damaging for small children to have secrets about who they are. I think the problem for my mother was not really being Jewish, it was being poor. Poverty, real poverty was a major issue for her.{....}
>
> Then I had my own experiences of two things, which I think are inseparable in our world, but which people

don't adequately talk about together. One, experiencing what people might call distress. And then two, inseparable from that for most people, is the benefits system. I was reliant on the benefit system for about eight years, when we were bringing up small children. The benefits system was oppressive then. In more recent years, it's become much more oppressive and frightening. I think that the rather damaging childhood I had, and then the path that we had chosen where we didn't get funding [for our work], and we ended up on benefits for years are two key factors in why I ended up using mental health services.' 🗦🗦

Y.H. describes the events which led up to him being hospitalised after a breakdown in his mental health.

🗦🗦 I first got hospitalized when I was about 15 years of age, and there were a lot of things that were going on at that time which I think caused that breakdown. My mum fell very ill. One of my close cousins I grew up with was killed in New York. At the school I was at there was a lot of gang violence. I wasn't in a gang, I never really saw the point in that kind of stuff. I got set up by a girl and I got hammered in the face by gang members. This all happened within two or three weeks. I feel that all this kind of thing contributed to the mental health situation. 🗦🗦

Dr O.N. writes as a clinical psychologist but also from his experience of growing up as a second-generation immigrant in the UK. He thinks that not only do experiences of racism and trauma contribute to vulnerability, but when problems do arise it is hard for people to seek help due to their mistrust in the health service. This is something which research has found is higher among people with Black or mixed ethnicity, perhaps because of their experiences of unfair treatment and stigma (Henderson et al., 2015). This means that they may not seek help until they are at the point of breakdown.

🗦🗦 My experience growing up was completely different to the experience my dad had. There were always problems in relating because my dad never really understood why young people in the UK would act the way we do. If we experienced racism my parents would say, just ignore it, it's not important. They could do that because they had already developed their identities in the Caribbean. They knew who they were. They were strong and capable.

Whereas as a young black person growing up in London, I experienced all sorts of racism. I think there's a toll that it takes, all these traumas and microaggressions. It builds and it means that you don't really feel like you belong in the UK, but this is your home. If you ever got to the Caribbean they say – well my nickname over there was 'English boy'. So where do I belong? And parents don't really understand why you're struggling so much and these characteristics build and make us more vulnerable.

Then there is a mistrust in services and what they will do, so people don't feel able to approach their GP or talk about how people are feeling. It's quite complex. 🗦🗦

7.2 Making sense of distress

In Chapter 2 I discussed how the sense which is made of a person's mental health problems affects what interventions are offered. I introduced several different models of understanding mental health. On an individual level, the way a person understands their experiences can affect the help they seek, and what they find useful.

Again, people's experiences vary. Some find that a diagnosis provides welcome relief and means they can stop blaming themselves, whilst others reject that as an explanation. Some find that once they have had mental health problems, they are stigmatised by others. The first three accounts following come from service users, then there is one from a psychologist and two from psychiatrists.

The first account is by Josiah Hartley. He experienced depression for several years as an adolescent and young adult. He found that seeing a psychiatrist and being told he had an illness offered an explanation for his difficulties which helped him blame himself less (something which has been described as the brain or blame dichotomy; Boyle, 2013). He found the diagnosis of depression and understanding his problems as an illness (the medical model) extremely helpful and felt that it changed the way he thought about himself and his experiences. Josh did not find it helpful to be asked what happened to him or to look for social explanations, because he couldn't think of anything which had caused his depression.

🗦🗦 I didn't know what to expect from psychiatry, didn't know how it would be of benefit, but I honestly wish I had gone to see him sooner. He sat behind a desk and it felt more business-like than medical and that suited me. He was interested in my studies and spoke to me calmly like an equal. I trusted him; I guess that was the fundamental difference. He too asked me if there was any one thing that had happened, one traumatic event? One memory that scarred, something on which I could hang my illness, but again all I could do was shake my head and tell him that no, there was nothing … He then said: 'I bet you kind of wish there was because as terrible as that would be at least you and everyone else could understand it, relate to it. It would be a starting point.' 'Exactly.' He got it. He asked me about my medical history, my family history, explaining things to me on a biological level, to which I responded well. He then told me something that was simple and yet radical. It has stayed with me. It was the first time it had been said expressly and it altered the way I viewed my illness, he said: 'You know this isn't your fault, Josh, don't you?' I stared at him, a little overcome with emotion.

I nodded, only half believing him, despite our very factual discussion. 'Seriously, Josh' – he spoke more earnestly now, leaning forward to hold my eyeline – 'you have an illness and it is not your fault. Just like if you had a physical illness, cancer or whatever, you wouldn't blame yourself then, would you?' I shook my head again. 'Well, this is no different. You have an illness. You have severe depression. An illness. And just like any illness you need to be kind to yourself and give yourself time to heal and we can give you drugs that can help with that process. Okay?' 'Okay.' I cried again.

Now, it might sound odd, but until he said this to me, it did not fully occur to me that I was ill. I knew things weren't right, but I thought I was weak, going through a blip, a crisis, crazy … call it what you like, but ill? My God, that was it, I was ill! His words were like scissors cutting me free of some of the ties that bound me to my depression. I can now see that this was the start of what led to my recovery. A small beginning, like cracking open the window in a previously airless room, like shining a thin beam of light into a dark chamber, like removing a plug from my ear to allow the smallest sound to filter in where before there had only been silence. I can see his mouth forming the words, hear his voice sounding them and I realized that it was not my fault … It was not my fault … It was not my fault … 🙶

Chris Coombs's experience was quite different. Having started with the diagnosis of depression, he then started to feel differently about it. His understanding integrates biology with his experiences of disability, and he no longer finds the term 'depression' useful in describing his experience.

🙶 At the back end of 2015, as I started out on a new leg of my therapy journey, I looked at 'depression'. Where

did it come from? What was it about? Had I been honest to say it was simply a part of me? Yes and no…

It was everywhere, but it was borne out of much more than simple biology. Out of academic expectations not met, self-imposed rules and introjections, never really addressing some of the effects of being suicidal. A lack of direction, a lack of meaning, a lack of relationship, and, quietly in the background, a creeping realisation that all was not well with my view of my own body and disability and my actually diagnosable condition of cerebral palsy and the idea that my body was older than I felt. There was so much more to it even than all that, and the complex interplay is something I could never hope to translate fully, but all this led to a simple realisation. 'Depression' wasn't so much about my body and brain mechanics, but about what happened to me.

Part of the reason I think so many people cling to diagnostic labels is that they think their stories are unworthy of their feelings and emotions. A label takes that out of their hands. Labels mean that we don't have to question whether someone's mental health struggles are somehow legitimate or acceptable. We don't have to see if they tick enough boxes to be helped or treated. The label covers for that.

But, if we are any kind of caring society, should we even have to ask if someone's experiences and responses are somehow fair? The worst thing that happens to a person is the worst thing that happened to them. Who are we do say whether or not that qualifies for a label and a diagnosis? What experiences are toxic enough to 'need' treating and which ones are acceptable? Who are we to say when a grief or low mood is invalid because it has passed the sell-by date and is now a pathology? This shit is too damn personal for that. And because that is entirely personal, I now find the label of 'depression' cumbersome and unwieldy. I've not come to that overnight—it is a long journey that is not finished. But I have come to realize that, based on who I am, my reactions to everything were understandable and made logical sense. Those responses to trauma are mine and mine alone. My emotions and feelings and subsequent actions were not a result of being somehow 'disordered', but natural human reactions that had no need to be pathologized or placed in the box marked 'wrong'. 🙶

Y.H. was admitted to hospital and then discharged. He spoke about the way in which people around him understood his mental health problems, and how this affected his life. Here he describes the stigma he experienced after leaving a psychiatric hospital and how that affected him. This is an example of societal response, exacerbating the difficulties a person has because of the way they are seen by others.

" Once you've been inside a mental institution, people or even family members treat you differently. Like, you're finished in life. You can tell by the way they interact with you that they think that you're not ever going to come out of it.

I've seen that happen to a lot of people. Even though now they don't look at me like that, because I'm trying to do a lot of things. But it's the way you do things as well. Because sometimes, just because you've been in a mental institution, they might look at something that you're doing a little bit different.

They think 'You've been in a mental institution.'

For a lot of people, they think [that means] that you're finished, but that's not the case. **"**

Professionals understand people's difficulties in a variety of ways. This will then affect the way that they work with people. These three accounts, the first from a psychologist and the next two from psychiatrists, describes different ways in which health professionals make sense of the experiences of the people they work with.

Dr H.N. told me how she thinks about the psychological impact of human trafficking on the people she sees. These people have been through terrible experiences and have often lost their families and countries. She sees psychological therapy as a process of rebuilding a person's relationships with themselves.

" When I see survivors of very long-term trafficking and long-term imprisonment and torture, it can feel that they had years of blankness. They no longer talk to themselves, they no longer encourage themselves, they no longer may be accessing their memories of their family, they may have lost their relationship with their faith if they had one.

When I interview people who have been in domestic servitude for a long time I ask, 'How did you cope? What did you do at night? Did you pray?'

And some people say 'I don't know. I can't remember. I just think I was blank, you know, and it's just that awful.' Suddenly, they are out of it, and fifteen years have gone by. They say, 'I didn't think I was 40. I thought I was 25.'

Sometimes that's what you're trying to treat. You're trying to get the person to build their relationship with themselves again. I worked with a woman years ago and at the end of treatment, she said, 'I know now what happened to me, what my problem was—I had forgotten to love myself.' **"**

Dr Y.E. told me how she and the team she works with try to understand someone's difficulties. She described the pressure she sometimes feels from families to give a diagnosis and medication. She talks about systemic issues which she sees surrounding the young people she works with. A **systemic approach** means that the perspective is widened from the individual to seeing a person in context, which includes their family, their school, and their community.

" I don't see my role primarily as trying to stick a label on someone. We formulate things in terms of what the main difficulties are for the young person and the system in which they live, which may or may not fit neatly into a medical model. Normally, it doesn't.

We might see a young person and there's difficulties they're having at home or at school. The family are often really struggling. We sometimes have parents that are really keen for a diagnostic label, because that validates the struggle they've been having. It may also mean they get access to certain benefits. It would fit really neatly for some families, if a medication could be prescribed that would just solve everything for them. But more often than not, there's a lot of systemic issues going on. There are difficulties in the dynamic between parents or between parent and child.

So that wouldn't neatly fit into a medical model.

Diagnosis can be about clearly documenting the experience that the young person has had and I see that as a way of advocating for them. If they spent all this time telling me all this information, I don't want it to be wasted. I want the information to have been processed and assimilated and us to have reached that diagnosis, if that's what they need. **"**

Dr Sami Timimi is highly critical of the psychiatric diagnostic model. He explains his thoughts about the models used in the mental health system. He thinks that psychiatric diagnoses are understood as explanations when they are only descriptions.

" The models we use have all sorts of consequences in terms of our practice. One thing that has animated me is the fact that our psychiatric classification system is thought of as a diagnostic one when it isn't. It cannot be. Because diagnosis constructs a system of classification used in a technical sense to explain phenomena.

If I were to ask the question, 'What is diabetes?', I wouldn't answer it by describing someone's possible presentation. Fatigue and urinating a lot are common presenting symptoms of diabetes. But there's lots of other ways it could present, and also lots of other conditions can present like that. Diabetes is defined as an abnormality of sugar metabolism not as 'fatigue and urinating excessively'. It's defined by its proximal cause. We know what sort of 'thing' we are dealing with when we make a 'diagnosis' of diabetes.

There are areas in medicine where the proximal explanation isn't very clear, but generally speaking, a diagnostic system connects your experiences or what we call 'symptoms' with a particular cause. This is important, because it then defines what treatments we use

If I were to ask, 'What is depression?', I cannot answer that by relating it to some sort of proximal cause. I have to give you a description. I have to describe the presence of low mood and negative thinking. To say that this description has told me the cause of your low mood is a bit like saying that the pain in my head is caused by a headache. You can't use a description as an explanation. Our services are built around this idea that what we do is diagnose a condition and then follow a specific treatment pathway.

When people come to my service looking for a diagnosis, I talk about exactly this. I say, "Actually, there isn't such a thing as a diagnosis". I say, "I can't do any brain scan. I can't do any blood tests … In psychiatry, everything is subjective. It's all opinion. It's all clinical judgement. 🥇

7.3 Interventions

In Chapter 6 I described different interventions for mental health problems. Here, you can read some first-hand accounts of being on the receiving end of these interventions. You will also read some accounts by professionals of how they themselves intervene and try to help. These are individual accounts which should not be used to generalise about the effects of any particular intervention. The accounts reflect the complexity of people's experiences, and several people emphasise the importance of seeing individuals in context.

Peter Beresford told me about his experience of looking for help and being prescribed first a tranquilliser and then a residential group intervention. He also saw a psychologist individually.

🥇 I went to the GP. I was identified as someone with severe anxiety and depression. The GP said, 'In a few weeks' time there's going to be some sort of group opportunity to do relaxation exercises, which should help. Or there are these pills.'

Well, you can imagine in my state what I went for, so then began six years of purgatory on Ativan [a benzodiazepine].

The consequences for me of the combination of my distress and this medication was that I could barely go out. My life was absolutely inhibited. I remember well the experience of being on the pills, not being able to go out. When I did go out I would get into a terrible state, cringing at the side of the pavement, unable to get up.

After six years of this awfulness I was extremely lucky because the local teaching hospital had an integrated residential research programme to get people off these prescription tranquillizers. A small group of us went on this, and it was a wonderful opportunity. It meant I was able to start the process of change. 🥇

Y.H. was admitted to hospital, where he was given risperidone (an anti-psychotic) and then offered psychological therapy. He felt that the two together helped him but also reflects on the way that the medication made him feel different.

🥇 In hospital they put me on risperidone. When you come out, it's like you've come out into a new world. You feel calm. But the medication sedates you to a point where you feel like you're not yourself. You find it harder to laugh. I don't know why. It's because of the chemicals inside the drug. Certain things that you would laugh about on a normal daily basis, you don't end up laughing about. [...]

Talking therapy has helped me with understanding my behaviour and how people perceive me. I didn't understand how people perceived me, especially my mum. I would have had less hospital admissions if I had understood how my mum perceived my behaviour.

Therapy helped me to the point where I don't even think that negatively anymore. Before it was always at the back of my mind. "How do people perceive me? Be very careful how people perceive you, because you don't know how somebody is going to react." 🥇

7.4 Different ways to help

In the following section, professionals talk about what they do and how they hope to help. As you can see, mental health services are only one part of this. Those who work in the NHS talk about working with individuals using medication or therapy, whilst those outside it talk about using group work and forum theatre to explore issues of power and oppression, with the aim of promoting healing and empowering people.

Dr Y.E, working with young people and their families in a clinic setting, talks about the different ways in which medication is sometimes understood by families, and the way in which she understands it as a psychiatrist.

❝ I see part of my role as a psychiatrist as being really realistic with the team about the limitations of medication. Sometimes families can think, 'Well, we've tried everything. And maybe now it's time to try medication'. But medication isn't a last resort. There are specific criteria someone needs to fulfil to be suitable for medication. There's no point giving someone an anti-depressant if actually, they're not having symptoms that medication would help with.

I'm always very clear with people that the evidence shows that medication works best alongside talking therapy. If you're saying you don't believe in talking therapies, but you're asking me for medication I need to be realistic and say, 'You're going to have limited improvement with it. We can try it, but you need to think about the side effects and decide if it is really what you want.' As a psychiatrist, you should be very aware of what the current NICE guidelines are and what the recommendations are. **❞**

Dr Sami Timimi also works in a clinic setting. He describes how he offers alternative ways of thinking about their difficulties to the families he works with.

❝ As the consultant psychiatrist, I tend to see people who are a few years down the line in treatment. Mostly they have already had the experience that a diagnosis has not actually led to long-term change. It might have led to a kind of short-term relief, but it does become more difficult as you get cultured into that way of thinking about your problems. It can be really hard when I then come along and say, 'Well, that way of thinking might not be true about you and your problems'.

What I find is that a problem once it establishes itself can start to cause itself. It feeds upon itself. This is the process that I call 'the problem becomes the problem'.

Let's take the example of insomnia. Insomnia is usually caused by something upsetting. After many nights of not being able to sleep, what do you think the research shows is now on your mind? It's not being able to sleep. So now the fact that you've got insomnia becomes the cause of your insomnia. Now that it's defined as a problem you try to find a solution. You might try some apps. You might try a different routine at night. Once you've tried these few things, and they've helped for a bit, but the insomnia keeps coming back, then each time it doesn't help 'solve' the insomnia, you become more preoccupied with it. It starts creeping into your day with worrying about whether you're going to sleep that night. At some point, you might go to a doctor and soon you might find yourself on medication. Medication works for a while, but then it causes its own problems. You're now in an antagonistic, tortured relationship with insomnia that builds every time a solution doesn't 'work'.

I talk about this idea [with families], in terms of their relationship to the problem. What if you've defined this as a problem that needs a solution before your life can improve, and the solution refuses to come? The odd thing is that your attempts to solve the problem are now driving the problem.

So this prepares people for the possibility that I'm not going to be suggesting medication or a new diagnosis, because that will just further embed the idea that they have a problem that needs solving.

To go back to the insomnia example, my aim is now to help them stop trying to solve it, but to see insomnia in ordinary terms, rather than in terms of a problem needing a solution. You will still get terrible sleep some nights but may also have better sleep on other nights. The bad nights just become irritating rather than torture. And the better nights are just better nights. **❞**

Dr. O.N., working in large NHS hospitals, describes working within multi-disciplinary teams and how different professions work together, integrating their different perspectives.

❝ One of the things I've always been keen on as a psychologist is really engaging the whole team. I work very hard with the psychiatrist to get them to think psychologically. One example would be, we've got this patient who is on a high dose of lithium. Clearly lithium has not had any effect on this person's mental health and she's been on lithium for six months now. The psychiatrists would argue, well, she's got a diagnosis of bipolar, she needs to be on lithium. And I would argue, well actually the lithium has no effect on her and it may not actually be bipolar. It might be that she's just depressed or something else. The lithium is having such an impact on this person's ability to cope, because it's really toxic medication. It makes them feel awful. So, if anything, the lithium is having a bigger impact on that person's ability to cope and function. I would be encouraging the psychiatrists to look at reducing medication or giving them a break, whilst I might see them more intensely during that time as a psychologist.

One of the things I would be trying to do is to get the psychiatrist to open their eyes to the person in front of them as opposed to hanging onto, 'This is a diagnosis and the treatment for that is this drug'. I'm trying to work with the team as a psychologist and developing a holistic formulation of what's going on with this person. But the team are still looking at the manual and due to the power of the medical model they don't want to take the risk, because if anything happens they will be asked why they deviated from the standard treatment. It's about trying to empower psychiatrists to think more psychologically so that we can provide better treatment together. That's the way I've tried to influence the system from within. **"**

Farzana Khan describes her work with Healing Justice London. This is a very different approach to both conventional psychology and psychiatry, rooted in a social justice approach to mental health and healing. She told me about their ethos which aims to increase agency and capacity in the people they work with.

" At Healing Justice London we are looking at how we build the kind of ecosystems that are needed for health and thriving and wellness, and how we understand and respond to how oppression intersects with that. We draw on our cultural and spiritual and ancestral traditions, and from non-Eurocentric paradigms or frameworks of health and healing. We look at creating capacity for transformation.

What all forms of harm and violence and oppression do is reduce capacity and reduce agency. So we look at the strategic intervention points where we can create capacity in, with, and for our communities, in our own bodies, in our own beings in the infrastructure around health, and then also what it means to sustain capacity, to feel resourced, to feel stable and to be able to navigate our lives and be well.

Healing Justice London emerged out of practice and grassroots work. understanding the nuance that, actually, this is survival work. This has to do with health. Race is

a health issue. What does it mean to show up, beyond representation, but actually to be present? **"**

Another approach taken by Heather Hunt, a clinical and child psychologist, is the use of forum theatre as a powerful and participatory way in highlighting psycho-social issues community members want to address. She emphasises the importance of understanding how power operates in a community. Her approach could also be described as rooted in a social justice model but is different again to Healing Justice London.

" I listened to women, mothers of young children about their lives and asked the question 'What's needed round here so that your children can flourish?' A strong and consistent message was not to take domestic violence for granted. So, with two male actor colleagues we developed three forum theatre pieces based on stories from women who had survived domestic violence and how they had tried to protect their children. We then showed the plays to community audiences comprising local women, health visitors, social workers, and teachers. In a forum theatre piece the audience are 'spectators' and can come and take a role to see if they can make a difference. In these plays we had neighbours, mothers, social workers, teachers etc.

So much surprising and useful learning took place as local women showed the very different ways they wanted support people to act. The other amazing surprise was how professional people on first seeing the plays said they were too distressing to show to women who had been affected but on showing the plays often those very women laughed and were delighted that 'We had got it!' As a psychologist I am learning how important it is to really validate a person's experience rather than interpret it. **"**

7.5 Going forward

What happens after a person has had a mental health problem? Moving on will often involve a complex mixture of changes, including on a biological, psychological, and social level. Some feel that receiving their diagnosis was a turning point, whilst others think that leaving that diagnosis behind was when things started to improve. Some attribute their recovery to the interventions they received, whilst others think that making a change in the circumstances of their lives or their religious faith is responsible.

The concept of recovery is itself a contested one within the survivor-led movement, with its implicit reference to a disease model of mental health. Some argue that they have learnt to relate to their problems in a different way, rather than recover from an illness. Others feel that they have been harmed by their experience in the mental health system, and that they need to recover from that just as much as from their mental health problems. Y.H. has found that his religious faith helped him take a different perspective on life.

❝ One thing that I've noticed is that you always have to look on the other side of it, because you're not dead if you're in a mental institution. If you're at your lowest, you realize that you can't stay low forever. Nothing's perfect. No situation is permanent. Maybe two months down the line, things will have drastically changed. You are who you say you are. If you feel that you are somebody great, you can become somebody great. Through God, Jesus Christ really helped me. All the glory to God. ❞

Josh Hartley tried anti-depressants and then came off them gradually. For him, he felt that deciding to leave university (for the second time) was a turning point.

❝ It would be nice if I could say my energy returned overnight or that I crawled into bed one night without the strength or inclination to turn off the bedside light and woke the next morning with the energy and motivation of an athlete, double high-fiving the beam at the bottom of the stairs and cartwheeling along the hallway, but no, this was not how it was. It was more of a slow stretch, a gradual awakening; so gradual in fact that I barely noticed it at first. But then one day I realized I was a little more engaged, my focus better, I could hear and retain what people were saying as long as they were brief and this was how it continued. My eyes seemed to open more fully, as opposed to the half-lidded haze that had filtered my world for as long as I could remember. And when I realized what was happening it gave me the confidence to look for more positives, to try more, do more as it felt like everything was heading in the right direction.

I can only liken it to any physical injury when suddenly you realize that it doesn't hurt quite so much and you are not quite as preoccupied with it every minute of every day and the pain of it does not keep you awake all night. Normality creeps in until it is possible not to think about the injury at all. ❞

Fran Stalley saw ten therapists before she found one who helped her by offering trauma-focused therapy (in her case this was EMDR). She felt that this focus on trauma is what made the difference.

❝ He was my eleventh therapist and the first therapist who understood complex trauma. He encouraged me to go and read about trauma to understand myself better. He treated me like someone whose emotional reactions were normal for a person who had gone through trauma. He really understood it. He knew how to treat complex trauma and he also knew how not to make it worse, unlike the other therapists that I had had.

Having had this therapy, targeted at my complex trauma, I feel very different now. I rarely get flashbacks. When I do, they are years apart. I don't tend to dissociate anymore. If I do, I can get myself out. My mood on a day-to-day basis is fine, I'm not depressed or particularly anxious. If I feel my mood sliding, I take prompt action to prevent it from getting worse.

Even though I now feel better, the abuse has negatively impacted every area of my life: I don't have a partner, a house, a car, a career, savings, a pension, nor family (I didn't want children, but I don't speak to my family because of the abuse). If I had been able to have trauma-focused therapy when I was in my 20s, maybe I would have been able to focus on living my life rather than overcoming the complex trauma and my life would now be easier. ❞

7.6 The future

There are many calls for better and more effective support for those with mental health problems, but people disagree on what this would look like and where extra funding should go. These are the thoughts of some professionals, all with years of experience of working in very different settings. Dr H.N. thinks it would be helpful to be able to offer a more long-term relationship.

❝ Our services are not designed for the idea that people could come back time after time. I have a lot of experiences of people ringing me years later asking for help with something and I'm not really supposed to devote any time to that. For some people maybe a better model for a service or an intervention would be something more like a lifelong friend or support worker, who keeps at a bit of a distance when we're not needed so much. This might work in terms of people rebuilding their trust in humanity. ❞

Dr Y.E. wishes that help could be offered earlier, before things have gone so badly wrong.

❝ We would love to work with families a lot earlier on in the difficulties. The threshold is so high that they are often at the end of a journey by the time they come in. There's a lot of interventions and work we could do much earlier on. But we're not seeing those children because there's just not capacity. **❞**

Farzana Khan told me of her vision of the ways in which she thinks we need to change the way we respond to people in distress.

❝ First and foremost, [we need] embodied or somatic rules that help us to inhabit our bodies, feel agency through our bodies, and to create capacity and safety. Because you can't just be in your body, especially if you've experienced violence and harm. There's no way to do embodiment work without also understanding and redressing eugenics, understanding the relationship to race or the social construct, but also how our bodies are brutalized and who benefits from the brutality of our bodies and the mobility of our bodies.

A second strategy is centring Disability Justice, Disability Justice, distinct from disability rights, which is much more concerned about policy and particular kinds of services and access. Disability Justice looks at whose bodies are desirable, valued, and whose are disposed of. It really connects the societal and structural implications and the ways our environments and cultures are designed and cultivated.

A third is participatory and co-production, so the dynamic between doctor and patient isn't one of a power dynamic, but one more like, what is it that I can know about my body? And how can you help my body towards health and wholeness?

And then the last I would say is trauma-informed. Trauma-informed is essential because we come from communities that experience profound forms of trauma and we do not want to reproduce harm. And we also want to understand how we don't reproduce harm on those that we are trying to support. What can traumatize us is so vast and varied. The nuance and skill that's needed to build that resilience is slow and deep work that needs to be accessible and resourced. Being able to have a trauma-informed approach also allows those that want to participate, but whose trauma responses may deny them the ability to access their wholeness. **❞**

Dr O.N. told me that he thinks professionals need to open up to an awareness of racism and diversity when thinking about mental health.

❝ We don't talk about racism in society. I think that is something that we as a profession [clinical psychologists] could do better. When we're developing a formulation, it needs to incorporate those kinds of traumas. There's nothing in DSM that acknowledges any of this. So people would say, 'Oh yes, it's psychosis'. They wouldn't say 'Oh, this person's experienced a great deal of racism in their life'. It's always thinking about reasons and context because that enables us to take a wider lens on what's going on for people.

I think we need to work hard to make people feel safe. One of the problems is that we have a very non-diverse clinical psychologist population. One of the challenges for a Black person going into the clinic is that they are really scared, because maybe they will increase your meds or whatever. So then you are meeting someone [the psychologist] who doesn't understand why you are in this state. You wouldn't feel safe, and it shouldn't be your role to educate white people.

We need more training on all levels, so that all staff really understand the experience of the whole community, including those from ethnic minorities. I'm interested in how we can develop new roles for those people who are in their local communities, who would never go and become clinical psychologists because they can't even think of going a whole year without a salary. They don't have the resources or the knowledge of how to get on the process. I would like to try and develop a whole new career which is embedded in the community, for people from the community to provide psychological interventions at a level between primary and secondary care. It would be more pulling people from the community and training them up. **❞**

Chapter Summary

- The stories you have read here represent only a few people's perspectives. Even just in the stories here, you can see the rich diversity of experiences and opinions.
- It is no longer possible for researchers and health professionals to continue their work without listening to the perspective of service users and those with lived experience.

- Lived experience is extremely complex and many people hold directly opposing perspectives based on their lived experience.
- There is no such thing as one 'expert by experience' voice and a person with lived experience cannot be assumed to represent the experience of others. It is important to always ask whose voices are not heard and to ensure that a diversity of viewpoints is included. This may mean looking particularly for those who have found non-diagnostic explanations for their difficulties, as their voices are less likely to be counted as 'lived experience'.

- The experience of experts can help to broaden understanding as they are able to compare and contrast the lived experiences of the many different people that they see.
- The models which people use to understand mental health will affect what they think is necessary and what they think is lacking. Holding different perspectives, including those which are incongruent with our own, is part of the complexity of continuing to try to understand mental health.

 ## END OF CHAPTER QUESTIONS

1. Why might psychologists seek out lived experience accounts of mental health difficulties? What are the advantages and disadvantages of doing so?

2. What are some of the challenges in incorporating an expert by experience voice into research and service provision? How might these be addressed?

3. What is the benefit in including the experience of professionals alongside the lived experience of those with mental health problems? How can the two sets of experience complement each other?

4. Marginalisation comes up in several of these accounts. What are the different ways in which being marginalised may affect a person's mental health? Use examples from the text to illustrate.

 ## FURTHER READING

Cohen, B. (2007). *Mental Health User Narratives: New Perspectives on Illness and Recovery*. London: Palgrave Macmillan.

An academic text which uses the stories of mental health service users to illustrate how they see their difficulties and recovery.

Hartley, J., and Prowse, A. (2020). *The Boy Between: A Mother and Son's Journey from a World Gone Grey*. Seattle: Little A.

A personal account of depression by a young man and his mother.

Watson, J. (ed.) (2019). *Drop the Disorder! Challenging the Culture of Psychiatric Diagnosis*. Monmouth: PCCS Books.

A collection of essays by professionals and service users which argues that we need to move away from seeing distress and unusual experiences as medical disorders.

 ## REFERENCES

Beresford, P. (2023). *A Straight Talking Introduction to Emotional Wellbeing: from Mental Illness to Mad Studies*. Monmouth: PCCS Books.

Boyle, M. (2013). The persistence of medicalisation: Is the presentation of alternatives part of the problem? In S. Coles, S. Keenan, and B. Diamond (eds), *Madness Contested: Power and Practice*. Ross-on-Wye: PCCS Books, pp. 3–22.

Coombs, C. (2019). Disability, depression and the language of disorder. In J. Watson (ed.), *Drop the Disorder! Challenging the Culture of Psychiatric Diagnosis*. Monmouth: PCCS Books, Chapter 14.

Hartley, J., and Prowse, A. (2020). *The Boy Between: A Mother and Son's Journey from a World Gone Grey*. Seattle: Little A.

Henderson, R., Williams, P., Gabbidon, J., Farrelly, S., Schauman, O., Hatch, S., … Clement, S. (2015). Mistrust of mental health services: Ethnicity, hospital admission and unfair treatment. *Epidemiology and Psychiatric Sciences*, 24(3), 258–265. doi:10.1017/S2045796014000158

Read, J. (2020). Bad things happen and can drive you crazy: The causal beliefs of 701 people taking antipsychotics. *Psychiatry Research*, 285, 112754. doi:10.1016/j.psychres.2020.112754

Stalley, F. (2021). *Childhood Trauma Recovery: The Email Conversations with My Therapist That Helped Me Overcome Childhood PTSD*. Kindle Direct.

Chapter 8
Technology and Global Mental Health

Learning objectives

When you have completed this chapter, you should be able to do the following:

8.1 Explain some of the ways in which the internet has changed the landscape of mental health, and evaluate its impact.

8.2 Describe how social media may be instrumental in social contagion and the implications of this for mental health.

8.3 Evaluate the assumptions of the movement for global mental health.

8.4 Outline the concept of decolonising mental health and critically discuss what this means for psychologists.

Introduction

The final two chapters of this book are about the ways in which the psychology of mental health is being transformed by the technological and social changes of the 21st century. They are about emerging frontiers and future directions. In this chapter, I will start by talking about technological advances and the opportunities and risks which these may pose to mental health. Advances in technology have made it possible for ideas and models of mental health to spread wider than ever before, and this chapter will turn there next, when discussing the movement for global mental health.

8.1 The internet

In the early 1990s, the arrival of what was then called the 'World Wide Web' heralded the start of a dramatic chance in people's lives. It's now hard to imagine a world without computers and mobile devices, and the instant diffusion of information to millions of people across the globe is taken for granted. Before the 1990s, however, this was the stuff of science fiction.

The effect of this new connectivity on mental health was unpredictable. Would it change the way people thought and felt about their lives, being able to connect with others so fast? There were many possibilities. Some were concerned about the harmful effects of so much information available so fast, and about the potentially addictive nature of the new technology. Others were enthusiastic about the possibility of reaching many more people who needed help and of building communities independent of location.

Concerns about the impact of the internet

Fears about the impact of the internet and use of technology were quickly reflected in the media with the use of terms such as 'internet addiction' or 'pathological internet use'. These positioned technology use as an addictive behaviour, on a par with substance misuse. The most recent version of ICD includes the diagnosis of '**Gaming Disorder**', which is given to people whose use of video games is so excessive that it impairs their ability to engage in the rest of their life.

Clinics sprang up offering private treatment, often following the models of addiction developed for drugs and alcohol. This applied the medical model to technology use. Even without a psychiatric diagnosis, many people are afraid of the impact of society's increased dependence on technology. There is particular concern about the effects on children and young people. Parenting books blame too much 'screen time' for children's problems, and regular articles are published in the mainstream media which focus on the negative impact on the developing human brain of spending too much time on a computer (e.g. Chadwick, 2020).

What does the research tell us? Findings in this area are inconsistent and largely correlational (meaning that they cannot establish causality). Some large-scale population studies have found associations between mental health problems and 'screen time' (Twenge and Campbell, 2018) whilst others have not (Orben and Przybylski, 2019).

Thinking critically, we need to ask what is it that the rather vague terms 'technology' or 'screen time' include. One of the problems with the research is that technology is a means of access, not an entity in itself. As handheld tablets and smart phones are more widely used, more activities are accessed through a screen. Screen time can now include time spent reading, writing, talking to friends via text or video link, browsing the internet, playing board games, exercising, playing video games, watching documentaries and following online courses. During the COVID-19 pandemic many young people accessed all their education via a screen.

This makes the concept of 'screen time' an extremely wide one which is likely to mean very different things for different people.

Accessing mental health support over the internet

Apart from all the fears about how destructive this new technology might be, it's indisputable that the internet has great potential in improving communication and access to help. Computer programs and apps have been developed which enable people to access self-help material at home. Websites such as Living Life to the Full (lltf.com) and MoodGym (moodgym.com.au) provide free-to-access self-help courses which use principles from cognitive behaviour therapy. Computerised CBT (cCBT) courses are recommended in the NICE guidelines and there is evidence that they can be effective in reducing symptoms of depression and anxiety (Andrews et al., 2018). Critics say, however, that it is less clear whether these are effective when used in day-to-day clinical practice. The REEACT study, a large scale randomised study of two cCBT programs as used in 83 different GP practices, found that despite phone support only 16–18% of participants completed either of the cCBT programs, with the most common number of sessions accessed being only one out of a total of six or eight (Gilbody et al., 2015). This study found little or no effect of cCBT on symptoms of depression at four-month follow-up, as compared to GP care as usual. These studies raise questions about the difference between a research study and the real-life application, something which it is always important to consider in mental health research. An intervention may be efficacious, meaning that it works under ideal conditions, but not effective when it is applied outside those conditions.

Technology-based interventions are increasingly used for more serious mental health problems. Cognitive training apps are in development for use with people diagnosed with schizophrenia (Krzystanek et al., 2020), and virtual reality programs have successfully been used to treat agoraphobic avoidance with people with psychosis (Freeman et al., 2022). The idea is that by using virtual reality, people can practise encountering feared social situations and build up their tolerance, something which they might not be able to do in real life due to their severe anxiety. This is an exciting possibility, providing a safe environment for people to experiment and challenge their thoughts.

Critics of internet-based approaches say that they reduce psychological therapy to a set of techniques, and that there is no replacement for a personal relationship with a therapist. They also argue that claims about the cost-effectiveness of computerised therapies may be over-stated. The high drop-out rates for those accessing cCBT suggest that access to a computer program is not sufficient; it is necessary for a person to be supported and encouraged to use the program as well. This then makes use of the programs more expensive as support staff need to be employed.

The internet has the potential to increase accessibility to mental health care. The increased affordability of smart phones and mobile devices have meant that even people without computers can access the internet and video conferencing platforms. People in remote rural areas as well as those with illnesses, disabilities, or caring responsibilities can access psychological interventions or see a psychiatrist without leaving their homes. The COVID-19 crisis resulted in a near universal shift of psychotherapeutic work from in person to online. Circumstances rather than the evidence base necessitated the change, but early studies conducted during the pandemic indicate that online psychological therapy can be as effective as in person (Nguyen et al., 2022). Remote therapy is different to the computerised programs discussed above because it refers to traditional psychological therapy delivered over video-link, rather than apps and programs developed to be used alone or with minimal support.

8.2 Social media

How about social media use specifically, something which many argue is damaging to mental health? The research is inconclusive. Some researchers suggest that heavy use of social media can contribute to anxiety and depression, whilst others argue that the relationship could be the other way round—i.e., people who are anxious or depressed are more likely to spend lots of time on social media. One longitudinal study did not find a relationship between anxiety, depression, and social media use in adolescents (Coyne et al., 2020) but systematic reviews have found correlations between problematic social media use and depression (Shannon et al., 2022). Another longitudinal population survey found that use of social media was a protective factor, with those who used the internet for social networking less likely to report an increase in

severe psychological distress over time, when compared to those who do not use social network sites (Hampton, 2019). 'Social media use' is a complex factor with different effects on different individuals.

A difficulty in this area is that technological developments are moving so fast that by the time research studies come out, they are already out of date. Smart phones only became widely available in 2007, and so young people born around that time are the first generation who have grown up with constant access to the internet, even when out of the house. There is no way to tell what the long-term effects of this might be in advance and by the time those studies are in, there will be new developments and new ways to interact with technology.

Moving beyond simply looking at quantity of time spent online, researchers have become interested in what is happening when people connect over social media—and what impact this might have on their mental health. Researchers have long been interested in the idea that emotions and mood can spread between people who are in the same place, a process called emotion or social contagion. They use statistical models similar to those used for infectious diseases to track this.

This led researchers to wonder whether the same might be true over social media—and whether therefore emotions might spread to millions via their social media newsfeeds, sometimes called Digital Emotion Contagion (Goldenberg and Gross, 2020). It appears that it does. Reading emotionally laden content—both negative and positive—affects how people feel and what they do. This has been demonstrated in massive studies on social networks such as Facebook (Kramer, Guillory, and Hancock, 2014) and Twitter (Ferrara and Yang, 2015). These Facebook studies raised many ethical issues. It has been claimed that researchers manipulated and monitored the Facebook feeds of hundreds of thousands of participants without informing them in advance, using as their justification the fact that at the time the basic terms of service for Facebook included consent for users' data to be used for analysis and research (Meyer, 2014). These studies looked at deliberately manipulating emotions over social media networks for marketing or political purposes, something which many find unethical.

Influence and the internet

In 2020 and 2021, lockdown due to the COVID-19 pandemic meant that many adolescents were spending extended periods of time on social media.

By 2021, psychiatrists and neurologists in the United States reported that they were seeing a steep increase in the number of young people presenting with Tourette-like symptoms (Pringsheim et al., 2021). **Tourette's Syndrome** is a childhood onset tic disorder characterised by involuntary movements or noises.

The young people who were presenting to clinics had been diagnosed with Tourette's, but when seen at specialist clinics it was clear that there were significant differences in their presentation to those with classic Tourette's. Onset was in adolescence rather than childhood, came on rapidly and the nature and course of their tics was different. In Germany, a clinic reported that young people were presenting with symptoms which appeared to be related to a single YouTube channel called *Gewitter im Kopf* (Thunderstorm in the Brain). This channel featured a young man with Tourette's who made many videos featuring different tics. His videos were viewed by millions. One German study found that all the young people they saw with these new tic symptoms had watched this YouTube channel prior to the start of their symptoms and there was an overlap between the tics demonstrated by their patients and those shown on the YouTube channel (Müller-Vahl et al., 2022). This spread of symptoms between people without an organic or biological cause is called a **sociogenic** or **psychogenic** illness. There are examples of this transfer of symptoms happening through history, usually in social settings such as a school or church (Weir, 2005).

Müller et al. propose a need for a new category which they called a **mass social media-induced illness**. Sociogenic illness was previously understood to be transmitted by physically being with other people who were exhibiting symptoms, but the social media-induced illness theory suggests that symptoms can spread via contact on the internet, meaning that a single social media influencer can spread symptoms to a very large number of people, as appears to have happened with Tourette's.

There is no suggestion that young people were intentionally mimicking the symptoms they saw on the videos. It appears that they were being influenced by what they saw without being consciously aware that this was happening. Many young people will have watched the videos without developing symptoms, but when millions are watching, some will be susceptible and will develop symptoms.

The internet has irrevocably changed the availability of information but has also made it harder for people to distinguish between trustworthy information and that which is designed to influence them. If an individual suspects that they may meet criteria for a mental health diagnosis, they can now take online screenings and look through the diagnostic criteria themselves long before they see a mental health professional. They can join online support groups and discuss their symptoms with others. In these groups, people sometimes share experiences of what should be said to a professional in order to increase the chances of receiving a diagnosis. By the time a person sees a professional, they may be sure that they should receive a diagnosis and some have already taken it on as part of their identity. They may disagree if told that they don't meet diagnostic criteria. Doctors describe how individuals come in asking for a specific diagnosis and refuse to accept the opinion of the professional in a way which was far less common before the internet.

This new access to information brings with it a vulnerability to influence. There is a profit motive for pharmaceutical companies in encouraging people to seek diagnoses which could lead to them being prescribed medication, and the pharmaceutical industry funds apparently 'grass roots' awareness campaigns which encourage people to see their problems in medical terms and to seek treatment (Kaczmarek, 2022). This **disease mongering** is discussed in Chapter 4. Diagnosis is presented as the answer to a person's struggles and people are encouraged to see everyday behaviours and emotional reactions as symptoms. It can be hard for an individual to discern whether the information that they are finding online is reliable and unbiased.

Self-diagnosis has pitfalls. Individuals do not have a reliable way to compare their experiences with those of the wider population, so they are not able to judge how their symptoms compare to others. An individual may be convinced that their difficulties reach diagnostic threshold, whilst a professional who sees thousands of people will have a different perspective on how severe those difficulties are.

It isn't just pharmaceutical companies who are monetising mental health. Psychiatric diagnoses including dissociative identity disorder, obsessive compulsive disorder, and bipolar disorder are common as hashtags on social media platforms such as TikTok, as social influencers make highly successful videos showing symptoms (Haltigan et al., 2023). These videos are viewed millions of times, which brings in money for their creators. Online communities have formed around these hashtags. Haltigan et al. point out that some of these online communities are creating their own definitions of concepts which they describe as 'liberated from conventional **psychiatric nosology**'. In other words, within these communities concepts such as 'dissociative identity disorder' are not defined by the official diagnostic criteria but instead by the lived experience of those within the community. One such example is the 'Plurals' online community which has its own way of understanding dissociated identities which may be far from the understanding of most professionals (Christensen, 2022). In the environment of online communities diagnostic criteria can become increasingly irrelevant. People identify with a diagnostic term such as 'dissociative identity disorder' and define this in a way which reflects their lived experience. This may be very different to how a clinician would understand the term.

The recent research on social media-induced illness (discussed above) suggests that symptoms themselves as well as awareness can spread over the internet. When a diagnosis brings social benefits such as community, status, and identity, this will influence both how people see themselves and the symptoms that they experience. It will lead to increasing numbers seeking diagnosis and identifying themselves by a diagnosis.

Another aspect of the technological advances of the last 30 years has been that people living in parts of the world which were relatively cut off can now access the internet. This has implications for mental health interventions across the world, and that is what I will talk about in the next section.

8.3 Global mental health—'scaling up'

For most of this book, I have focused on the psychology of mental health in higher income countries (**HIC**), countries such as the UK and the USA, where both psychiatry and psychology are well-established and where mental health services are in place, even if not at adequate levels to meet the need in the population.

These countries are in the minority in the world. The World Bank divides countries up into higher income, middle income, and low income. 75% of the world's population live in middle income countries, ranging from huge countries such as Brazil and China to tiny

countries such as Belize. A further 9% live in low-income countries, which include Afghanistan and Zimbabwe. These countries are sometimes combined in the acronym **LMIC** (lower- and middle-income countries). In many of these countries, mental health care is often not well funded or widely available, particularly in rural areas. Distressing experiences and unusual behaviour may be understood in very different ways. There are usually few psychiatrists or psychologists.

Global mental health is a term used to describe the efforts of organisations such as the World Health Organization (WHO) and non-governmental organisations across the world to improve the mental health of people in LMIC—or to 'close the gap' as it is sometimes phrased. Through programmes such as mhGAP (Mental Health Gap Action Programme) the WHO campaigns for mental health to be integrated into general health care and for it to be made more of a priority.

Scaling up mental health services is a challenge. Psychiatrists and psychologists are expensive to employ and take a long time to train, and so in many LMIC primary care workers are trained and then supported to work with people in their community. Studies of such workers have found that the amount of training they get varies from two days to a few months (Shahmalak et al., 2019). This is clearly very much cheaper than the decade or so of higher education required to produce a psychiatrist. These 'lay health workers' work under the supervision of a team of specialists and their role is often to visit families, to offer support, and to encourage people to continue to take drugs prescribed by the psychiatrist which are provided for free. Models like this appear to be effective at reducing symptoms and improving quality of life at a relatively low cost (Malia et al., 2019).

Mental health literacy

Lack of services is not the only reason why people in LMIC do not seek professional help for mental health problems. Many people across the world do not think of their emotional experiences as belonging in the realm of health. Psychosocial, moral, or spiritual explanations are often favoured, and people who understand their problems in these terms are not likely to go to a clinic for help. Even when services are there, people may not see the need for them (Roberts et al., 2022).

For this reason, scaling up mental health services usually goes hand in hand with **psychoeducation** and awareness programmes. These have the aim of changing the way in which people think about distress and unusual experiences. These programmes are sometimes called '**mental health literacy**' which is defined as knowledge about mental health disorders which enables 'recognition, management, and prevention' (Furnham and Swami, 2018).

Critics say that this equates being literate (a basic skill) with identifying distress and unusual behaviour as mental disorders and encouraging people to seek medical help (the medical model). They argue that it assumes that the psychiatric framework is applicable universally (rather than culturally specific) and superior to local understandings of mental distress (Mills, 2014). The model used by the WHO frames mental health problems as 'an illness like any other', an approach which some argue can lead to increased stigma (Read et al., 2006) and which is often quite different to the psychosocial or spiritual explanations favoured by many before they have contact with mental health services. Mills points out that the 'illness like any other' model is profitable for pharmaceutical companies as it creates new markets for their drugs.

Different outcomes

Outcome studies for scaling up have produced some unexpected results. At the end of the twentieth century, large-scale studies conducted by the World Health Organization (WHO) compared the outcomes of people who fit the criteria for a diagnosis of schizophrenia in countries across the world (Jablensky et al., 1992). Somewhat to everyone's surprise, they found that outcomes were better, particularly in terms of functioning and symptoms, for people who lived in LMIC when compared to HIC. This was particularly evident in India. These were people who were experiencing the most severe mental health problems, who were generally not treated with drugs, and many of whom were not receiving what would be considered to be proper 'mental health care' by a psychiatrist or psychologist. This finding has led to much discussion of why this might be, with suggested explanations including different societal responses, family situations, and cultural factors (Luhrmann, 2007) or even natural selection, with the hypothesis being that those who suffer from severe mental health problems are more likely to be abandoned at times of famine (and therefore tragically to starve), thus meaning that their

IN THE REAL WORLD 8.1

Farmer Suicides in India

Vidarbha is an area of India which is known for the cultivation of cotton and soybean, and also, tragically, for its very high incidence of suicide among farmers (Bomble and Lhungdim, 2020). It isn't the only 'suicide district' for farmers in India, and in fact farmer suicides are elevated across the Asia-Pacific region.

Farming in India has changed since the 1970s. At that time, farmers used indigenous seed varieties which were low cost and locally produced. After 1970, hybrid, genetically modified seeds started being produced by large, private companies. These had higher yields and in order to keep up the farmers had to use them. They cost much more money. This meant that in order to plant a crop, a farmer had to have access to money up front, often borrowed from moneylenders. Farmers became particularly vulnerable to crop failure, or to the falling price of their crops on the world market. Each year, they could not know if the price of their crop would cover the cost of the cultivation, and whether they would be able to repay their debts (Mills, 2014).

When farmers themselves are asked why they think there is a high rate of suicide among other farmers, they cite debt,

addictions, poor prices for crops, environmental problems, government apathy, private money lenders, and crop failure (Dongre and Deskmukh, 2012). They therefore give mostly social explanations.

From a mental health perspective, suicidal thinking and behaviour can be framed as an illness or disorder. With this in mind, teams of psychiatrists have been sent to visit farmers whilst articles argue that 'psychological counselling' from volunteers should be made available to suicidal farmers and can prevent suicides (Kant, 2019). This frames the problem as a psychological or psychiatric one, rather than as the result of systemic changes within which farming is becoming unsustainable as a way of life.

Prof Sarabjeet, principal investigator on a farmer suicide prevention study sums it up '…the efforts of increasing production, developing new varieties and techniques can bring desired results only if the farmers are vibrant and have a healthy and stress-free mind' (quoted in Kant, 2019). The virtual impossibility of staying 'healthy and stress-free' whilst falling into debt and losing your livelihood is hidden by the mental disease narrative.

genes were not passed on (Thirthalli and Jain, 2009). These are all hypotheses and it is still not clear why this discrepancy exists. However, it does indicate that a degree of caution might be indicated when attempting to spread a Western model of mental health across the globe.

Another criticism of the global mental health movement is that it has the potential to depoliticise events and to obscure the consequences of government policies which cause extreme human distress. Serious systemic issues can be framed as a problem of individual wellbeing. This is illustrated in the case study in Box 8.1, of farmer suicides in India.

8.4 Decolonising mental health

Critics of the global mental health movement sometimes draw an analogy between the worldwide proliferation of a Western model of mental health and oppressive ideologies, such as racism and colonialisation. They say that the concept of 'mental disorder' can be used to control and oppress groups of people, in the same way as racist ideas are. In the wake of the murder of George Floyd and the **Black Lives Matter** movement, some called on psychologists and psychiatrists to 'decolonise mental health' (Weine et al., 2020). Others argue that framing distress as an illness locates the problem in the victims of oppression rather than in the oppression itself and that the training for psychiatrists needs to challenge fundamental assumptions (Bracken et al., 2021). Some argue that the very concept of 'mental health' needs to be rethought when thinking about oppressed people, as it has the potential to take further power away from people who are already in a less favoured position in society (Nelson, 2012).

Others argue that decolonising is an **ideological** framework which can distract us from the task of alleviating mental health problems and distress. Some psychologists argue that bringing social justice theories into psychology leads to division and could be harmful (Sherwood, 2022). Others say that psychologists and psychiatrists should stay out of politics and focus on their core work, which they see as working with individuals to improve their lives. They point out that psychologists need to work with everyone, no matter what their beliefs, and that if (for example) social justice becomes a focus, this ties a political agenda with psychological therapy. This could lead to some people having the perception that psychology is not for them and creating barriers to accessing therapy.

Chapter Summary

- Technological advances are happening so fast that the evidence base often lags behind.

- There has been fear about the impact of the new technology on mental health, particularly video games and social media, but also excitement about the opportunity for people to access treatment via technology.

- There is emerging evidence that emotions and mental health symptoms may spread over social media, a process some have termed 'mass social media-induced illness'.

- 'Scaling-up' mental health across the world brings practical issues but also raises questions about whether the psychiatric system is universally applicable and useful.

? END OF CHAPTER QUESTIONS

1. What does it mean when a diagnosis is 'liberated from conventional psychiatric nosology' by internet support groups and communities? Is this a good thing? Why or why not?

2. Is influence via the internet something which psychologists should be concerned about? Give some examples of the different ways in which this happens and discuss what the consequences might be (e.g. social media-induced illness, disease mongering).

3. 'The medical model of mental health depoliticises oppression.' What does this mean? Do you agree or disagree?

FURTHER READING

Lewis, H. (2022). The Twitching Generation. *The Atlantic*. https://www.theatlantic.com/ideas/archive/2022/02/social-media-illness-teen-girls/622916/

Long-form article by a journalist about the spread of tics and Tourette's through TikTok.

Living Life to the Full (www.llttf.com) A free to access educational self-help website by Dr Chris Williams.

This includes online courses using computerized CBT for a range of psychological problems.

Mills, C. (2014). *Decolonizing Global Mental Health: The Psychiatrization of the Majority World.* Abingdon: Routledge. ISBN 978-1-135-08043-3.

This book by a researcher in public health looks at the way in which diagnoses travel around the world and how global mental health policies promote a particular way of understanding behaviour and distress.

Summerfield, D. (2012). Afterword: Against 'global mental health.' *Transcultural Psychiatry*, 49(3–4), 519–530. doi:10.1177/1363461512454701

REFERENCES

Andrews, G., Basu, A., Cuijpers, P., Craske, M.G., McEvoy, P., English, C.L., and Newby, J.M. (2018). Computer therapy for the anxiety and depression disorders is effective, acceptable and practical health care: An updated meta-analysis. *Journal of Anxiety Disorders*, 55, 70–78. ISSN 0887–6185. doi:10.1016/j.janxdis.2018.01.001

Bomble, P., and Lhungdim, H. (2020). Mental health status of farmers in Maharastra, India: A study from farmer suicide prone area of Vidarbha region. *Clinical Epidemiology and Global Health*, 8(3), 684–688.

Bracken, P., Fernando, S., Alsaraf, S., Creed, M., Double, D., Gilberthorpe, T., Hassan, R., Jadhav, S., Jeyapaul, P., Kopua, D., Parsons, M., Rodger, J., Summerfield, D., Thomas, P., and Timimi, S. (2021). Decolonising the medical curriculum: Psychiatry faces particular challenges. *Anthropology and Medicine*, 28(4), 420–428. doi:10.1080/13648470.2021.1949892

Chadwick, J. (2020).'Green time' spent outdoors in nature is better for children's mental health and academic achievement than 'screen time', study shows. *Daily Mail* online. Retrieved 4 September. https://www.dailymail.co.uk/sciencetech/article-8698091/More-green-time-screen-time-helps-childrens-mental-health.html

Christensen, E. (2022). The online community: DID and plurality. *European Journal of Trauma and Dissociation*, 6(2), 100257. doi:10.1016/j.ejtd.2021.100257

Coyne, S., Rogers, A., Zurcher, J., Stockdale, L., and Booth, M. (2020). Does time spent using social media impact mental health?: An eight year longitudinal study. *Computers in Human Behaviour*, 104, 106160.

Dongre, A., and Deshmukh, P. (2012). Farmer's suicides in the Vidarbha region of Maharastra, India: A qualitative exploration of their causes. *Journal of Injury and Violence Research*, 4(1), 2–6.

Ferrara, E., and Yang, Z. (2015). Measuring emotional contagion in social media. *PLoS ONE*, 10(11), e0142390.

Freeman, D., Lambe, S., Kabir, T., et al. (2022). Automated virtual reality therapy to treat agoraphobic avoidance and distress in patients with psychosis (gameChange): A multicentre, parallel-group, single-blind, randomised controlled trial in England with mediation and moderation analyses. *The Lancet*, 9(5), 375–388. doi:10.1016/S2215-0366(22)00060-8

Furnham, A., and Swami, V. (2018). Mental health literacy: A review of what it is and why it matters. *International Perspectives in Psychology: Research, Practice, Consultation*, 7(4), 240–257.

Gilbody, S., Littlewood, E., Hewitt, C., Brierley, G., Tharmanathan, P., Araya R., et al. (2015). Computerised cognitive behaviour therapy (cCBT) as treatment for depression in primary care (REEACT trial): Large scale pragmatic randomised controlled trial. *BMJ*, 351, h5627.

Goldenberg, A., and Gross, J. (2020). Digital emotion contagion. *Trends in Cognitive Sciences*, 24(4), 316–328.

Haltigan, J.D., Pringsheim, T.M., and Rajkumar, G. (2023). Social media as an incubator of personality and behavioral psychopathology: Symptom and disorder authenticity or psychosomatic social contagion? *Comprehensive Psychiatry*, 121, 152362.

Hampton, K. (2019). Social media and change in psychological distress over time: The role of social causation. *Journal of Computer-Mediated Communication*, 24(5), 205–222. doi:10.1093/jcmc/zmz010

Jablensky, A., Sartorius, N., Ernberg, G., Anker, M., Korten, A., Cooper, J., … Bertelsen, A. (1992). Schizophrenia: Manifestations, incidence and course in different cultures: A World Health Organization ten-country study. *Psychological Medicine: Monograph Supplement*, 20, 1–97. doi:10.1017/S0264180100000904

Kaczmarek, E. (2022). Promoting diseases to promote drugs: The role of the pharmaceutical industry in fostering good and bad medicalization. *British Journal of Clinical Pharmacology*, 88(1), 34–39. doi:10.1111/bcp.14835

Kant, A. (2019). Counselling can prevent farm suicides. *The Times of India*. Retrieved 10 September 2019. https://timesofindia.indiatimes.com/city/chandigarh/counselling-can-prevent-farm-suicides/articleshow/71061751.cms

Kramer, A., Guillory, J., and Hancock, J. (2014). Emotional contagion through social networks. *Proceedings of the National Academy of Sciences*, 111(24), 8788–8790. doi:10.1073/pnas.1320040111

Krzystanek, M., Krysta, K., Borkowski, M., Skałacka, K., Przybyło, J., Pałasz, A., Mucic, D., Martyniak, E., and Waszkiewicz, N. (2020). The effect of smartphone-based cognitive training on the functional/cognitive markers of schizophrenia: A one-year randomized study. *Journal of Clinical Medicine*, 9(11), 3681. doi:10.3390/jcm9113681

Luhrmann, T.M. (2007). Social defeat and the culture of chronicity: Or, why schizophrenia does so well over there and so badly here. *Culture, Medicine and Psychiatry*, 31, 135–172. doi:10.1007/s11013-007-9049-z

Malia, A., Margoob, M., Iyer, S., Majid, A., Lal, S., Joober, R., and Mansouri, B. (2019). Testing the effectiveness of implementing a model of healthcare involving trained lay health workers in treating major mental disorders among youth in a conflict-ridden, low-middle income environment: Part II, Results. *The Canadian Journal of Psychiatry*, 64(9), 630–637.

Meyer, R. (2014). Everything we know about Facebook's secret mood-manipulation experiment. *The Atlantic*, 28 June.

Mills, C. (2014). *Decolonizing Global Mental Health: The Psychiatrization of the Majority World*. Abingdon: Routledge.

Müller-Vahl, K.R., Pisarenko, A., Jakubovski, E., and Fremer, C. (2022). Stop that! It's not Tourette's but a new type of mass sociogenic illness. *Brain*, 145(2), 476–480. doi:10.1093/brain/awab316. PMID: 34424292; PMCID: PMC9014744.

Nelson, S. (2012). *Challenging hidden assumptions: Colonial norms as determinants of Aboriginal mental health*. National Collaborating Centre for Aboriginal Health. https://www.researchgate.net/publication/341244879_Challenging_hidden_assumptions_Colonial_norms_as_determinants_of_Aboriginal_mental_health

Nguyen, J., McNulty, N., Grant, N., Martland, N., Dowling, D., King, S., … Dom, G. (2022). The effectiveness of remote therapy in two London IAPT services. *The Cognitive Behaviour Therapist*, 15, E23. doi:10.1017/S1754470X22000198

Orben, A., and Przybylski, A.K. (2019). Screens, teens, and psychological well-being: Evidence from three time-use-diary studies. *Psychological Science*, 30(5), 682–696. doi:10.1177/0956797619830329

Pringsheim, T., Ganos, C., McGuire, J.F., Hedderly, T., Woods, D., Gilbert, D.L., Piacentini, J., Dale, R.C., and Martino, D. (2021). Rapid onset functional tic-like behaviors in young females during the COVID-19 pandemic. *Movement Disorders*, 36, 2707–2713. doi:10.1002/mds.28778

Read, J., Haslam, N., Sayce, L., and Davies, E. (2006). Prejudice and schizophrenia: A review of the 'mental illness is an illness like any other' approach. *Acta Psychiatrica Scandinavica*, 114, 303–318. doi:10.1111/j.1600-0447.2006.00824.x

Roberts, T., Miguel Esponda, G., Torre, C., Pillai, P., Cohen, A., and Burgess, R. (2022). Reconceptualising the treatment gap for common mental disorders: A fork in the road for global mental health? *The British Journal of Psychiatry*, 221(3), 553–557. doi:10.1192/bjp.2021.221

Shahmalak, U., Blakemore, A., Waheed, M.W., et al. (2019). The experiences of lay health workers trained in task-shifting psychological interventions: A qualitative systematic review. *International Journal of Mental Health Systems*, 13, 64. doi:10.1186/s13033-019-0320-9

Shannon, H., Bush, K., Villeneuve, P.J., Hellemans, K.G., and Guimond, S. (2022). Problematic social media use in adolescents and young adults: Systematic review and meta-analysis. *JMIR Mental Health*, 9(4), e33450. doi:10.2196/33450

Sherwood, C. (2022). Critical social justice is more likely to lead to division and victimhood than equality. *PsychReg* published online. https://www.psychreg.org/critical-social-justice-more-likely-lead-division-victimhood-than-equality/

Thirthalli, J., and Jain, S. (2009). Better outcome of schizophrenia in India: A natural selection against severe forms? *Schizophrenia Bulletin*, 35(3), 655–657. doi:10.1093/schbul/sbn012

Twenge, J.M., and Campbell, W.K. (2018). Associations between screen time and lower psychological well-being among children and adolescents: Evidence from a population-based study. *Preventive Medicine Reports*, 12, 271–283. doi:10.1016/j.pmedr.2018.10.003

Weine, S., Kohrt, B.A., Collins, P.Y., Cooper, J., Lewis-Fernandez, R., Okpaku, S., and Wainberg, M.L. (2020). Justice for George Floyd and a reckoning for global mental health. *Global Mental Health*, 7, e22, 1–5.

Weir, E. (2005). Mass sociogenic illness. *Canadian Medical Association Journal*, 172(1), 36. doi:10.1503/cmaj.045027

Chapter 9
Biological Advances and Dimensionality

Learning objectives

When you have completed this chapter, you should be able to do the following:

9.1 Outline recent neuroscientific advances and explain what the advent of fMRI could mean for mental health.

9.2 Explain how the field of behavioural genetics has developed and discuss some of the complexities, including polygenic indices and gene–environment interactions.

9.3 Describe why transdiagnostic classification systems are being developed and explain the different assumptions and priorities of RDoC, HiToP, and the complex systems approach.

9.4 Explain how transdiagnostic interventions work and evaluate whether these represent an advance on what went before.

Introduction

This final chapter is about the ways in which advances in neuroscience and behavioural genetics are revolutionising the way that scientists think about mental health problems. I'll talk about the current frontiers of biological research, and then move on to the new systems which are being developed to reflect current thinking. I'll discuss transdiagnostic models and finish with a brief discussion about transdiagnostic interventions.

9.1 Neuroscientific advances

The early years of the twenty-first century saw dramatic breakthroughs in the understanding of the biology of mental health problems. With the advent of functional brain imaging and genome-wide association studies, it became possible to look at the biological correlates of mental health problems in a way which was previously impossible. This led to optimistic predictions that the very professions of psychiatry and psychology would become unnecessary. The argument was that psychiatry, in particular, would inevitably become more biological in focus, and as this happened, it would merge with other areas of healthcare such as neurology (Fitzgerald, 2015). Others strongly disagree with this prediction, arguing that the distinctly different approaches would always be necessary (Pies, 2005).

Up to 1991, much of the way in which the brain was understood came either from post-mortem examinations or from studies of people who had experienced traumatic brain injury. Neuropsychologists would draw conclusions about what different areas of the brain did by examining the impairments seen in people with brain damage in a particular area. Then came the development of **functional magnetic resonance imaging (fMRI)**, a non-invasive technique which allows scientists to map brain activity in a living person through measuring changes in cerebral blood flow. Changes in blood flow are related to neuronal activation, meaning that by tracking blood flow, scientists could see which area of the brain was in use.

fMRI was a game-changer for neuroscience in mental health. Researchers could now look for specific differences in the brains of people who report psychological distress, comparing the patterns of neuronal activation with control groups who do not report distress. Reviews of the neuroimaging research suggests, for example, that suicidal thoughts and behaviours are associated with abnormalities in the ventral pre-frontal cortex, an area of the brain known to be involved in cognitive control and self-reflection (Schmaal et al., 2020). These neuroscientific studies are part of the search for **biomarkers**—biological correlates of mental health problems. Researchers hope that identifying biomarkers for mental health problems will facilitate targeted interventions, either through medication or through techniques which directly target the brain, such as transcranial magnetic stimulation (Lefaucheur et al., 2020).

Transcranial magnetic stimulation (TMS) is a non-invasive procedure which uses an insulated coil placed over the scalp. This generates repetitive magnetic pulses (called rTMS) which induce changes in neuronal activation in the brain. A meta-analysis found that 29.3% of those who received rTMS for major depression showed a response (defined as 50% or greater reduction in scores on depression scales post-treatment) as compared to 10.4% of those who received a sham (placebo) version of rTMS (Berlim et al., 2014). Other reviews have found similar results.

rTMS is now used for severe depression and is recommended in the NICE guidelines. It is available on the NHS in a very few trusts, as well as through a host of private providers. Some enthusiasts suggest it could be used for a wider range of mental health problems, but here in the UK research is in the early days. A recent meta-analysis found that whilst it appeared to be an efficacious treatment for bipolar depression, there was an absence of adequately powered trials (Nguyen et al., 2020).

Not everyone is enthusiastic about the research focus on neuroscientific biomarkers and neurological interventions. Critics argue that a narrow focus on biomarkers ignores the way in which people's internal experiences are related to the events and circumstances of their lives (Borsboom et al., 2018). They argue that brains are, of course, involved with every aspect of mental health, but that identifying biomarkers may tell us little about a person's distress and how to alleviate it if we ignore psychological and social factors. They also point out that neuroscience research is extremely expensive, and that a lot of money is spent on looking for biological correlates of mental health problems, when many of the environmental causes (such as poverty and trauma) are well understood but there is little political will to address them.

9.2 Behavioural genetics

Behavioural genetics is an area where biology and psychology intersect. It has undergone dramatic changes in the last forty years. Research in this field looks at the associations between genes and complex behavioural traits, including mental health problems. I introduced behavioural genetics and the concept of heritability in Chapter 3. Here, I am going to give more of an overview of the field of behavioural genetics.

Twin and adoption studies

Up to the end of the twentieth century, work on the genetics of behaviour had to be done indirectly. Researchers ran twin and adoption studies, looking at the differences between those who were genetically related and those who weren't (adoption studies) and those who were genetically identical and those who only shared some of their genes (twin studies). These studies allowed researchers to look at the overall role of genes and environmental influences on behavioural traits. Twin and adoption studies established the importance of genetic influences on complex behavioural and developmental traits and some have continued to the next generation. One example is the 'children of TEDS' study which looks at the children born to the 20,000 twins who participated in the Twins Early Development Study (TEDS), a large-scale study which has been running since 1994 (Ahmadzadeh et al., 2019). These studies make it clear that genetic influences cannot be separated from the environment, and that genetic influences are significant across a wide range of behavioural traits and outcomes.

Monogenic theories and candidate genes

As technology developed, it became possible to scan the genome for specific genes. Interest moved beyond the question of whether something was heritable (since the answer was generally that almost all behavioural traits were to some degree), to asking *which* genes were involved, and exactly *how* they were involved. Research initially focused on the possibility of finding a single gene mutation which, it was thought, would explain the incidence of a mental health problem, something known as the **monogenic model**. It is now clear that this is not the case (Henriksen, Nordgaard, and Jansson, 2017).

The monogenic model suggested that a single **gene mutation** might be found which explained why some people developed severe mental health problems, the 'gene for schizophrenia' idea. This was disproved for schizophrenia early on when it became clear that the transmission patterns could not be explained by a single major gene (Tsuang, Bucher, and Fleming, 1982). Given the increasing evidence that the diagnostic categories of DSM and ICD do not reflect homogenous or distinct groups, it is unsurprising that no genes were identified which could predict who would get such a diagnosis. There are a very few disorders which are monogenic in origin, the most common of which is Huntington's disease, a progressive condition which affects movement, learning, and emotion, and which is caused by a single defective gene on chromosome 4.

On a molecular level, in the early 2000s behavioural genetic research focused on looking for **candidate genes**; specific genes which caused disruptions in particular processes. These studies were hypothesis driven. A diagnosis of schizophrenia has often been associated with differences in the dopamine pathway, so candidate genes would be selected which were known to be involved with this pathway. Studies were designed to look at whether people who had a diagnosis of schizophrenia also had differences (called **polymorphisms**) in those specific genes. There was hope that identifying the genes which were implicated would enable genetic therapies to be developed.

Thousands of candidate genes studies were carried out, but no 'faulty genes' were found. Some studies found associations with particular polymorphisms, but these have generally been small in size and have failed to replicate (Johnson et al., 2017).

Polygenic scores

In 2003, the Human Genome Project was completed and the field changed radically. 99.9% of the human genome was sequenced and it became possible to scan the entire genome of a person relatively cheaply. This made a new area of research possible: **genome-wide association studies (GWAS)**. These studies are not hypothesis driven in the same way as candidate gene studies. They do not look at what particular genes might be doing in the brain. They look at the association between a very high number of tiny DNA differences, called **single nucleotide polymorphisms** (**SNPs**, pronounced snips), and behavioural traits in a very large number of people. The most important thing about these SNPs is that they are all part of normal genetic variation. They are not 'faulty', and the studies do not suggest how they might be affecting a person's behaviour and experiences. Looking at the quantity of these tiny variants produces a '**polygenic risk score**'. It is now widely accepted that complex behavioural traits such as mental health problems are **polygenic traits** (Anderson et al., 2019).

A polygenic score is made up of multiple common genetic variants. Differences between those who develop mental health problems and those who do not are quantitative rather than qualitative (Plomin, 2018). This means they are about the *number* of SNPs, rather than exactly *which* SNPs. It appears that these polygenic risk scores are **transdiagnostic**, with some researchers suggesting that there is an underlying 'p' factor which summarises risk for all forms of common mental health problems, including those which are considered to be neurodevelopmental, such as ADHD and autism (Caspi et al., 2014). This has potentially very important implications for how we conceptualise mental health, indicating as it does that any biological risk factors may be general rather than specific. This is the opposite of what was expected at first, when researchers thought that genetic research would enable us to identify the different biological causes of different diagnostic categories. Instead, the genomic analysis research brings together diagnostic categories, indicating that any underlying genetic risk is shared (Selzam et al., 2018).

Polygenic risk scores do not inform us about mechanisms. 'Mechanisms' in this sense mean the way in which one variable (the **genotype**) causes a change in another variable (the **phenotype**). Phenotypes are the characteristics which we can observe about a person, and are almost always due to a combination of genes and environment. Even something as highly heritable as height is influenced by environment. When a population do not have enough to eat, children's growth will be affected and their height in adulthood will be less than it might have been. Many factors which are associated with mental health will be modifiable by behavioural or environmental effects rather than due to a direct biological effect, something which has important implications for healthcare and the development of interventions. For example, there is growing evidence that cannabis use may cause psychotic symptoms, but it is not well understood who is most at risk (Gage et al., 2016). Understanding these causal pathways is highly complex and this is likely to become more so as ever larger studies are completed.

Currently, polygenic risk scores are not very useful in clinical practice or research. They only account for a very small amount of the variance in diagnosable mental health problems—the best available predicts 7% of the variance for schizophrenia, and only 3% of the variance for depression. They have not led to the development of any new interventions. What these polygenic risk scores could mean for psychology is controversial. Some envision a world where polygenic risk scores predict more and more of the variance in behavioural traits. Genes do not alter over time—so in theory a person could have their polygenic scores calculated at birth, and would then know immediately what problems they might be at a higher risk of developing in later life. This could enable psychologists to move towards working on prevention and to the development of interventions tailored specifically to a person's genetic vulnerability. Some studies look at differential responses to interventions such as CBT, finding polygenic differences between those who improve and those who do not, raising the possibility in the future of targeting interventions based on someone's genotype (Keers et al., 2016). Critics argue that a genotype will never be a better predictor of how someone responds to therapy than interacting with and assessing the person themselves.

Some also warn of the possible negative consequences of families being told that their babies are at genetically high risk of developing serious mental health problems. They point out that since polygenic risk scores tell us nothing at all about the mechanisms, planning individualised prevention programmes will be impossible. It's possible that telling someone they are very likely to develop serious mental health problems later in life could become a self-fulfilling prophecy, making things worse rather than preventing future problems. Others argue that the power of polygenic scores might really emerge when combined with environmental factors—perhaps then we might become able to predict who could be vulnerable to specific environmental events, something which is called **differential susceptibility** (Belsky, 2013).

Recently, there has been a growing awareness that GWAS have been carried out on populations which are not representative of the whole world (being almost entirely based in the USA, Australia/New Zealand, or Europe, on populations with European ancestry), and that this means that findings are not generalisable to other populations (Duncan et al., 2019). A polygenic risk score which predicts something in a sample of European ancestry may not do the same in a sample with African or Asian ancestry. Results from a GWAS are not transferable and findings from one group cannot be expected to apply to another group. If you're interested in finding out more about GWAS and their strengths and limitations, I'd recommend *The Genetic Lottery, Why DNA Matters for Social Equality* by Kathryn Paige Harden (Harden, 2021).

Gene–environment interactions

Another reason to be cautious about the power of new genetic techniques to predict our futures is just how complex the interactions are. Perhaps the most surprising finding in behavioural genetic research is that many aspects of the environment are heritable. How much TV children watch has been shown to be heritable (Plomin et al., 1990), as is getting married or divorced (Jerskey et al., 2010). This makes sense if you consider that people are always active participants in their environment. People literally shape their environment, at least partly because of their genetic make-up. Then, of course, they will have different experiences to other people who have created different environments for themselves, and these different experiences will affect how their lives develop.

These are called **gene–environment interactions** and there is now extensive research into the different ways in which these can occur (Musci et al., 2019).

These findings have transformed the way we think about nature and nurture, because it is clear that the two can never be separated. Our genetic heritage affects our experience of our environment and the way in which we interact with it, and the environment affects how our genes express themselves.

Why is this relevant to mental health? Because it influences the way in which we think about the heritability of mental health problems. Let's take one example. Being of Black Caribbean ethnicity in the UK is associated with a higher risk of developing psychosis (Radua et al., 2018). Ethnicity and skin colour are genetic. For this reason, there will be an association between the genes for darker skin and psychosis in a sample of people from the UK. However, being of Black Caribbean ethnicity in the UK is also associated with an increased risk of experiencing racial discrimination, as well as a higher chance of living in poverty as a child. These things are associated with a higher risk of developing psychosis. Therefore, a link which is apparently biological (between genes and psychosis) could be caused by structural differences in the environment. The association does not mean that the genes which are responsible for skin colour directly cause neurological or psychiatric differences between people. In an environment without racial discrimination or income inequality, it is highly probable that the association between darker skin and psychosis would disappear. Yet a simplistic understanding of genetics could lead to the conclusion that the relationship between those genes and the risk of psychosis means that those genes directly cause psychosis, when this is not the case.

One clear and consistent finding from the biological research is that the diagnostic categories in DSM and ICD are not mirrored by simple biological differences. Researchers have become increasingly frustrated with the limitations of the psychiatric diagnostic system, with some arguing that it is holding back scientific progress. The next section of this chapter outlines way in which researchers and clinicians are trying to address and overcome these limitations.

9.3 Transdiagnostic classification systems

Concerns about the way in which the diagnostic system is limiting progress come both from those who are engaged in biological research, and those whose focus is clinical. Researchers increasingly found that the diagnoses they were researching did not correspond to biological categories, calling many findings into question. If a research study compares those with a diagnosis of autism (for example) with those who do not receive a diagnosis, then there is an inherent assumption that the diagnosis represents something meaningful which is shared by all those in the diagnosed group (and not by those in the undiagnosed group). There is little evidence for this. Differences within the same category are a feature of the diagnostic system, since a diagnosis is given when a person has met a specified number of a list of criteria, the specific content of which can vary greatly. The assumption of the diagnostic system is that these varied presentations all reflect a similar underlying problem or disorder. If this isn't true and all the people with a diagnosis of schizophrenia (for example) *don't* share a core issue, then constructing and testing hypotheses which assume that they make up a homogenous group isn't going to lead anywhere helpful.

Clinicians come at this from a different angle. Whilst some psychological therapies (like CBT) have manuals which are developed along diagnostic lines, in everyday clinical practice therapists adapt their treatment plan to the person in front on them. It makes no sense to spend hours of therapy addressing a problem that a person doesn't have, just because it's in the treatment manual for the diagnosis which they have received. It's also possible for a person to have several experiences which are categorised as symptoms of different mental health problems, meaning that they are highly distressed but don't fit criteria for any single diagnosis. This means that there is a disconnect between the research—which mostly focuses on testing the efficacy of a particular therapy with a group of people with the same diagnosis (and usually only one diagnosis)—and routine clinical practice, in which many people have several diagnoses or (particularly in the UK and other countries where access to healthcare is not dependent on a diagnosis) none at all.

These frustrations have led to a growing clinical and research interest in developing transdiagnostic approaches to categorising and treating mental health problems. These interests come from different starting points, and thus they have come up with very different solutions. The term 'transdiagnostic' simply means something that is used across diagnostic categories. However, new dimensional models of mental health are being developed which involve rethinking the categories entirely, instead focusing on how particular experiences vary across the population. Behavioural genetic research has increasingly pointed towards a genetic transdiagnostic risk factor 'p' (or psychopathology) rather than specific genes being associated with different diagnostic categories (Caspi et al., 2014). Another recent arrival is the complex network model of mental health (Fried, 2022). This uses computational modelling to look at how different symptoms and experiences interact.

There are currently two main different transdiagnostic dimensional models of mental health in development, RDoC and HiToP. These have been developed as alternative classification systems to DSM and ICD. Moving away from a categorical diagnostic system is not the same as rejecting the biomedical model. Whilst the psychiatric diagnostic system is built on a biomedical model, it is only one way of applying the medical model to distress. It's possible to think that distressing experiences and unusual behaviour are still best conceptualised as medical disorders, but that the diagnostic system does a poor job of classifying these disorders and that another method of categorisation would be better.

Research Domain Criteria (RDoC)

The scientists behind RDoC were frustrated with the lack of biological correlates for mental health diagnoses because this limited their research. They did not think that this meant that mental health was not biologically determined. Instead, they thought this was due to the inadequacies of a diagnostic system which was based on behaviour and experiences, rather than on biological processes. Current diagnostic systems start with observing behaviour and categorises that. RDoC turned the system around, starting from neurobiology rather than from behaviour. The key idea is that the same neurobiological factor might result in a range of different behaviours or emotional reactions. In the present diagnostic system these would be placed in different categories, thus limiting the ability of researchers to identify the underlying neurobiological factors.

RDoC assumes that by linking biology and behaviour, valid and reliable phenotypes will be constructed from the 'bottom up'. They predict that this will enable targeted or precision treatments to be developed (Insel et al., 2010). This model was developed by, among others, Thomas Insel, the ex-director of the

National Institute for Mental Health (NIMH) in the USA, a leading organisation which funds research into mental health.

RDoC is not intended as a clinical alternative to diagnosis, but as a framework for research. As an approach, it is firmly rooted in the biomedical model of understanding mental health, perhaps even more so than the traditional diagnostic approach. The core principle of RDoC is that mental health problems are due to dysfunctions in neural circuitry and that any effective, scientific classification system should start there (Lilienfeld and Treadway, 2016). RDoC has seven key pillars, one of which is that dimensionality (rather than discrete categories) should always be assumed, both between different mental health problems and between those who have mental health problems and those who do not (Morris et al., 2022). You can find out more about RDoC on the NIMH website.

Hierarchical Taxonomy of Psychopathology (HiTOP)

RDoC focuses on basic biological processes. Clinical researchers felt that this meant that clinical phenomena were not adequately addressed and that another framework was needed to classify clinical constructs. They set out to develop a transdiagnostic dimensional model of mental health starting at the level of experiences and behaviour (Kotov et al., 2017). They looked for higher-order dimensions which transcended diagnoses.

This framework describes higher-order 'spectra' of experiences. These spectra include **internalising**, **thought disorder**, disinhibited **externalising**, antagonistic externalising, and detachment. 'Super-spectra' are above those, and are made up of 'emotional dysfunction', 'externalising' and 'thought disorder'. Research has found that that all these spectra are correlated with each other, and thus suggests the presence above the super-spectra of a higher order 'p' (for psychopathology) factor. This 'p' factor is supported by the genetic research (Caspi et al., 2014). The suggestion is that this single general factor predicts the propensity of a person to develop a wide range of problems, across diagnostic categories.

Figure 9.1 outlines this framework.

Like RDoC, HiToP is intended for research use rather than as a clinical tool.

Accepting that mental health is best understood in a dimensional rather than categorical way has profound

Figure 9.1 HiToP (From Kotov et al., 2017).

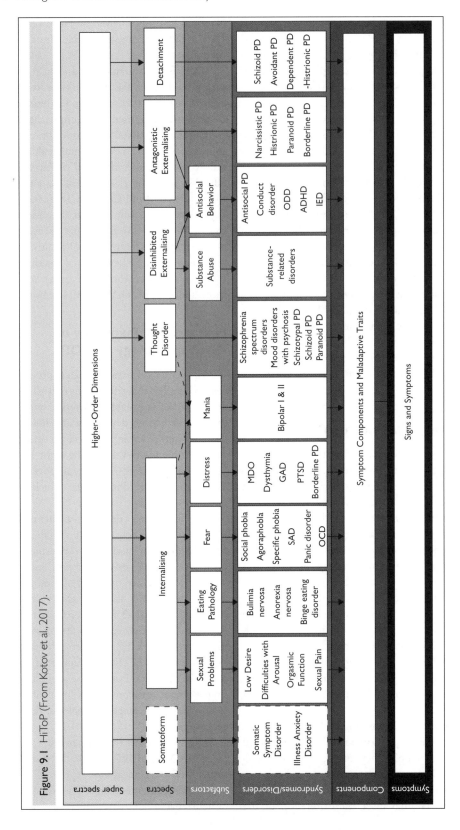

IN THE REAL WORLD 9.1

Eye Movement Desensitisation and Reprocessing (EMDR) therapy is a form of psychological therapy which helps people come to terms with traumatic events from their past. After a trauma, people have a range of different responses. The PTSD diagnostic criteria only recognise some of these responses. Other responses are categorised differently, and these people will get a different diagnosis.

EMDR is recommended by NICE for PTSD and most of the evidence is with people who have received this diagnosis. In order to get a diagnosis of PTSD, one must have been exposed to a 'Criterion A' event—an event which involves death, threatened death, actual or threatened serious injury, or actual or threatened sexual violence. Many NHS services restrict access to EMDR to people who have a diagnosis of PTSD.

People find all sorts of experiences traumatic which do not come under 'Criterion A'. In particular, emotional neglect or verbal abuse in childhood, bullying at school, or abandonment by a parent can cause ongoing distress in a very similar way to a Criterion A event. From a psychological perspective, the responses could be treated in the same way. However, because the evidence base is diagnosis focused, those who have not experienced a Criterion A event may not be allowed access to EMDR or other forms of trauma-focused therapy.

If, instead, difficulties with traumatic memories were seen as a transdiagnostic symptom which can exist in those with and without a PTSD diagnosis, then it would make sense to offer EMDR or another trauma-focused therapy to anyone who had these problems, rather than restrict it to those who have a diagnosis of PTSD. But the evidence base is based on diagnosis, and thus clinical practice is also limited by those diagnostic categories.

implications for the evidence base and how it is used. The NICE guidelines are based on categories. NICE recommends particular treatments for some diagnostic categories and not others, because this is the way the research has been done. The example in the Box 9.1, of EMDR therapy, describes how this can restrict the treatment that people are offered.

Complex systems

Many of the models used by psychiatrists and psychologists to understand mental health aspire to simplicity. Researchers and clinicians seek to identify the underlying cause of a person's problems, whether they think about that in biological, social, or psychological terms. A complex systems approach turns this around and starts with the assumption of complexity. It suggests that mental health problems arrive from an interacting set of elements which include the biological, psychological, and social, connected together in a complex web of interactions (Fried and Robinaugh, 2020). From these systems, various presentations emerge which we may then see as a diagnostic category, but these categories are constructed or manufactured rather than natural categories.

The implication of this is that we cannot hope to understand mental health by only investigating single components or by separately focusing on different areas. We need to understand individual components *and* the complex interactions between them. **Complex systems modelling** is used by scientists to understand phenomena such as climate change where it can enable researchers to identify early warning signs such as the environmental changes which take place just before ecological collapse occurs. Complex systems researchers suggest that their modelling could enable us to identify these early warning signs for mental health problems, meaning that we could intervene before someone is in a state of crisis. Eiko Fried, a complex system scientist in the Netherlands, is currently working on developing a personalised early warning system for depression which people could have available on their smartphone, using network models. He suggests that embracing complexity means that we can bring in insights from fields such as geophysics and ecology, which will enable us to think about mental health in new ways (Fried, 2022).

All of these transdiagnostic models are currently conceptual rather than applied. Critics point out that they have as yet made little difference to what actually happens in mental health clinics across the world, and it isn't clear when that will change. Complexity and dimensionality are both major shifts in thinking, and it isn't obvious how they could be easily matched with the interventions currently available—if a drug is licensed for use with depression, for example, what happens if the category of depression is dropped in favour of a more complex, non-categorical way of thinking about mental health? What is it now licensed for? The status quo is that treatments have been developed along diagnostic lines and research is usually done on this basis.

There is an increasing cultural gap between the changing scientific understanding of mental health and how the general population understands it. As scientists move towards transdiagnostic and dimensional frameworks, specific diagnostic categories are important to a large number of people who feel they are part of their identity. Online discourse often assumes that there is an underlying biological and psychological difference shared by all those with a particular diagnosis (or even, all those who identify with a diagnosis) and that those diagnoses are clear and distinct categories. These beliefs are not borne out by the research but may be strongly held by members of an online community which defines itself by a diagnostic category. This raises the interesting question of who leads change—if clinicians and researchers move towards dimensional ways of understanding mental health, but the population at large identify with discrete categories and diagnostic labels, communication between the two may become increasingly difficult.

9.4 Transdiagnostic interventions

Alongside these new models of mental health, transdiagnostic interventions are being developed (Newby et al., 2015). These therapies focus on processes rather than diagnosis. Whereas a diagnosis-specific intervention might be designed for depression, a transdiagnostic intervention might start with a problem experienced by many people (some of whom may have diagnoses of depression but others of whom will not), such as repetitive thinking or self-criticism. These interventions have been developed both for use by individual therapists and computerised therapy programmes. CBT programmes have been developed where a therapist chooses specific modules to target

the problems that a person is bringing, and these have been found to be as effective as diagnosis-based interventions (Newby et al., 2017).

Third-wave CBT therapies, such as **Acceptance and Commitment Therapy (ACT)** target transdiagnostic processes, for example the tendency some people have towards 'experiential avoidance' where people make choices based on trying to avoid emotional distress, rather than because the choice itself has value for them. People who engage in experiential avoidance may have a range of diagnoses or no diagnosis at all. ACT takes a values-based approach, helping people identify what matters most to them and work out ways to do more of the things they value.

Critics say that a transdiagnostic approach is not new—early pioneers of psychological approaches such as Freud and Rogers saw their role as working with whatever a person brought, regardless of whether it fitted into a diagnostic category or not. Nevertheless, in recent years diagnostic categories have had a major influence in how health systems are organised and how research is carried out, and therefore the move to transdiagnostic intervention represents a significant shift.

Chapter Summary

- Neurobiological and genetic research does not support the existence of distinct diagnostic categories at a biological level.
- Researchers are moving to dimensional models as an alternative.
- A complex systems approach is another alternative suggested by researchers.
- In clinical practice, new transdiagnostic models are being developed with promising results.

? QUESTIONS

1. Are advances in neuroscience and behavioural genetics likely to mean that psychologists of the future will be working on prevention and prediction rather than intervention? Why or why not?
2. Are researchers likely to find a gene for schizophrenia or autism if the studies are large enough? Why or why not?
3. 'The environment is heritable'. What does this mean? Why is it important when understanding behavioural genetics?
4. Why is there so much research interest in developing a transdiagnostic model of mental health? What are the challenges in using transdiagnostic models in clinical practice?

FURTHER READING

Fried, E. (2022). Studying mental health problems as systems, not syndromes. *Current Directions in Psychological Science*, 31(6). doi:10.1177/09637214221114089

This paper explains the complex systems approach to understanding mental health problems.

Harden, K.P. (2021). *The Genetic Lottery: Why DNA Matters for Social Equality*. Princeton, NJ: Princeton University Press.

This book by a psychologist and behavioural geneticist gives a good overview of the way in which genetic research has evolved, and argues that we must acknowledge human genetic variation in order to create a more equal society.

Hayes, S., with Smith, S. (2005). *Get Out of Your Mind and Into Your Life: The New Acceptance and Commitment Therapy*. Oakland, CA: New Harbinger.

A self-help book which makes the ideas of acceptance and commitment therapy (ACT) accessible to a wider audience. This is an example of a transdiagnostic therapy.

REFERENCES

Ahmadzadeh, Y., Eley, T., Plomin, R., Dale, P., Lester, K., Oliver, B., … McAdams, T. (2019). Children of the Twins Early Development Study (CoTEDS): A children-of-twins study. *Twin Research and Human Genetics*, 22(6), 514–522. doi:10.1017/thg.2019.61

Anderson, J., Shade, J., DiBlasi, E., Shabalin, A., and Dochery, A. (2019). Polygenic risk scoring and prediction of mental health outcomes. *Current Opinion in Psychology*, 27, 77–81.

Belsky, J. (2013). Differential susceptibility to environmental influences. *International Journal of Child Care and Education Policy*, 7, 15–31. doi:10.1007/2288-6729-7-2-15

Berlim, M.T., van den Eynde, F., Tovar-Perdomo, S., and Daskalakis, Z.J. (2014). Response, remission and drop-out rates following high-frequency repetitive transcranial magnetic stimulation (rTMS) for treating major depression: A systematic review and meta-analysis of randomized, double-blind and sham-controlled trials. *Psychological Medicine*, 44(2), 225–239. doi:10.1017/S0033291713000512. Epub 2013 Mar 18. PMID: 23507264.

Borsboom, D., Cramer, A., and Kalis, A. (2018). Brain disorders? Not really: Why network structures block reductionism in psychopathology research. *Behavioral and Brain Sciences*, 42, E2. doi:10.1017/S0140525X17002266

Caspi, A., Houts, R.M., Belsky, D.W., Goldman-Mellor, S.J., Harrington, H., Israel, S., Meier, M.H., Ramrakha, S., Shalev, I., Poulton, R., and Moffitt, T.E. (2014). The p Factor: One general psychopathology factor in the structure of psychiatric disorders? *Clinical Psychological Science: A Journal of the Association for Psychological Science*, 2(2), 119–137. doi:10.1177/2167702613497473

Duncan, L., Shen, H., Gelaye, B., Meijsen, J., Ressler, K., Feldman, M., Peterson, R., and Domingue, B. (2019). Analysis of polygenic risk score usage and performance in diverse human populations. *Nature Communications*, 10, 3328.

Fitzgerald, M. (2015). Do psychiatry and neurology need a close partnership or a merger? *BJPsych Bulletin*, 39(3), 105–107. doi:10.1192/pb.bp.113.046227

Fried, E. (2022). Studying mental health problems as systems, not syndromes. *Current Directions in Psychological Science*, 31(6). doi:10.1177/09637214221114089

Fried, E., and Robinaugh, D.J. (2020). Systems all the way down: Embracing complexity in mental health research. *BMC Medicine*, 18(1), 205. doi:10.1186/s12916-020-01668-w

Gage, S.H., Hickman, M., and Zammit, S. (2016). Association between cannabis and psychosis: Epidemiologic evidence. *Biological Psychiatry*, 79(7), 549–556. doi:10.1016/j.biopsych.2015.08.001. Epub 2015 Aug 12. PMID: 26386480.

Harden, K.P. (2021). *The Genetic Lottery: Why DNA Matters for Social Equality*. Princeton, NJ: Princeton University Press.

Henriksen, M.G., Nordgaard, J., and Jansson, L.B. (2017). Genetics of schizophrenia: Overview of methods, findings and limitations. *Frontiers of Human Neuroscience*, 11,322. doi:10.3389/fnhum.2017.00322. PMID: 28690503; PMCID: PMC5480258.

Insel, T., Cuthbert, B., Garvey, M., Heinssen, R., Pine, D.S., Quinn, K., Sanislow, C., and Wang, P. (2010). Research Domain Criteria (RDoC): Toward a new classification framework for research on mental disorders. *American Journal of Psychiatry*, 167(7), 748–751.

Jerskey, B., Panizzon, M., Jacobson, K., Neale, M., et al. (2010). Marriage and divorce: A genetic perspective. *Personality and Individual Differences*, 49(5), 473–479.

Johnson, E.C., Border, R., Melroy-Greif, W.E., de Leeuw, C.A., Ehringer, M.A., and Keller, M.C. (2017). No evidence that schizophrenia candidate genes are more associated with schizophrenia than noncandidate genes. *Biological Psychiatry*, 82(10), 702–708. doi:10.1016/j.biopsych.2017.06.033

Keers, R., Coleman, J., Lester, K., Roberts, S., Breen, G., Thastum, M., Bögels, S., Schneider, S., Heiervang, E., Meiser-Stedman, R., Nauta, M., Creswell, C., Thirlwall, K., Rapee, R.M., Hudson, J.L., Lewis, C., Plomin, R., and Eley, T.C. (2016). A genome-wide test of the differential susceptibility hypothesis reveals a genetic predictor of differential response to psychological treatments for child anxiety disorders. *Psychotherapy and Psychosomatics*, 85, 146–158. doi:10.1159/000444023

Kotov, R., Krueger, R., Watson, D., and 17 other authors (2017). The Hierarchical Taxonomy of Psychopathology (HiTOP): A dimensional alternative to traditional nosologies. *Journal of Abnormal Psychology*, 126(4), 454–477.

Lefaucheur, J., Aleman, A., Baeken, C., Benninger, D.H., Brunelin, J., Di Lazzaro, V., Filipović, S.R., Grefkes, C., Hasan, A., Hummel, F.C., Jääskeläinen, S.K., Langguth, B., Leocani, L., Londero, A., Nardone, R., Nguyen, J.-P., Nyffeler, T., Oliveira-Maia, A.J., Oliviero, A., Padberg, F., Palm, U., Paulus, W., Poulet, E., Quartarone, A., Rachid, F., Rektorová, I., Rossi, S., Sahlsten, H., Schecklmann, M., Szekely, D., and Ziemann, U. (2020). Evidence-based guidelines on the therapeutic use of repetitive transcranial magnetic stimulation (rTMS): An update (2014–2018). *Clinical Neurophysiology*, 131(2), 474–528.

Lilienfeld, S.O., and Treadway, M.T. (2016). Clashing diagnostic approaches: DSM-ICD versus RDoC. *Annual Review of Clinical Psychology*, 12, 435–463. doi:10.1146/annurev-clinpsy-021815-093122

Morris, S.E., Sanislow, C.A., Pacheco, J., et al. (2022). Revisiting the seven pillars of RDoC. *BMC Medicine*, 20, 220. doi:10.1186/s12916-022-02414-0

Musci, R.J., Augustinavicius, J.L., and Volk, H. (2019). Gene–environment interactions in psychiatry: Recent evidence and clinical implications. *Current Psychiatry Reports*, 21, 81. doi:10.1007/s11920-019-1065-5

Newby, J.M., McKinnon, A., Kuyken, W., Gilbody, S., and Dalgleish, T. (2015). Systematic review and meta-analysis of transdiagnostic psychological treatments for anxiety and depressive disorders in adulthood. *Clinical Psychology Review*, 40, 91–110. doi:10.1016/j.cpr.2015.06.002. Epub 6 June 2015. PMID: 26094079.

Newby, J.M., Mewton, L., and Andrews, G. (2017). Transdiagnostic versus disorder-specific internet-delivered cognitive behaviour therapy for anxiety and depression in primary care. *Journal of Anxiety Disorders*, 46, 25–34. doi:10.1016/j.janxdis.2016.06.002. Epub 23 June 2016. PMID: 27396841.

Nguyen, T.D., Hieronymus, F., Lorentzen, R., McGirr, A., and Østergaard, S.D. (2020). The efficacy of repetitive transcranial magnetic stimulation (rTMS) for bipolar depression: A systematic review and meta-analysis. *Journal of Affective Disorders*, 279, 250–255. doi:10.1016/j.jad.2020.10.013

Pies, R. (2005). Why psychiatry and neurology cannot simply merge. *The Journal of Neuropsychiatry and Clinical Neurosciences*, 17(3), 304–309.

Plomin, R., Corley, R., DeFries, J.C., and Fulker, D.W. (1990). Individual differences in television viewing in early childhood: nature as well as nurture. *Psychological Science*, 1(6), 371–377.

Plomin, R. (2018). *Blueprint: How DNA Makes Us Who We Are.* London: Allen Lane.

Radua, J., Ramella-Cravaro, V., Ioannidis, J.P.A., Reichenberg, A., Phiphopthatsanee, N., Amir, T., Yenn Thoo, H., Oliver, D., Davies, C., Morgan, C., McGuire, P., Murray, R.M. and Fusar-Poli, P. (2018). What causes psychosis? An umbrella review of risk and protective factors. *World Psychiatry*, 17, 49–66. doi:10.1002/wps.20490

Schmaal, L., van Harmelen, A.L., Chatzi, V., et al. (2020). Imaging suicidal thoughts and behaviors: A comprehensive review of 2 decades of neuroimaging studies. *Molecular Psychiatry*, 25, 408–427. doi:10.1038/s41380-019-0587-x

Selzam, S., Coleman, J.R.I., Caspi, A., Moffitt, T.E., and Plomin, R. (2018). A polygenic p factor for major psychiatric disorders. *Translational Psychiatry*, 8(1), 205. doi:10.1038/s41398-018-0217-4. PMID: 30279410; PMCID: PMC6168558.

Tsuang, M.T., Bucher, K.D., and Fleming, J.A. (1982). Testing the monogenic theory of schizophrenia: An application of segregation analysis to blind family study data. *British Journal of Psychiatry*, 140, 595–599. doi:10.1192/bjp.140.6.595. PMID: 7104548.

Glossary

Abnormal Deviating from what is typical or normal.

Acceptance and Commitment Therapy (ACT) A form of psychological therapy which focuses on acceptance of difficult thoughts and feelings rather than on trying to change them.

Active interactions Interactions which the individual shapes by choosing features of their environment.

Addiction A physical or psychological inability to stop using a substance or doing an activity, even though it causes physical and psychological harm.

Adverse childhood experiences (ACEs) Stressful events occurring in childhood which may be chronic and ongoing. There is an extensive field of research into the impact of ACEs on later life.

Adversity Serious or continuous difficult or challenging events which happen in a person's life.

Anorexia nervosa A type of eating disorder where the person severely restricts their food intake, sometimes to the point where their life is put at risk.

Anti-depressants Drugs used to treat depression.

Anti-psychotics Drugs used with people experiencing psychosis. First generation anti-psychotics include chlorpromazine and haloperidol. Second generation (or atypical) anti-psychotics include olanzapine, risperidone, and quetiapine.

Anxiety An emotional reaction characterised by feelings of tension and worried thoughts. It may also include physiological reactions such as the heart beating fast or sweaty palms.

Applied psychologists People who have completed an undergraduate degree in psychology, followed by a postgraduate degree in using applied psychology with different groups of people. This can include clinical psychologists, counselling psychologists, occupational psychologists, forensic psychologists, educational psychologists, and more.

Atypical Statistically unusual.

Autism A lifelong diagnosis given to children and increasingly adults who demonstrate differences in social interaction, communication, and repetitive behaviour. It is considered to be a 'neurodevelopmental disorder' according to DSM.

Behavioural activation A therapeutic approach in which therapists help clients engage in more valued activities.

Behavioural genetics The study of the way in which genetic variation affects behavioural and psychological traits. This includes mental health, cognitive abilities, and personality.

Behaviourism A theory of learning which sees behaviour as being a response to environmental stimuli and therefore modifiable by altering the contingencies. Behaviourism is concerned with what can be observed.

Binge-eating disorder A diagnosis given to those who eat large quantities of food in a short period of time and feel that they are unable to stop.

Biomarkers A naturally occurring biological characteristic by which a particular process can be identified.

Biomedical model A model which suggests that mental health problems are brain disorders or diseases, and which sees mental health as directly analogous to physical health. This is the dominant model of mental health in the Western world and has been so for several decades. The psychiatric diagnostic system is based on the assumptions of the biomedical model but is not the only way that the biomedical model can be expressed.

Biopsychosocial model A model of health (all health, not just mental health) conceptualised by Engel (1977). He suggested that the psychological and social factors should be considered alongside biological factors when seeking to understand (and treat) a person's problems.

Bipolar disorder A diagnosis which was formerly called manic-depressive illness or manic depression. This describes unusual shifts in a person's energy levels and mood, sometimes from very high (the 'mania' phase) to very low (depression). These episodes can last days or longer.

Black Lives Matter (BLM) a decentralised social and political movement which started in 2013 following the acquittal of a police officer who shot dead African-American teenager, Trayvon Martin. BLM advocates for non-violent civil disobedience in protest against police brutality and racially motivated violence against black people.

Blind (in the context of a clinical trial) Clinical trial in which the participants do not know if they are receiving an actual drug or a placebo.

Brain–gut axis A bidirectional communication network linking the central nervous system with the enteric nervous system. The enteric nervous system governs the function of the gastrointestinal tract. This means that the brain can influence intestinal function but there are also indications that the gut microbiome can produce neuroactive substances and may affect brain functioning.

Bulimia nervosa An eating disorders diagnosis in which a person eats large quantities of food and then uses ways such as vomiting and laxatives to prevent weight gain.

Candidate gene approach Research which focuses on looking for genetic differences in pre-determined genes of interest.

Case-control study A research design which compares two groups of people who are matched in as many ways as possible, differing only in that one group have a diagnosis of the condition under study. Members of the group who have a diagnosis are considered 'cases' whilst the 'control' group should be very similar, except for the absence of the diagnosis.

Categories Separate and distinct groups

Categorise Dividing experiences up into separate groups or disorders which are seen as separate.

Causality A type of relationship between two variables. Establishing causality means to demonstrate that change in the independent variable reliably leads to change in the dependent variable and that other factors are not responsible for this relationship.

Chemical imbalance theory The idea that mental health problems are caused by a chemical imbalance in the brain which drugs act to correct.

Client An individual who is using the professional advice or services of another.

Cognitive behaviour therapy (CBT) Psychological therapy which focuses on the way that people think and behave, particularly the meaning they ascribe to events. Originally created by Aaron Beck in the 1960s.

Cognitive conceptualisation (or case conceptualisation) The formulation framework in CBT used for understanding a person's problems. It relates a person's thoughts, feelings and behaviour to their experiences.

Cognitive models Theories which seek to explain and predict a person's internal experience in terms of their thoughts, feelings, behaviour, and physiological responses.

Cohort studies Research studies where the same group of people (the cohort) are followed over time, sometimes for decades.

Community psychology Community psychology studies individuals within their context and seeks to improve community functioning in order to improve wellbeing.

Complex systems approach (in mental health): An approach which suggests that mental health problems can be conceptualised with multi-factorial computer models of mutually reinforcing symptoms and experiences.

Complex systems modelling A scientific framework which investigates how the relationship between a system's parts give rise to phenomena, and how the system interacts with the environment around it. It uses mathematical, statistical, and computational techniques to generate insight into how complicated systems function. It is widely used including in ecology, neuroscience, communication systems, and social and economic organisations.

Conversion therapy A now discredited form of therapy which attempts to change someone's sexual orientation through aversive behavioural techniques.

Coping mechanism A psychological strategy or adaptation which a person develops in order to manage their distress. This can be conscious or unconscious.

Core deficit A model or hypothesis which tries to explain all the different behavioural, cognitive, and neurobiological phenomena seen by individuals within a particular diagnostic category by finding a single shared underlying impairment.

Counselling Talking therapy which is generally shorter-term and less structured than psychotherapy. It is usually focused on reflection and insight rather than symptom reduction.

Culture-bound syndrome A particular set of behaviours and experiences which is seen only in a specific culture and which is recognised in that culture as unusual.

Dementia A general term for the impaired ability to remember, think, or make decisions which has an impact on the person's ability to do everyday activities. It is usually associated with aging but does not affect all older adults.

Dependent variable The variable being tested in an experiment, which may be affected by the independent variable (e.g. scores on a depression questionnaire, diagnosis of mental health problems).

Depersonalised When a person is treated as if they have no humanity or individuality.

Depression A diagnostic category which is characterised by persistent sadness and a loss of interest in activities which were previously enjoyable. This term is also used colloquially to mean low mood.

Deterministic The idea that if something happens, something else will inevitably follow. For example, this could mean that a particular genetic mutation would always lead to a person developing depression, no matter what the other circumstances.

Developmental task A task that arises in a certain period of life. Frequently, if a person does not achieve a developmental task, this will mean they cannot perform the tasks associated with the next stage of life.

Diagnosis Identifying an illness or disorder by comparing the person's presentation with a list of symptoms or by carrying out a diagnostic test. In mental health this is formally done with a diagnostic manual which lists the criteria for each diagnosis. There are currently no biological diagnostic tests for the mental health problems listed in the manuals, although biological tests may be done in order to exclude physical health conditions.

Diagnostic manuals Books produced at regular intervals by the American Psychiatric Association (DSM) and the World Health Organization (ICD) which define 'mental disorders' using lists of symptoms.

Diagnostic and Statistical Manual of Mental Disorders (DSM) Currently in its fifth edition, a system for diagnosis published by the American Psychiatric Association which lists symptoms for at least 157 different 'mental disorders'.

Diathesis Greek word meaning predisposition or vulnerability.

Differential susceptibility The idea that people with particular genotypes respond in a different way to environmental factors, which affects their outcome.

Dimension A continuum on which a person can have various levels of a characteristic, rather than being seen as either having a disorder or not.

Dimensional framework An approach to mental health which focuses on how different experiences vary on a continuum across the whole population, rather than on assigning people to categories.

Disease mongering The practice of widening the diagnostic boundaries and promoting public awareness in order to expand the market for treatment.

Disease-centred model The theory that drugs used in mental health are curing a biological disorder.

Disordered Not working in a way which is considered to be normal and healthy.

Distress The experience of mental or physical suffering, such as extreme anxiety, pain, or sadness.

Dopamine A neurotransmitter involved in several different pathways in the brain, in particular a pathway associated with reward-motivated behaviour.

Dose-response relationship A relationship between two variables where the quantity of the independent variable directly affects the quantity of the dependent variable.

Double-blind clinical trial Clinical trial in which neither the participants nor the researchers know who is receiving active treatment and who is getting the placebo until the study is finished. In a triple-blind trial, the researcher is also kept ignorant of who is in which group.

Down Syndrome (Trisomy 21) A condition when a child is born with an extra copy of chromosome 21. This can affect both a person's intellectual ability and physical growth, and cause developmental and health issues.

Drug-centred model The theory that drugs have an effect on how people think and feel but that this does not mean they are curing a disease.

Ecologically valid The extent to which the findings of a research study can be generalised to people in real-life settings. Studies which are well designed may still have poor ecological validity. This can be a particular problem for experimental or laboratory studies in psychology.

Effectiveness How well an intervention performs in the real world.

Efficacy The performance of an intervention under ideal and controlled conditions.

Equitable Dealing fairly with all concerned.

Evidence-based medicine Medical practice which is based on integrating three components: the best scientific research, individual clinical expertise, and the patient's preferences.

Evocative interactions Interactions where the individual evokes a response in others by their behaviour.

Experimental studies (in psychology) A research design which applies experimental research methods to human behaviour. Experimental design involves manipulating one variable (called the independent variable) in order to see if it causes changes in another variable (called the dependent variable).

Explanatory power The ability of a theory to explain the concept which it describes. For example, if a diagnosis has explanatory power, it should explain *why* this person is having these problems, and therefore provide indications of what could be done to help.

Externalising symptoms Behaviours which are outwardly expressed such as aggression, impulsivity, and anti-social behaviour.

Eye Movement Desensitisation and Reprocessing (EMDR) A psychological therapy used to treat the symptoms of trauma.

Formal diagnosis Diagnosis made by a qualified professional according to the strict criteria outlined in a diagnostic manual. This may be done using a structured interview.

Formulation A collaborative effort between a psychologist and an individual to summarise difficulties, make sense of them, and explain why they may be happening.

Functional magnetic resonance imaging (fMRI) A type of brain scan which measures small changes in blood flow in the brain and which can therefore look at brain activity in living people.

Gaming disorder A recent diagnostic category defined by the WHO as 'a pattern of persistent or recurrent gaming behaviour so severe that it takes precedence over other life interests'.

Gender dysphoria Diagnosis which describes the distress or unease felt when a person feels that their identity is at odds with their biological sex.

Gene mutation A change in the DNA sequence of an organism.

Gene–environment interactions The interplay of genes and genomic function with the physical and social environment. These interactions influence the way in which phenotypes are expressed.

Genome-wide association studies (GWAS) Large-scale research studies which scan the entire genome looking for multiple common genetic variations which are associated with different characteristics.

Genotype The set of genes of an individual.

Hallucinations The experience of perceiving objects, events, or sensory experience which do not have an external source. For example, an auditory hallucination could include hearing voices when no one is there.

Heritability The proportion of variation which is accounted for by inherited rather than environmental factors. Heritability is often misunderstood. It is a population-level concept, not an individual one. It is a measure of how well differences between people are accounted for by differences in their genes. It is not a measure of how much of a person's individual characteristics are accounted for by their genes.

Heritable Capable of being inherited.

HIC Higher income country such as the UK and USA.

Hierarchy of evidence A hierarchical model used to rank the relative strength of results obtained from different scientific research methods.

Humanistic psychology A movement in psychology which focuses on facilitating optimal human development rather than treating psychopathology. Also called person-centred psychology.

Hypervigilant Being highly alert to potential threat or danger.

International Classification of Disorders (ICD) Currently in its eleventh edition, it is the global system for diagnosis, an alternative to DSM-5. Published by the World Health Organization. ICD includes physical diseases alongside mental health problems, unlike DSM.

Ideological Based on or relating to a system of principles and beliefs, with the implication that it is not open to scientific or other alternatives.

Incidence The number of new cases which arise within a specific time period.

Independent variable The variable which either changes on its own (e.g. age, or time) or because a researcher changes it (e.g. by assigning groups to different types of intervention).

Informal diagnosis Diagnosis used in practice or for communication between professionals without a formal assessment having been made. This sometimes might be called a 'working diagnosis'. Informal diagnoses are given by a wide range of people and may be based on limited knowledge of the person and their situation.

Insight Having an accurate understanding or appraisal of a situation.

Internalising symptoms Experiences of distress which are directed inwards such as anxiety and depression.

Intersectionality A term coined by American lawyer Kimberlé Crenshaw to describe the ways in which Black women experience specific discrimination which was not experienced by either Black men or white women and which could be missed by focusing on race or sex discrimination separately.

Intervention Action taken to change a situation, usually with the aim of improvement.

Labelling theory A theory developed by sociologists which states that when a person is given a label, this will change how others behave towards them and how they see themselves, and that this may have negative effects.

Level of analysis The level focused on when examining a complex situation. Levels can be biological, psychological, or societal.

LMIC Lower- and middle-income countries, in which 85% of the world's population live.

Lobotomy A neurosurgery used in the 1950s as a treatment for a wide range of mental health problems. It involved severing nerve fibres in the prefrontal lobes of the brain.

Longitudinal cohort studies See *Cohort studies*.

Madness A term used to describe those who have lost touch with reality. Now most often used colloquially and in a derogatory way, although in recent years there has been a move to reclaim the word with activists organising 'Mad Pride' demonstrations. 'Madness Studies' is a developing field of work, led by people with lived experience.

Manualised (in therapy) A therapy for which a manual has been written, laying out in advance what therapists should do in each session.

Mass social-media induced illness The spread of illness symptoms through a large population via exposure due to social media.

Medicalised When something (for example, distress or unusual behaviour) is perceived and framed as a medical problem.

Mental health The state of a person's psychological and emotional well-being.

Mental health literacy A term used for psychoeducation which is usually about recognition of different mental health problems and knowledge of how to seek help.

Mental health problems When people are experiencing difficulties with their emotional wellbeing. This term is often used instead of 'mental disorders' which is the term used by the diagnostic manuals as it is perceived to be less stigmatising.

Mental illness Used by some instead of 'mental health problems' to refer to those whose are experiencing severe changes to their emotions, thinking, and behaviour which are affecting their ability to function.

Meta-analysis A study which brings together the data from multiple independent studies on the same topic to look at overall trends.

Microaggressions A term used for verbal, behavioural, or environmental events which subtly convey prejudice or hostility towards a group of people, whether this is intentional or not.

Model A theoretical framework which outlines a way of understanding a phenomenon which cannot be directly observed.

Monogenic model The idea that a particular problem is caused by variation in a single gene.

MRI Magnetic resonance imaging, a form of brain scanning.

Neurone A specialised cell which transmits nerve impulses within the body and brain.

Neuroplasticity The ability of the brain to reorganise in response to experiences and learning, or following injury.

Neurosis An historical term used for people in distress who are not experiencing reality in a different way to other people (i.e. who are not experiencing psychosis). This term is rarely used now.

Neurotransmitters Naturally occurring substances in the brain which transmit nerve impulses across a synapse.

Normal What is expected. A term often used to describe the conventions of most of a population. 'Normal' will vary between different cultures and times.

Obsessive-compulsive disorder (OCD) A diagnosis given to those who have uncontrollable and recurring thoughts (obsessions) and/or behaviours (compulsions) which the person feels the urge to repeat over and over.

Organisation for Economic Co-operation and Development (OECD) An intergovernmental economic organisation of 37 countries who describe themselves as committed to democracy and the market economy. These are mostly higher-income countries.

Panic disorder A diagnosis of a type of anxiety disorder where people have unexpected and repeated episodes of intense fear which is accompanied by physical symptoms.

Paranoid delusions When a person thinks and feels that they are being threatened in some way, even when there is very little or no evidence that they are. This is often experienced in an episode of psychosis.

Passive interactions (in behavioural genetics) Gene–environment interactions which happen without any input from the individual (for example, the environment that parents provide for their genetically related offspring).

Pathological Caused by a disease or disorder.

Pathologising Seeing behaviour or experiences as an indication of disease or disorder, rather than as part of the normal range.

Patient An individual who is receiving medical care and treatment.

Perinatal period The time before and after the birth of a baby.

Personality disorder A set of ten different diagnostic categories which are given when a person's long-lasting way of thinking, feeling, and relating to others deviates significantly from the expectations of their culture, causing distress and problems functioning. These are among the most stigmatised diagnoses. They are considered to be lifelong and sometimes untreatable.

Phenotype The observable characteristics of an individual.

Phobia An extreme or irrational fear of something.

Polygenic index/score A number which summarises the estimated effects of many different genetic variants on an individual's phenotype. A polygenic score gives an estimate of the genetic risk of an individual developing a particular disease or exhibiting a particular trait.

Polygenic Due to multiple genetic variants, usually thousands or more.

Polygenic trait A characteristic which is influenced by two or more genes. Polygenic traits do not follow Mendelian inheritance patterns because multiple genes are involved.

Polymorphism A genetic variation which means that different forms of the gene exist in a given population.

Post-traumatic stress disorder (PTSD) A diagnosis of an anxiety disorder which develops following a traumatic (and often life-threatening) event, such as violent or sexual assault, natural disaster or military combat.

Power Threat Meaning Framework (PTMF) An alternative to traditional perspectives on why people experience disturbing emotions and unusual behaviour, which starts from the premise that many 'symptoms' can be understood as responses to threat arising from the impact of power.

Predictive power The ability of a theory to predict what will happen in the future.

Presenting problems The problems or difficulties which have led a person to seek help.

Prevalence The proportion of a population who have a particular characteristic during a given time period.

Probabilistic The idea that an event or experience can make an outcome more or less likely, without the outcome being certain.

Progressive (when applied to illness) Gradually getting worse over time.

Protocol (in therapy) A detailed plan of the therapy procedure.

Psychiatric nosology The grouping of mental health problems into diagnostic categories based on criteria set out in the diagnostic manuals.

Psychiatric services An umbrella term for the clinical services which are also sometimes called 'mental health services'. These include out-patient clinics and psychiatric hospitals and will usually involve the input of many health professionals alongside psychiatrists.

Psychiatrists Medical doctors who have trained in general medicine and then have specialised in mental health.

Psychiatry Medical speciality which deals with the diagnosis, treatment, and prevention of mental health problems. Psychiatrists often use diagnosis as a way to plan treatment and are able to prescribe drugs.

Psychoanalysis A school of psychotherapy developed by Sigmund Freud which focused on the role of the unconscious mind and which was a radical change from what had come before.

Psychodynamic An approach originating in the work of Freud which emphasises unconscious psychological processing, suggesting that events occurring in childhood remain in the unconscious and shape the life of the adult. This term refers to both Freud's theories and those of the people who built on his work.

Psychoeducation Giving people information about mental health and psychological therapy, usually through direct teaching or information leaflets.

Psychological therapy The use of psychological methods and theory to help a person change their behaviour and overcome distress. This can include methods outside of individual talking therapy, including family interventions.

Psychologists People who have studied psychology, the academic study of mind and behaviour. They may not have any training in applying this practically. This term is not regulated.

Psychology The academic study of mind and behaviour, in particular through understanding mental processes and how they affect behaviour and experience.

Psychopathology A dysfunctional psychological response, often used to describe mental health problems.

Psychosis A term used for people who have experiences such as hearing voices and seeing things that other people do not hear and see. It also includes unusual beliefs, such as thinking that your thoughts are being broadcast on loudspeaker or that you are being followed by secret agents.

Psychosocial The interrelationship of social factors and individual psychological processes.

Psychotherapy Talking therapy aimed at helping people with a broad range of difficulties. The term 'psychotherapy' is often used to mean psychoanalytic and longer-term psychotherapy but is also used as an umbrella term, including psychological therapy and counselling.

Qualitative (in research) Research which looks to develop insight into subjective experiences, opinions, and feelings. This usually involves a process of collecting non-numerical data through interviews, open questions, and content analysis.

Quantitative (in research) Research which uses methods and techniques to measure and quantify human behaviour. This process will usually involve collecting numerical data which can be analysed statistically.

Quasi-experimental design An experiment to investigate causality which is designed without randomisation, often by using a naturally occurring difference between groups of people.

Randomised control trial (RCT) A research design where participants are randomly assigned to different groups. One group will usually be given a clinical treatment whilst the other group are not given any treatment and act as the 'controls'. By comparing the two groups, the effect of the treatment can be seen.

Reductionism Describing a complex phenomenon in terms of simple constituents, particularly when this is said to provide a sufficient explanation. Biological reductionism therefore focuses solely on biology as the level of explanation, whilst ignoring other factors.

Reliability A measure of whether something is consistent. There are three types of reliability, over time (test–retest), internal consistency (across items), and across different researchers or clinicians (inter-rater reliability). An investigation or diagnostic process is said to be reliable if the results are similar every time that it is carried out.

Schizophrenia A diagnosis given to those who are experiencing disruptions in their thought processes, perceptions, emotional responsiveness, and social interactions. It is considered to be severe and enduring in many cases.

Scientist-practitioner A model of training where practitioners take an evidence-based approach to professional practice. They apply empirical findings to their work and also take a scientific approach within their work, using the logic of hypothesis testing in their decision making.

Selective Serotonin Reuptake Inhibitors (SSRI): Class of drugs used for depression and a wide spectrum of other mental health problems. Commonly used SSRIs include citalopram, fluoxetine, and sertraline.

Service user A term for a person who receives or uses mental health care services.

Sick role Term used in medical sociology for the behaviour expected from a person who is considered to be ill. These expectations can be the individual's own or those of their family and the wider community.

Single nucleotide polymorphism (SNP) Pronounced 'snip', it is the most common type of genetic variation. Each SNP represents a difference in a single DNA nucleotide. These can be in the DNA between genes or within a gene. Most SNPs have no effect on health or development.

Social anxiety A diagnosis given to those who experience an intense, persistent fear of being watched and judged by others, affecting their daily life.

Social causation model The theory that social circumstances, particularly adversity, can cause mental health problems.

Social constructionism A theoretical model which holds that the ways in which we understand the world are always culturally and historically specific.

Social justice model A model which focuses on the concept of promoting a fair society by challenging oppression and injustice.

Social theory A theory which seeks to explain a person's experiences and behaviour by looking at the world around them and their social context.

Societal response/reaction The way in which society responds to a person, particularly one who is behaving in an unusual manner.

Socio-cultural model A model which sees an individual as embedded in their cultural context.

Socio-ecological model (Bronfenbrenner, 1989) A nested model which attempts to capture some of the complexity of people's lives by placing them in a wider context.

Socioeconomic status (SES) A measure of combined social and economic status.

Sociogenic or psychogenic illness The spread of illness or psychological symptoms through a population where there is no infectious or organic agent responsible for contagion. The spread is therefore considered to be through social contagion.

Stigma Negative societal attitudes towards someone based on a characteristic such as a mental health problem or disability.

Strengths approach Focuses on a person or community's strengths and building these up rather than focusing on deficits, weaknesses, or problems.

Stress–diathesis model The theory that psychological problems result from an interaction between a person's vulnerability (diathesis) and the stressors in their environment.

Substance use Taking a substance such as a drug or alcohol.

Survival response The natural reaction by an animal to a situation perceived as a threat to its existence. This involves physiological changes, preparing the animal to deal with danger by fighting, running away, or freezing. This is sometimes called the Fight, Flight, or Freeze response (FFF).

Survivors A term to describe themselves used by people who have had (generally negative) experience of the mental health system.

Survivor movement A broad term for associations of individuals who have experience of mental health services and who see themselves as survivors of the interventions they underwent.

Survivor-led research: Research designed and led by people who have lived experience of the mental health system themselves.

Symptom pool The set of culturally acceptable features which people (usually unconsciously) draw on when expressing distress.

Symptom (in mental health) Behaviour or an emotional response which is considered to deviate from what is considered to be 'normal' and thus is taken as a possible indication of a mental health problem. A pattern of symptoms is used to decide if a person meets the criteria for a given diagnosis.

Systematic review The process of collecting and evaluating all the available evidence on a particular topic.

Systemic approaches (in psychology) Therapy or interventions which focus on the interactions and relationships between people, often within a family but also in wider systems such as a school or workplace.

Therapeutic relationship A professional relationship between a client and a therapist which creates a sense of safety and therefore enables the client to engage in therapeutic work.

Thought disorder symptoms A disorganised way of thinking which can include hearing voices and difficulties in interacting with others.

Tourette's Syndrome A condition in which a person makes involuntary sounds and movements called tics. It usually starts in childhood.

Transcranial magnetic stimulation (TMS) A non-invasive treatment which uses electromagnetic induction to cause an electric current in specific areas of the brain and which may improve symptoms of depression.

Transdiagnostic An approach which focuses on processes and mechanisms across diagnoses rather than on specific disorders. For example, self-criticism or rumination could directly be addressed in a transdiagnostic approach, rather than being seen as part of a disorder.

Trauma-informed approach The understanding that trauma is common and will often affect a person's physical, social, and emotional development, and that symptoms may be best understood as coping mechanisms developed in order to manage adversity.

Treatment Medical care given to a person for a disease or disorder.

Triangulate (in research) Using multiple methods to test the same underlying hypothesis.

Unconscious bias Underlying attitudes and stereotypes which people unconsciously attribute to another group of people.

Unusual experiences and behaviour A non-medicalised term for behaviours and experiences which the biomedical model calls 'symptoms'. This includes hallucinations and delusions.

Utility (in psychology) The worth or usefulness that something has. For example, a diagnosis may have high utility even without high validity or reliability.

Validity (in psychology) A measure of whether a test or assessment measures what it is intended to measure.

Index